Where's Daddy?

Where's Daddy?

The Mythologies behind
Custody-Access-Support

K. C.

Harbinger Press
Richmond, Virginia
2000

DISCLAIMER

The author and publisher of this book cannot be held liable for error, omissions, or any actions that may be taken as a consequence of using it.

HARBINGER PRESS

2711 Buford Rd. #383. Richmond, Virginia. 23235

Library of Congress Cataloguing-in-Publication Data
K. C.
    Where's daddy? : the mythologies behind
    custody-access-support / K. C. – 1st ed.
    p. cm.
    LCCN: 99-65844
    ISBN: 0-9674736-5-9

    1. Children of divorced parents. 2. Child
custody. 3. Fatherless family. 4. Father and
child.   I. Title.

HQ777.5.K22 2000   306.89
                    QB199-1453

Printed in the United States of America
Published simultaneously in Canada.

10 9 8 7 6 5 4 3 2 1

For all the children.

Acknowledgments

This book would not have been possible without the many and varied contributions of these people. Thank you.

Ken Larkin	Dr. Richard McCall
Trevor Berry	Tom Williamson
Jill Curtis	Shelley Sapyta
Tim Rait	Karen Waters
Dan Poynter	Dina Fullerton
Stephen Solghoian	Karen Stedman, research

The following have kindly permitted reprinting of copyrighted material.

Testament. The Bible and History. John Romer. Michael O'Mara Books Ltd. ISBN 1-85479-005-6.

Beyond Culture by Edward T. Hall. Copyright © 1976, 1981 by Edward T. Hall. Used by permission of Doubleday, a division of Random House, Inc. ISBN 0-385-12474-0.

Generation of Vipers, Philip Wylie. Dalkey Archive Press. ISBN 1-56478-146-1.

Children's Rights Council. Web page from www.vix.com/crc.

A Family Divided, Robert Mendelson. Prometheus Books. ISBN 1-57392-151-3.

Portions from *A Course in Miracles*® copyright 1975, 1999, reprinted by permission of the Foundation for *A Course in Miracles*® - 1275 Tennanah Lake Road - Roscoe, NY 12776. ISBN 0-670-86975-9.

Appendix I is the preface from *The Evolution of Cooperation* by Robert Axelrod. Copyright© 1984 by Robert Axelrod. Reprinted by

permission of Basic Books, a member of Perseus Books, L.L.C. ISBN
0-465-02121-2.

The Way of the Warrior Trader, Richard D. McCall. McGraw-Hill.
ISBN 0-7863-1163-0.

Divorced Dads: Shattering the Myths, Sanford L. Braver with Diane
O'Connell, Jeremy P. Tarcher/Puttnam, 1998, ISBN 0-87477-862-x

Preface

I grew up in Canada near enough the U.S. border to watch "cowboys and Indians" on American television, back when that was half the programming. When very young, our (North Europeans') ability to "beat them up" was sufficient proof what we were doing was right, and meant to be, they misguided to resist our "superior" civilization.

When a little older, I noticed the depth of these people: the calm, the wisdom in their eyes, the larger purpose to their word and action. What did they know that I did not? What were they seeing that my culture's eyes kept from me? Why were we so different, and who was "superior"?

We are the ones who are different. Very different from any society to have existed. What makes us so? Are we the ones missing something?

This book is but a corner of that personal quest for that understanding, formally called cultural anthropology. Cultural anthropology should be understood as trying to see that through which one sees, the ultimate self-exploration.

The other dimension to this book is social comment. Somehow one begets the other, but I don't know which the begettor and which the begettee. So I humbly submit this work as but the ruminations of one common man.

Table of Contents

Insets

Introduction

Except for problem definition in the first chapter, this book does not dwell on the problems with Custody-Access-Support. As an irritated Winston Churchill once demurely murmured, "Any idiot can see what's *wrong* with something."

There being something wrong is not the point. It is assumed any thinking person knows something is very wrong with the Custody-Access-Support (CAS) structure currently imposed. For one, to be as nice as possible about it, CAS "tends to exclude fathers from the raising of their children." Or, more to the point, tends to tear a parent (of whichever gender) from children's lives. Which is a horrible trauma, a horror to both parent and child, committed by this society to huge numbers of its members. Entire families are destroyed in the name of "protecting" something or other, only because the adults wish to part. "Parentectomy," Dr. A. Frank Williams of Cedars-Sinai Hospital in Los Angeles calls it. Do even women think they are better off? That is, when they are the custodial parent, not reacting any better to being non-custodial than do men.

Knowing the Wrongs hardly makes its replacement clear.

Nor will this book attempt to describe another Utopian divorced family, which does not and never will exist. You should know up front that the author personally favours what he calls a "co-parenting" structure, and at the end even offers some operational suggestions for its implementation. But that is not the point of this book nor its body of work. Others have already treated the rights and wrongs to considerable degree, and written doctoral theses on what might replace it. Yet little has been done.

Besides, take any position on any issue and you can find at least one study and reams of anecdotes to "prove" it. Studies, anecdotes, and ideals are others' domain. Three insets and the last two appendixes have been filled with facts and studies; this book offers no new ones.

That co-parenting is well established by all research as highly desirable is not the point. Why those recommendations remain ignored, is. Because all arguments hinge on what is perceived by our formal culture,[1] this week, as *being* the "best interests of the child," few bothering to ask the children. What drives us to the "facts" that most convenience us?

With that, we get closer to the material of this book.

As for scope of the problem, what do you need? Statistics, which vary from year to year, jurisdiction to jurisdiction, and how the data is collected? "One in every three Canadians divorce," or, "50 to 60 percent of U.S. marriages end in divorce," or, "43 percent of children are without fathers." Statistics are notoriously subject to selective presentation or misrepresentation to suit the purposes of the presenter, this author clearly having his own. For instance, notice how the first statistic above is a measure of people who experience divorce, the second a measure of marriages. Do they say the same thing or something different?

Scope and relevance are measured by our lives. Are you divorced? Will you ever face it? Ever known anyone who has been through it, a member of your family? Were your parents divorced? Faced with your own or someone else's – and their stories! – how did you react? If you are like most, it was with some amount of bewilderment, confusion, maybe anger, likely a dose of numb denial. Perhaps you hardly knew how to react, what to believe of what you were hearing or what done to you. How to take it or what to do.

That is what this book is about. That bewilderment. The confusion and anger on all sides. That it has long been taken for granted that Custody-Access-Support is "sensible," yet when we come up against it, feels so at odds with our nature and only results in greater problems.

From where did the present system of custody and visitation come? Why has it been imposed for so long; why does it linger? Why have and do so many think it natural or right or in the best interests of anything, only to

---

[1]A society's *in*formal culture exists among intimates. It is more intelligent and humane, existing among those with whom we are most comfortable. A society's *formal* culture exists with acquaintances and strangers. It is the realm of stereotypes, social conventions and laws. A lower common denominator prevails.

As the gap between the two increases, the work for comedians increases, because the mission of humour is to break the tension between individual and group. Humour is always either taking something conventional (from the formal culture) and showing how ridiculous it is, or taking something personal (from the informal) and showing how normal it is.

find it so unnatural when themselves subjected to it? Is our society insane or am I?

Until we can honestly answer those questions, until we understand from where CAS comes and what still holds it in place, there are three very real dangers:

1) We will waste considerable energy believing we contest the care of children while in fact arguing more basic assumptions about the nature of social man.
2) Whatever new laws will make the same mistakes. Existing traps, dangers and inequities will simply take new form.
3) We may fail to distinguish when to apply what structure, every case having its idiosyncrasies.

We need to know what we are correcting, or we won't.

If you have to endure divorce, do you want it a trauma disrupting every facet of your life for years, degrading your children's forever? Or as easy a step for all parties as what is already a personal tragedy can be kept?

This book will not attempt to "lead the reader" to an "obvious and inevitable conclusion," the way people in literature describe what non-fiction is "supposed" to be like, as though the reader was stupid. Anyone seeking easy or inevitable answers can watch the news or other gossip media, not read a book. Not this book. Rather, the idea is to present certain perspectives and ideas which the reader may not have considered, to better think out the issues yourself and come to your own conclusions. Something many are inclined to anyway, despite the efforts of many to the contrary. The author claims no recent conversation with a burning bush. It is up to the reader to decide what he likes and will take with him, and what to reject. It always is; nothing is inevitable; all is up to you.

Before we begin, three things should be mentioned. First, this book is about some of Euro-rooted culture's social myths, not what some academics have concluded. It is about what is commonly experienced by real people in real society and the mythologies or beliefs that continue to shape this society.

For instance, while John Locke in the 1600s and others since wrote more eloquently than I on intolerance, this did not end slavery, prevent Nazi Europe nor Joe McCarthy America. And while few social scientists today subscribe to the "survival of the fittest," society is not comprised of social scientists. If anyone thinks this refrain dead just because some academics discredited it, they need only examine strong elements of the Republican Party of the U.S., the Reform Party of Canada, the Conservative Party of Margaret Thatcher, and miscellaneous rightist parties throughout the rest of Euro-rooted civilization. Survival of the fittest, "natural" competitiveness, and other forms of Social Darwinism, live in even subtle ways, believing the strong must thrive at the *expense* of the weak, that a society's strong are all that matter. To the extent it contributes to CAS, it is addressed.

This book is not about the "advances in thinking" of the few and learned. It makes no pretense to startling new academics; it is not an academic work. This book is about real life in our society. It is for the common man, about the common man, by a common man. In many ways, it strives to be the voice of the common man regarding some of these myths which, irrespective of The Few "knowing better," continue to drive our social processes; to voice some of the anguish and outcry commonly felt as their result.

Certainly anyone hoping to replace CAS had better have a very clear idea of what they are up against: why it is there; what holds it in place.

Second, when I say, "our culture" or "our society," I am referring to what I define as North Europe-Rooted Civilization. This includes the United States, Canada, Germany, England, Australia, Scandinavia, and so forth. It is a domain with common history, traditions, and culture that spread from Northern Europe during its expansionist period of the last 350 years, a very short part of its total history. I treat it as a single entity. According to my thesis (with which I will not much longer bore the reader) it is related to but distinguishable from Southern European (which spread to South America) and Eastern European societies, having distinguishable histories and traditions. Its principal feature is the Industrial Revolution, which began some 250 years ago and continues to this day. So strong is the identity between them, industrialization became its carrier. Granted, all three cited European cultural groups break down into sub-cultures, but all that is needed for this presentation is the commonality of North Europe-rooted or -origined people. (Admittedly, civilizations are more readily identified when dead.)

While most references are to the U.S., that body of resources being handiest to the author, this book is written for that international audience. Even a compromise of printing and spelling conventions is used. (Enough "errors" to satisfy everyone!) Indeed, a hidden agenda to this work is to help non-North Europe-origin people understand us; understand why we are how we are; make us a little more predictable.

The last item is somewhat of a warning. This is not a politically correct book (political correctness among its subjects, a phenomenon of our culture). For instance, while "women's lib" of the 1970s had legitimacy in seeking the end to Victorian stereotypes about woman – providing for their return to the economic life of society – like many men and women, I have by now not simply lost sympathy with feminism, but all patience. Lost patience with its lies about what women were like before "our enlightened era," with its chauvinistic projections of its own political agenda onto other cultures and times, with its grammar hang-up as though "chairperson" constituted social progress, with its distortions of history, and with its campaigns, not against violence, but only violence to women, as though women should enjoy some special status rather than be an integral part of society. By now, feminism embodies the very elitism and bigotry, the very "sexism" it initially opposed. Female violence, against men or other women, in whatever form, is as bad and pervasive as that by men, the feminist movement itself by now a fine example. Violence and bullying are social issues, not gender ones, and trying to make them gender-centric is sexist, done to bully.

Like many popular social movements, feminism quickly became but a power-grab of the few calling themselves progressive. Many socio-political movements have claimed progressiveness, only to use half-truths and distortions to bully and exploit, only to turn out regressive in terms of democracy and fairness. My disenchantment with feminism is rooted in a lifelong commitment to truth, humanism, socialism, and fairness. *Any who, like feminism, obsess over "other's" power, are obsessed with power. Not fairness.*

And that completes my political-correctness-hyphen-feminism tirade. The reader is forewarned. If some are offended by a lack of political correctness, they are having their own offensiveness with it, returned. If some call this backlash, they might examine their own excesses for need. Reaction is warranted, and overdue.

But take heart. Others are offended by a book by a socialist! :-)

1) The Problem, What Fails, What Works

*T*he Problem

One measure of an idea – not much loved by experts – is if it works. Custody-Access-Support (CAS) is documented to be producing:

- Single-parent families (an industry in itself).
- Female children denied unconditional male acceptance (a permanent, involved father), who grow up with confusions about acceptance and sexuality.
- Male children who grow up having problems with authority and limits.
- Children with lifelong abandonment scares.
- Child abductions.
- "Deadbeat daddies" (who do not pay support).
- Children denied monetary advantages they would otherwise enjoy (same thing).
- Very angry men, even homicidal.
- Women tied down to sole responsibility, angry and frustrated.

Can this idea be said to work?

CAS is not known to be producing much joy for anyone. Some may enjoy some temporary prurient satisfaction in getting everything on divorce: the children and a large part of the ex's assets and income. However hollow, it is the only satisfaction accorded by this structure, therefore pursued by both parties with all the intensity divorce usually produces on its own. But it commonly only increases even the "winner's" sense of loss.

The above list is not the result of divorce. At the human level, divorce is simply an acknowledgement of changing relations. (There may be strong feelings, but what divorce is, is acknowledging something already broken;

FIGURES

While 43% of U.S. children are fatherless,

- 90% of homeless and runaway children are from fatherless homes. Source: U.S. D.H.H.S., Bureau of the Census.

- 80% of rapists motivated with displaced anger come from fatherless homes. Source: Criminal Justice & Behaviour, Vol 14, p. 403-26, 1978.

- 71% of pregnant teenagers lack a father. Source: U.S. Dept. of Health & Human Services press release, Friday, March 26, 1999.

- 63% of youth suicides are from fatherless homes. Source: U.S. D.H.H.S., Bureau of the Census.

- 85% of children that exhibit behavioural disorders come from fatherless homes. Source: Center for Disease Control.

- 71% of high school dropouts come from fatherless homes. Source: National Principals Association Report on the State of High Schools.

- 75% of adolescent patients in chemical abuse centres come from fatherless homes. Source: Rainbows for all God`s Children.

- 70% of juveniles in state-operated institutions have no father. Source: U.S. Dept. of Justice, Special Report, Sept 1988.

- 85% of youths in prisons grew up in a fatherless home. Source: Fulton Co. Georgia jail populations, Texas Dept. of Corrections, 1992.

Also see Appendix III.

a faith lost.) The above is the result of the structure society imposes on any family where the parents are not, or are no longer, married. Just the parents. One partnership of the many comprising a family.

Do we do this when one of the children grows up and moves from home: impose restrictions on their contact with and involvement in the lives of the others, eliminate their contribution to decisions, eliminate all consideration of them, simply because they are no longer living there? And make them pay rent?

A few jurisdictions in North America and Europe have made some adjustments. Often they are merely token, though not all. For instance, there are attempts to say both parents must have equal say in significant matters (various forms of what, in the U.S., is call joint legal custody).

Worthy though this is, it can produce its own problems. Without very specific definitions of "equal say" and "significant matters," as long as one can whine or bully or raise more stink than the other, the one-parent structure remains. If there is any degree of conflict, we may have simply provided both opportunity and means, feeding the arguments of those opposing more than one parent. (The problem, as we shall see, may be in understanding operational equality and its *structural* implementation.)

Any degree of what still amounts to CAS produces proportionate amounts of the same problems, so we will deal with the pure model. By structure alone, irrespective of honeyed words and how "sensible" we make it sound, it is a denial of the parenthood of one of the parents. All decisions are made and carried out by one; the other pays. And the children are aware of this denial to them, but cannot even describe what is being done to them, usually until well into adulthood, if then. They commonly blame the parent denied them, cementing the gap we imposed.

Under CAS, there is one parent who decides everything and has all involvement in the child's life, making it a burden. We consider this one household and one parent a Good Thing. Necessary. Even obviously so. The other party "left" (or so we like to assume), so has to pay for (often more than) half of all of someone else's decisions, and a household in which he has no role. This in exchange for regulated visits with no guarantee they will actually occur or be hassle-free, and during which he is instructed to "obey the instructions" of the "real" parent. This is a one-parent structure. Period. No non-custodial parent, male or female, can long maintain a pretense otherwise as it takes too much effort. Direct, constant, material involvement is clearly and permanently denied. Just pay. This, punishment for "leaving," even when you were pushed out.

Twenty years ago I dated a non-custodial mother, divorced already a year. A nurse. She got every second weekend and every Wednesday night. Her daughter was five. It was very difficult watching her desperately cling to an attachment ebbing from lack of daily involvement and regulated contact. The child knew who her mother was, but was clearly confused over what to expect from her, how she should respond to this occasional, total separate experience. The tension among all three and conflict between the parents had no end, no chance to abate. How could it, unless the mother gave up all claim? Did anyone remove the source: a relationship without material expression, without normal liberties, with unnatural restrictions?

Do you suppose it any different for a father? (Ninety-five percent of non-custodial parents are men.) Or are we simply more confident of a more ready resignation: they know better what is expected of them? Does our forced loss of a parent of either gender help the children, or are we simply confident in their lack of voice?

Parental contact in families with married parents is not so strictly regulated. Why not; how do we know they are any less criminal, less irresponsible, that either parent is less caring of their children than separated ones? "I went to court to divorce my wife, not my children," cried Dr. Michael Nieland in *A Family Divided*.[2]

Support is unparalleled responsibility without authority. Whatever clothing, medical or dental care, schooling or anything else you decide on, I pay at least half. I have no say in what or how or even whether the money is actually spent, except whatever is allowed by the One Parent; the payer has no say in any decision except by subversion or additional expense. "She won't get you a bike even though I'm providing the money?" One parent is strictly regulated in making payments, the other, totally unaccountable for its use or in making anything near the same contribution. In the annals of human endeavour, no such blatant responsibility without authority, much less one-sided enforcement, would ever be proposed much less tolerated. Were anyone put in such a structure, what would you expect as the response?

If you wanted a conflict-*generating* structure, you couldn't do better than CAS. As long as everyone knows there will only be one parent – that it's all or nothing, winner take all – obviously they will be each other's enemy. How are we expecting them to act? When we make the children, the prime expression of the relationship, into the prime issue of contention by virtue of exclusive dominion, when we make *parenting* a divorce issue, not simply separation of the adults, how do the adults have a chance to simply and quietly come their own terms with their own feelings about only their own relationships? The children are sure to be bear the full expression of

---

[2] Robert Mendelson, *A Family Divided*. (Prometheus Books, 1997). ISBN 1-57392-151-3.

each side's vulnerability and duress. It usually means people never divorce; can never truly go on to a new life, the previous one a constant cloud of issues. Unless they totally abandon.

Two years after divorce, over fifty percent of children only see their non-custodial parent once or twice a year, or less. (*See Appendix III, p 202.*)

Is this the situation you, or any reasonable person, would have defined were it up to you, starting from scratch? Would you put anyone through this? Surely children and parenting should never be a divorce issue. If there are issues about the children's care (if!), surely they must have an avenue independent of parental marital status. How can we make that the case?

Unfortunately, some fathers' assertions for a meaningful role with their children take the form of nostalgia for the "good old days" of the male (figure-) head of the family and no divorces. But that structure also included, even relied upon, total female financial dependence on that figurehead. While the nostalgia may reflect a valid desire for a return to what, indeed, was a more solid and stable family, that structure was also unfair to women, removing them from society's economic life when its economic life became all that mattered to it. Clocks do not move backward, nor is it necessarily desirable.

But if it is bad for women to be totally dependent financially on their husbands in a money-only society, surely it is just as bad for men to be totally dependent on their (especially ex-) wives for anything to do with their own children.[3] How is it progress to replace one oppression with another, one denial of human dignity with another, one abject subordination with another?

Yet the greatest cop-out from a presumption of co-parenting takes the guise of either,

------

[3] While women's forced financial dependence on husbands is long gone, support payments instead of equal involvement with the children evidences continued female expectancy. Complete independence from a husband seems not completely convenient.

"Only if both agree."

Which is to say, only if the mother agrees, which amounts to the same presumption of one parent: Only the mother decides whether and to what degree the child has a father

or,

"Only if there is no conflict."

Which is the same thing, conflict easy to produce when sole custody is at stake, and what is divorce but a conflict when, as in 90 percent of the cases, it is the inclination of only one? On the first date, everyone is falling all over each other to get along. Not on the last.

There appears no presumption of equality – of a child being equally entitled to both parents – except whatever is allowed by the mother. It would seem some are more equal than others.

This despite the fact well defined co-parenting arrangements have been shown to *reduce* conflict.   Indeed, all studies show that even in high-conflict cases, joint custody is no worse than sole custody. (*See Appendix IV,* Studies.) As easy as it is to create conflict when you know sole custody is at stake, so it is to eliminate when nothing is. On that last date, if there is anything to fight over, they will. Current structures give a couple *everything* to fight over: exclusive dominion; ultimates and absolutes.

If we allow joint parenting before divorce, why are we so anxious to prevent it, after?

The material is voluminous, from Judith Wallerstein in the 70s,[4] to John Guidubaldi in the 80s,[5] and Sanford Braver in the 90s, to mention but a few. Most recently, Dr. Braver of Arizona State University headed a large team of researchers, from economists to psychologists, in the largest study of divorce and all its aspects ever done in the U.S. After submitting their learned papers, he and Diane O'Connell wrote an excellent book for the

---

[4]The California Children of Divorce Project, 1971 – 1977, produced dozens of papers throughout its life. Judith Wallersten and Joan B. Kelly also compiled a book for the public, giving many of their findings. *Surviving the Breakup.* One edition is by BasicBooks, ISBN 0-465-08345-5.

[5]*Growing Up in a Divorced Family: Initial and Long Term Perspectives in Children's Adjustment* (1987). Also see appendix III.

public about what they had discovered: *Divorced Dads: Shattering the Myths*. Among their findings:

> Our research has unravelled the mystery and resolved the paradox of the disconnected dad. Divorced fathers disengage when they are driven away, made to feel like they don't matter. Yet they almost always act like good fathers when they are empowered, made to feel that their fatherhood is still necessary in bringing up their children.[6]

Why has so little been done? Is a red herring preoccupying us?

Pride and Prejudice: The Failure

Here we discuss what does not work with respect to any social policy, yet is most commonly applied and most favoured by our beloved media: the red herring, righteousness. We examine only one result of CAS: failure to make support payments, actually not as rampant as believed.[7] But let us assume that even the worst stories about its failure are true.

The only interest CAS takes in a divorced man (the only role assigned) is paying for (often more than) half of the assumed expenses of the custodial parent. And when faced with any failure of this arbitrary, unilaterally imposed arrangement, how has society reacted? Force it all the more.

The state of Colorado is a typical example. It had a Child Support Enforcement Agency since the early 1970s. (The only institutions society has in place with respect to CAS are to enforce support and custody. No jurisdiction has any agency or mechanism to ensure what little the non-custodial parent is accorded. There is no enforcement of visitation short of expensive, toothless court appearances where the judge might wag his

---

[6]Sanford L. Braver with Diane O'Connell, *Divorced Dads: Shattering the Myths* (Jeremy P. Tarcher/Puttnam, 1998), pp 179. ISBN 0-87477-862-x.

[7]Ibid, chpt. 2.

finger. Could society make a stronger statement that it considers money, not simply an adequate substitute, but preferred replacement for a father? Could any man hold any delusions about the hope for his relations with his children?[8])

In 1994, Colorado began reporting delinquency to the credit bureau and added garnishing workman's compensation and unemployment benefits. (Not yet got 'round to welfare.) The next year they suspended driver's licenses. In 1997, commercial driver's licenses came under suspension. (Other jurisdictions suspend trade, professional and business licenses. Always a good way to raise money!)

Few beat the Province of Ontario where, starting in 1993, all (all!) support orders instantly convert to permanent garnishments against wages, tax returns, benefits, etcetera, irrespective of the wishes or preferred arrangements of either parent. This along with suspension of licenses, and even passports on non-compliance.

Forcing-what-fails is usually comical. Except when there are destroyed lives. A father not living with the mother is a criminal. No trial, just force. Make sure he fulfills his presumed only value (money), and nothing more.

Clearly some are resisting payment. (And with all the forcing, we could only be hoping to increase their numbers.) But many more are unemployed or less gainfully employed.[9] This is never allowed as an excuse. There is no allowance for temporary, much less long-term, financial setback: What is owed, accumulates. One must prove a permanent change in earning ability,

---

[8] In 1995, U.S. President Clinton directed federal agencies to "strengthen the role of fathers in families." By 1999 the U.S. Department of Health and Human Services made a token $10 million available to the states for access and visitation programs. As of this writing, none have claimed it.

"Dads Matter" campaigns by the very agencies appointed to enforce their humiliation is the height of cynicism. The problem is not with the public. It is with Officialdom. We do not need another "attitude transplant." We need fundamental structural change. Put your money where your mouth is.

[9] In one sample, 95 percent of fathers having no employment problems for the past five years paid regularly; 81 percent, always in full. But among those having experienced any unemployment, one-third paid nothing. Once you're in over your head, that's it. Source: Judi Bartfeld and Daniel R. Meyer. "Are There Really Deadbeat Dads? The Relationship Between Ability to Pay, Enforcement, and Compliance in Normal Child Support Cases." *Social Service Review 68*, (1994).

usually only disability, certainly not a selfish career change that happens to pay less. Moreover, a permanent change in circumstance can only be proven well after it's been the case, and reduction is not retroactive. Everyone is treated as dodging.[10]

Consider those who *are* resisting outright. Has anyone wondered whether they have a legitimate complaint? Have we given them just cause? Is every case the archetype we imagine; is any? Or are they making a statement, "You can't have it both ways. When you insist these children have no father, you have no right to take any more from me."

When the thirteen American colonies were faced with taxation without representation (support payments to their parent without a voice regarding its use), they did something drastic. Something to do with not sending it. In 1215, Magna Carta was signed in England because the nobles would not tolerate taxation without a say in its amount or spending; it was the beginning of Parliament. Responsibility without authority is normally considered an injustice. One normally expects a reaction.

In similar contexts, we call such people freedom fighters, standing up to injustice, courageously defying unreasonable authority. Would we prefer murder to civil disobedience? Sometimes we get that, then call it "men's brutality to women." Are fathers the ones being brutalized, we, somehow excusing it?

Better to weave a myth about irresponsible men, than let them face us with our own sins.

Colorado's and Ontario's escalation is typical. Society decrees a single structure imposed on all families upon divorce. Rebellion ensues, in some cases in the form of failure to comply (although a lot less than the hysterics would make you think). To society, the only visible failure of CAS is these damn men not paying support, the cries of fatherless children never heard above adults' holy wars. So the only "problem" is support not being paid. (Reductionism: isolate on one aspect, ignoring the context which is creating it.) Society reacts with anger at defiance, the anger of authoritarianism. "They're not behaving as we told them to." We increasingly try to force

---

[10] Only four percent are able to get a reduction when their earnings drop by over 15 percent. Source: Elaine Sorensen. "A Little Help for Some 'Dead-beat' Dads," *Wahsington Post* (November 15, 1995). pp A25.

them to our will, ignoring their objections, ignoring all other signs of failure, ignoring anything wrong with what we are forcing upon them and the legitimacy of their complaints.

Of course, more force simply drives more fathers further from their families, satisfying our worst suspicions, justifying our tactics. It's a jolly little self-fulfilling circus.

Fathers who fail to pay support for whatever reason make an unbeatable target. Everyone can jump in to morally condemn them, their victims innocent children. "However badly they feel treated, you'd think they'd at least care about their own children," the presumption that money is male caring. That humiliation alone can be sufficient motive to give up. It hardly occurs to us it was we who insisted these not be their children; their children and independent involvement expressly denied (not even their limited access assured in any form); "their children" in name only, support but a fine for having tried to have any.

This manufactured criminalization leaves single fathers especially vulnerable to charges of child abuse, a cry so popular in its own right today that reaction to it also far exceeds actual incidence.[11] It is all too common for mothers seeking their ex-partner's total elimination, or revenge, to make such accusations. (*See inset page 122.*) And it works. It works without recourse.

The crowning glory are the ploys to which agencies are now resorting. For instance, in Massachusetts starting in 1997, when a father is late with

---

[11] The facts about child abuse are readily available to anyone interested. Few have been. Those who are seem only interested in twisting them into "proving" some other agenda. I will not join in. Instead, we will examine the preconceptions that drive society to whichever facts convenience it.

Still, to what facts might I be referring about reaction to abuse out of proportion to what actually occurs? Start with the famous Los Angeles cases in the late 1980s where an overzealous district attorney got a lot of children to falsely accuse numerous daycare workers. And has anyone verified feminist claims of levels of wife-beating, or is feminism only proving the gullibility of the media, as did the military during the Cold War?

Perhaps the current hysterics about child abuse are not so much exaggeration as misplacement. Which this book is about: society's insidious abusiveness, of which the popular hysterics are both projection and example. For real examination of such facts, see *Ceasefire!* by Cathy Young. It is a level-headed assessment of both feminist and conservative claims. The Free Press, 1999. ISBN 0-684-83442-1.

a payment, the state sends him a letter. An upcoming birthday of one of his children is noted, so:

Now is a good time to renew your financial obligations.

Which is to say: We won't do a thing to assure your involvement in the child's life, even to assure you regular visits or any contact whatsoever. We won't even make sure you're able to talk to him by phone on his birthday. But hand over the dough or we'll tell everyone what an abuser you are.

The people doing this are sick. To a child, money is no substitute for a parent. We are obsessing on entirely the wrong end of the stick. Deadbeat daddies are targeted as a cause of family breakdowns rather than the most obvious and entirely predictable result.

But this is CAS's contribution. It is a system for producing supreme moral indignation. Society as a whole can feel holy and satisfied condemning, pursuing, and punishing Evil People it created, unfurling "best interests of the children" while trampling them, only satisfying themselves, not satisfying anyone subjected to it whether children, mothers, or fathers. CAS is a billion-dollar-a-year industry providing justified existence for social workers, bureaucrats, lawyers, and thousands of "churchladies." That's a lot of vested interest.

On the other hand, if we truly want to eliminate the "problems" with non-custodial parents, instead of just producing a segment for *60 Minutes*, we might consider eliminating non-custodial parenthood.

Righteousness is an agent of oppression. It is not an agent of change. It has never changed anyone, or anything.

Anatomy of Righteousness

The phenomenon of righteousness is so intrinsic to our culture, and has been made so much a part of this issue, that it warrants direct attention. It is always accompanied by its brother, bigotry: It is bigotry's voice. Most think bigotry what others are guilty of, which simply means we do not recognize our own.

The U.S. television series *All In the Family* is commonly thought to have been about "a bigot," Archie Bunker. It was a copy of similar shows in Europe. I suggest it worked as a comedy because it was about *two* bigots: the right-wing Archie, and left-wing Michael Spivak. Both were equally intolerant, equally narrow-minded, equally righteous in their beliefs, equally unwilling to listen to the other. Same structure, only the content differed.

North Europe-rooted society loves to produce people we can morally condemn. We withhold responsibility for ten or more years from those who acquire an adult mind and body (teenagers), then call them irresponsible. We finally accept alcoholism as a disease, but declare all other drug users criminals, then wonder from where came the greatest criminal empire to exist; it must be Bad People. To see ourselves Good, we make others Bad and systematically find or create as many "others" as we can.

- ▸ 400 years of Protestant versus Catholic
- ▸ The Tobacco Company Conspiracy
- ▸ The International Jewish Conspiracy
- ▸ Communist "Evil Empire"
- ▸ The International Male Conspiracy Against Women ("women have always been oppressed")
- ▸ Drug Addicts, and their inevitable supply chain
- ▸ Deadbeat Daddies

Which is your favourite? The common denominator, the driving force behind all the above as well as of Nazism, McCarthyism, racism, and apartheid, is righteousness. "My hatred is morally justified." Everyone's has been, the politically correct and feminists no exception. Our *nouveau* bigotries include tobacco, maleness, drugs, and some forms of violence, but not all. Good bigotries. Much better than those of previous generations, so we're progressive.

Feminists believe their sexism superior to or more justified than that of men. Many of us cannot distinguish them. "Zero tolerance" is *bragged* in social issues: we are proud of our narrow determinism, our continued insistence everyone be what suits my beliefs. We refuse to see social ills as the result of what we ourselves are doing, unwilling to accept our own responsibility by accusing others of not accepting theirs.

Righteousness is authority without responsibility. It presumes authority over decisions without the responsibility of being in the specific circumstance calling for them, and without having to live with their consequences. It insists others be responsible for a particular behaviour, robing them of that decision, when they are the ones in the specific instance requiring such a decision. Presuming authority without its incumbent responsibility is very immature. It denies others their opportunity to find their own answers and own way, denies that they are the ones who must, possibly afraid they may find something better than what we believe.

Righteousness is a replacement for – indeed, a perversion of – self-pride: it is pride at someone else's expense. It is robbing someone of their dignity and esteem to add to mine and make me feel important.

Given our predilection for it, it is hardly any wonder that in our society the slightest legitimate complaint suddenly turns into its own torrent of abuse. In the cases of apartheid, Nazism, McCarthyism and feminism, a people initially felt wronged or betrayed and found a scapegoat with which to make themselves as villainous as those they condemned. It quickly becomes a carry-over of a habit of hatred and suspicion, a desire to control others' lives instead one's own. We see almost anything others do as a personal violation. It is difficult to distinguish hatred from righteousness.

Righteousness is extremely powerful: You'd better be on the righteous side, or be yourself condemned. It has long been our culture's principal agent of its authoritarianism. Imposing one's will (vision, values) requires moral justification. It is our instrument of oppression, our mass addiction, and makes us dangerous, as much to ourselves as others. Righteousness is now a billion-dollar-a-year industry, from Fleet Street in the UK to *60 Minutes*, *Oprah*, and *Sally Jessy Raphael* in the U.S. Consider those making the use of tobacco a *moral* issue.

While all peoples exhibit prejudice of one sort or another, no other society with which I am familiar or have studied exhibit so many, so frequently (even consistently), nor with the fury as we. It starts with fear: a sense of threat or disenfranchisement, which seems easily provoked in us. It is a fear only soothed if all others are "like me" or on "my side" (our extreme tribalism). To accomplish this, I must have the One True Answer and Only Way. (Intolerance, narrow-mindedness, absolutes.) This issues forth the fire of morality.

Moral rage has become a habitual reaction to any perceived "bad thing," seeing almost anything as personal threat. We are all infected. Left wing, right-wing; socialist, capitalist; tinker, tailor, soldier, spy. The media fans it, for it sells better than anything. It is a cultural addiction.

Consequences

The results include social policies that simply go from one extreme to the other, each equally rammed down everyone's throat as one oppressed group then oppresses the others: From everyone should smoke to nobody should, ever, anywhere. A few years ago, all abortions were bad, now all are good, any is justified, everyone ought to on a whim. In each instance, dissent is hounded, any who argue are called backward, reactionary, or in some other way non-human, assigned to the opposite extreme whatever their true opinion. They are morally void, making it all right to "kill" (dismiss) them.

For instance, while the stigma Victorianism assigned an unwed mother was abominable (shaming, permanent social outcast, could never hope to marry), does that mean mother-only families are just as good for children or even better than multi-parent ones; that they should be promoted, fathers irrelevant?

All we have done is switch from shaming her to shaming him; from shaming single mothers to shaming single fathers, as though we still need someone to wag at. (The solution may have less to do with wedlock than ensuring two – or more – freely permanent parents. Stop preventing it. Stop shaming *him* by saying how meaningless *he* is.)

Until the current wave of women's movement (starting in the 1970s), a number of women who really had a penchant for running a business or desired a professional career, were frustrated trying to be exclusively a mother and housewife. Now, a different segment of women are shamed if they want to stay at home. We are no less narrow, only changing our focus. How are women freer when just a different group is repressed?

The abortion movement provides a study. One would think that if those professing choice about pregnancy really believed in choice, they would equally campaign for increased maternity homes so those who wanted to could *have* their children. But a 1992 survey by a group of social agencies in a major North American city found the majority of teenage girls who'd had abortions did not feel they had control over anything. It had not necessarily been their choice, nor had their views or feelings been considered. There had been little choice other than running away, same as there always has been for such people:

> Several [teen] mothers told stories about extreme pressure from boyfriends, family members and professionals to have an abortion. The pressure to choose abortion was experienced from school personnel and to the greatest extent from doctors and nurses.
>
> Parents, educators, doctors and social workers may have perfectly valid reasons why [*to believe that*] teenagers should not be parents. However, if society assumes control over their decisions about parenting or hurries them through the process, the young mother does not learn how to take control and responsibility for her own future – which is essential to her ability to eliminate the risk factors in her own behaviour or in her context.
>
> The combined effect of these internal and external forces undermines the sense of control over her body and her future which is necessary for the young mother to avoid risk and take advantage of opportunities.[12]

It would seem the abortion movement is only as interested in controlling others' lives and forcing their views on all society as those it claims to replace. Freedom and personal strength continue un-championed as we make the same mistakes with each social movement, each but a fashion.[13]

---

[12] *A Study Of Yong Mothers In Metro Toronto.* Young Mothers' Resource Group, April, 1993.

[13] Our adoption customs are second only to our divorce ones in inhumanity. If you are pregnant and know you cannot support the child, what is the difference between abortion and adoption? Both totally and permanently eliminate the child

(continued...)

So much for reform. So much for progress. The content may change (abortions good/bad), not the context: the structures implementing them, themselves the problem.

So you see the room for concern over changes to post-divorce childcare laws? We seem in the habit in our reforms, of not reforming. Of simply committing the same sins, only with this year's popular notions. In many ways we are as repressive, narrow, and intolerant as ever, just finding new toys. Last year's Victorian morality is this year's political correctness.[14] The content may differ (all abortions bad/good, women inferior/men evil, smoking good/bad), the structure is the same: use of social-shaming and self-appointment as society's conscience, a seat to which all must kowtow or be excommunicated.

"I have seen the enemy, and the enemy is ourselves."

Process Management: What Works

If our traditional response to social ills – righteousness and its "force to my will" – fails, and is simply the same bigotry we condemn in others, what might be more productive?

---

[13](...continued)
as far as you are concerned. Adoption is yesteryear's abortion. We retain that quality; there remains little choice about a pregnancy that cannot be handled. So by the same token, if those professing opposition to abortion really wanted to reduce the number performed instead of just forcing their values on everyone, they might campaign for broader choice in adoption arrangements.

[14] Coincidentally, Victorian morals and political correctness are both manifestations of the same European authoritarian *matriarchy* that has persisted throughout the generations. Our culture's brutality is culture-centric, not gender-centric, each simply finding its own expression. Don't forget, it was those "weak, helpless, docile, politically powerless" women of yesteryear who engineered Prohibition. That's power. It is interesting how only women today portray women of other eras and cultures as subservient. Men have rarely found them quite so agreeable.

> Man is not innately and solely aggressive or co-operative or loving or sexual or hard-working or playful . . . [he is] *situationally* loving, hard-working, hierarchical, etc. [*Italics mine.*][15]
>
> — Edward T. Hall, *Beyond Culture*, 1976

Righteousness is over the results of social processes. Process Management addresses the causes: the structures themselves which produce the ills. It addresses context, not the content.

When a truck is bearing down on you, ogling that pretty girl across the street somehow slips one's mind. Context (the structures or situations in which we find ourselves) dictates the vast majority of behaviour. Yet few sciences address it, none that are popular. It assumes some responsibility for what is being produced.

When anything is produced – a bridge, a bolt, a computerized system – *two* things are produced: the product, and the process to produce it. Indeed, first you create the process (context), which produces the product. Producing anything simultaneously produces both the means and its end.[16] So if you want to improve a product, improve the process producing it. Don't yell at the product, tend to what is producing it. The product will improve with improvement to its process.

In commercial enterprises we have learned that context (the process) is the only thing management can control (define, manage). Not the content

---

[15]Edward T Hall, *Beyond Culture* (Anchor / Doubleday, 1976). p 138, ISBN 0-385-12474-0.

[16] That both means and ends are equally produced by the same action makes it fallacious to attempt their distinction as in, "Do the ends justify the means?" If the end is "good" and the means "bad," you have a wash. Zero sum. Both are produced by the same action. Indeed, the process stands as precedent for re-use to similar ends. Attempting to distinguish means from ends is typical European reductionism: focus on small pieces in isolation. Context elimination. Since context determines what anything is – defines, even creates anything – eliminating it seems an obviously fallacy.

(the responses to and results of process).[17] In manufacturing, to reduce defects, improve the process: Increase training, define clear standards, rehearse procedures, improve equipment. Don't change the people doing the job (content), for if you put different people in the same situation to execute the same process, they will undoubtedly produce exactly the same results (number of defects). And don't just keep producing more or use more force hoping some will start to turn out "right." The system is producing whatever is getting produced, including the defects. Don't blame the results.

We can apply the lessons of process management to society. Society is a process. It is several processes, and may be taken as a whole. We go to school, assume jobs, marry, live, and must function in many of society's structures (corporations, unions, clubs, churches: legal and social structures). It is a process for producing its own members. And every year we produce increasing numbers of defects of all shapes and sizes: not just criminals and child molesters, but people who are obsequious and never stand up for themselves; obese people and other addicts; people overly aggressive who bully; people who cannot hold a job or a marriage; chronic meddlers and gossips; people carrying any one or combination of anger, pain, and loneliness.

We produce ourselves.

But the process is out of control (unpredictable variance of results). It is out of control exactly because everyone is running around tutting its results rather than improving the context producing them. Trying to "change people's attitudes," changes nothing; that is content. Real change is structural. Change that to which we must react.

How can we reduce the occurrence of a social ill? The same way you reduce the defects from any other process. Discover how we are producing them (which requires taking ownership of the fact we are) and correct or improve that context. Rather cynical to express deep concern over single-parent families while creating endless numbers. If we care so much, stop creating them. That is process management: determine how are we creating what we don't want, and stop it.

---

[17] Ref: W. Edwards Deming, *Out of the Crisis* (MIT, 1987). ISBN 0-911379-01-0

There is no cure-all. There will always be defects (misfits) of some sort or other. There being any defects is not by itself a symptom of a systemic cause. There will always be what the statisticians call "special cause." In the case of society, due to forces beyond our control (genetics, wars) we will always produce some people who do not fit in or cannot cope, no matter how much we improve or tune the context within which we live.

But there are precise definitions for "statistical significance," and when the occurrence of an undesired result falls within it, the cause is "common" (systemic, and ours), not special, not peculiar to the person committing it, not a happenchance of fate.

The advantage to statistical analysis is that it shows when it is our values and labelling that are out of whack. When it is not people who are odd, but those judging them. Homosexuality is an example. For centuries our culture (ours and the Middle East alone) called them deviant. But how can they be if every society and culture at every time in history has roughly the same proportion? This would seem a naturally occurring phenomenon, as much so as left-handedness. (Also persecuted by us until recently.) So one may reasonably conclude: if God didn't mean there to be homosexuals, there wouldn't be any. They seem neither man-made nor situation-induced.

On the other hand, serial killers are so rare, and their occurrence varies so wildly from society to society, they can only be special cases. And there are hints to their cause in what corresponds to their variance. Two causes are suggested: extreme alienation, and some freak biological imbalance.

Deadbeat daddies, single-parent families, hostile children, etc. There is nothing special about any of these. They are very common to our society; incredibly common, and increasing.

We are creating them. So, if Custody-Access-Support as the structure in which we place anyone who divorces is producing nothing but horrendous results, one would think changes to post-divorce family structure would be the only meaningful course. Not mindlessly forcing what obviously fails and is just as obviously inappropriate in the first place. And not just changing "people's attitude," which is trying to change social content, not the context in which we must live.

The difference between context and content is also why the profession of social work may be more harm than good, or at least cannot be counted on for much help.

1. The harm of any meddling (content management): dis-empowering the principles, and all the complications of introducing a third party's agenda. This is just another party for the principals to appease as though lawyers and judges were not enough.
2. Society believes something is being done about social problems, when it is not. Treating defects simply extends a system that is not working. Once a defect is created, it's too late. By and large, it is a waste to try to change what already exists. It is considerably more economical to not create them in the first place.
3. Instrument of conformance. When England decided to dump all orphans into Australia from the 1880s through the 1930s, tearing them from whatever family or home they had, social workers carried it out. When Canada and Australia adopted a policy of assimilation of native peoples (a formal policy of cultural genocide to "save" the natives) in the 1910s through 1970s, priests and social workers were the ones to take children as young as six from their homes, sending them thousands of miles to residential schools. (This context alone was telling them to be ashamed of being Natives.) There, they were often subjected to the normal European "suffering is good." (They were beaten: treated the way white people, especially then, treat their children, not the way Natives ever have.) In neither case did social work as a profession say, "This is wrong!" They were too busy doing it. (Individual professionals spoke out. The profession did not.)

   Having no mission statement, no principles or objectives or tests of success inherent to the profession,[18] the profession of social work is vulnerable to use by any socio-political interest as a tool to implement this year's expedience. Society's Enabler. Just a tool, as much a part of the divorce industry as lawyers.
4. "Your rewards will be in heaven." All "feel-good" professions are delighted when they see someone upset. They treat being upset, not the cause; switch the focus from outside one's self to inside; switch

---

[18] The only profession with any form of mission statement or written standard, is medical doctors. This has proved no guarantee of total or consistent professionalism, much less excellence, but at least they have some stated standard to which their performance may be compared.

from seeking solutions to learning to live with it. This is the modern version of, "Your rewards will be in heaven (so accept your lot)," needed to maintain a status quo.

If you are upset about how you are being treated in divorce, you are having trouble adjusting. Not that you *should* fight like hell if you have the slightest self-respect.

5. A vested interest in the status quo. Existing structures produce the reasons for their existence: their customers. It makes them indispensable. No profession is likely to advocate changes that would reduce their vitality to society. Social work may have more interest in *being* a social structure than correcting them.

Many individual social workers have, in fact, shown great courage in standing up against popular social programs or policies they know are harmful, CAS among them. Indeed, some of the strongest voices against custody, some of the best work uncovering its ills and alternatives, has come from its ranks. They are isolated voices, as the profession is silent. The profession as a profession has never stood for anything. Their lessons in making people "feel listened to" are used to get people to go along with whatever horror society is subjecting them to today, like the priest we send to walk the condemned man to the gallow. Yet they are promoted as experts. They may be expert at the wrong things.

Do-gooding is as unproductive as moral condemnation. They are opposite sides of the same coin: Both deal with results, not causes, simply in different ways. Both are cont*ent* management, addressing those affected by context. Neither have interest in nor put effort toward reducing the numbers of those condemned/treated, the status quo producing their grist and making them important.

Want to improve society? Instead of blaming or "adjusting" the people who comprise it and are simply its results, stop producing them. Improve the structures in which we ask people to live, in which people (we) must grow and find our way, that forge society's members. We do not define human nature (content). That is a given. Man is not infinitely malleable or there would be neither revolts nor revolutions. Define and improve that to which we are required to adjust. The responses will correspondingly improve, and we won't need so many feel-good professionals, as our context will no longer be so at odds with our nature.

Wrap-Up and Onward

Hopefully, we have laid some groundwork. Custody-Access-Support as a structure for non-marriage childcare is an unparalleled failure, only producing misery for all. Both righteousness and do-gooding treat the results, they do nothing to correct or stop or even identify the cause of any ills. Process management, however, is a tool for dealing with systemic problems because it focuses on finding their causes, hence on finding more appropriate structures within which to place people. It seeks to manage, not how people react, but to what they are required to react. Context, not content.[19] This, of course, assumes people are not inherently malicious and will respond positively when treated as though they matter. We will address this.

All this tells us *to* seek correction to post-divorce arrangements. It does not tell us what should replace CAS, nor where to look. To answer that, we need to know how our society came up with it. What has made it, for so long, seem right to so many; what led us to it; what keeps it in place; on what perceptions of mankind and family is it predicated? Is Custody-Access-Support predicated on anything close to the truth about humans? If not, what is – and how do we know what is – a more accurate image of humans and families? Only then can we consider what structures might more closely model such an image, more readily fit those involved in couple separation.

---

[19] An excellent book is undoubtedly to be had in fully applying the principles of Total Quality Management to social processes. For one thing, it calls for the direct involvement of those subjected to a process in its definition and maintenance. It is empowering. Alas, not this book. Process management was introduced as a tool for identifying and addressing systemic causes, as Edwards Deming estimates this the source of 94 percent of all defects, ills, problems, or undesired results. It is what should be applied to see if anything suggested here or anywhere else actually works. It now drops from sight; we proceed to our own mission: guidance on where and how to look for ideas for such improvements, and what to avoid.

Unless we clearly understand this, we will only make the same mistakes in whatever structures replace it, as we have done with so many "reforms" and "advances."

The following list is the author's personal conclusions, humbly submitted for consideration. It is a list of the five myths, still common to North Europe-rooted thinking, which seem to most contribute to the defence of CAS. After a chapter on the background of North Europe-rooted culture in general, each will be discussed. Each has corollaries.

1. Women have children.

    Not simply nurturing, but even having children is considered a "woman thing." It is not considered simply human, taking a couple. Having and nurturing children is another thing we have gender-fied, and any look at societies in general shows it to be decidedly unnatural, certainly uncommon.

2. Uni-paradigm-ism.

    One authority, one God, only one thing is right for all things at all times. So a child must have only one parent, and one household. This is possibly the greatest problem, being deeply ingrained.

3. Exclusive linear thinking.

    In this case: men take care of women, women take care of children. Straight line, one dimensional, non-systemic. This is a description of CAS itself: what it explicitly implements. The danger in this image of family is obvious. Should women stop needing men to take care of them, men are altogether out of family. Exactly what's happened. So extremely conservative men cling to the notion of female subordination (another myth with little truth) as their only way back into the equation, while many feminists bask in the notion of doing totally without men. Both only take the positions they do because of viewing family and its structure through the same narrow aperture.

4. Divorce is a sin.

    Despite this no longer being the public perception, it continues to haunt our legal processes and traditions. Something holy has been defiled; someone is shirking their responsibilities; something must be preserved at all cost. In many ways, we still do not allow marriages to end, children now providing the means. We wind up trying to preserve the wrong things, destroying family ties that should exist notwithstanding marriage.

5. No clear concept of social equality.

How do you treat a divorcing couple even-handedly? What is equality within a marriage, much less post-marriage? Equality still very much confuses us, it's rhetoric possibly preoccupying us more than other societies because we have long had so little. We still struggle with what it is in day-to-day life.

Note that only one expressly has to do with gender myths. While it is true that CAS is the most visible expression of North Euro-rooted society's general de-patrification of family (Disposable Daddy; the "family is female" motif which has been prominent here for centuries), some of our gender mythology itself, both pre- and post-feminism, is the product of other forces. Gender myths are as much result as cause.

Certainly if you want to accomplish de-patrification (eliminate fathers), CAS is the sort of thing to implement. It articulates the model for all families: one female parent. But many children never had a father, not because of divorce and CAS, but the sum of all five myths. CAS is an expression of de-patrification, which is itself a product.

Still, isolating simply on de-patrification, is it natural to mankind? Is a society of exclusively matriarchic families the kind of society that most promotes health? Is it common among all societies? Whether common or not, is that the kind of society in which we wish to live: where we eliminate male parents as thoroughly and quickly as we can irrespective of their own inclination? Or does it increase the chances of producing abnormalities and defects?

In what kind of society would you like to live, do you feel would be most natural to you? Well, it is up to you, as it is yours.

2) Background

From what fires are we forged? What forces produced North Europeans in the first place and continue driving us on?

Much of this chapter may seem removed from Custody-Access-Support. Bear in mind that the issue is not whether sole- or co-parenting is preferable. That is thoroughly addressed by others using all manor of science. The issue is, why is the evidence ignored? Clearly we are up against deeply ingrained biases well beyond most sciences. We are up against biases beyond righteousness, simply used to defend the irrational. We are after those biases. With respect to CAS, they most show themselves in the five myths listed, but we need to know in what they are rooted.

This chapter gives the critical context for examining any Euro-mythology. Academic completeness in that examination is not critical here, so academic perfection is sacrificed for brevity. The idea is to stimulate thought, not bore the reader with proofs. It is to broadly set a table, not be the definitive work on any of the matters touched upon in this chapter. The libraries teem with books that fully explore any of the things presented here, so thorough treatment and citing all evidence is not attempted. Some notions are simply offered; we seek only brush strokes.

Despite this, the chapter is long. There is much to cover. Hopefully, it is informative and to the point. But if you find one section bogging down, skip to the next.

The European migrations, and Rome, contributed most to building our basic perceptions of ourselves and the world in which we live. They most influenced us. They created perceptions that haunt us to this day, habits of thought, and reaction, and ways of seeing things passed from generation to generation, however long gone may be the contexts that bore them.

Migrations

It sounded innocent in school: migration. The Celts then Gauls then Huns and Goths and Norse, Romans, Moors, and Mongolians, just to lightly cover the last three thousand years. Wave after wave for possibly ten thousand years, mostly off the steppes of Asia, pushing those who came before them against the Atlantic Wall, each pushing the other. Until 1500 A.D. when the wall was meaningfully breached (and the violent migrations spilled to the Americas), once a people were against the Atlantic, that was it. Nowhere to go.

This is very different from the other side of the continent where human migration pushed people into either what we now call the Americas, or the Pacific islands. On the west side, there was one gaping ocean.

What did this "migration" and "Atlantic Wall" stuff really mean?

Consider what has recently been going on in the former Yugoslavia: tribal murder and turmoil, "ethnic cleansing," get out of my way. That is Europe. It has been for ten thousand years. Movements of peoples trampling those before: constant bloodshed, a human press. That the rest of Europe has now gone almost two generations without a major war is almost miraculous. As a transplant, for how long has the United States ever gone without a war?

U.S. anthropologist John B. Calhoun coined the term "behavioural sink."[20] Beyond a measurable point, population density causes normal social behaviour to short-circuit. Tension and conflict rises, behaviour deteriorates (sinks), society unglues. We see this in U.S. ghettoes, the cause being sheer population density: people effectively piling on top of each other without effective boundaries. They start to live only for territory.[21]

---

[20] Eugene L. Bliss edited, "A 'Behavioral Sink', " *Roots of Behavior*. (New York: Harper & Brothers, 1962).

[21] The exact "measurable point" at which breakdown starts will, like all things, change with other changes in context. For instance, one reason human societies now withstand the greater populations our increased food and sanitation produce is suburbia: spreading out, facilitated by our transportation. More important is apartment buildings. As long as the walls prevent sound intrusion (as long as!),

(continued...)

Those migrations were wave after wave of terror.[22]

What effect might that have? What would living thousands of years in a war zone, in almost constant fear for your life, make a people like? What perceptions and beliefs about the world and life and society would this leave those who remained, this uncommon sink?

Well, it would produce us: the most violent and brutal society to have ever existed. Attila the Hun and Genghis Khan were but a generation, even they hardly hold a finger to the atrocities we have committed: from the Inquisition, to slavery, to Native Americans, to European Jews, to our wars with ourselves. And ours have been systemic, not from only one person or time. For instance, almost every society has had slaves, including most Native Americans. But in most it has either been of specific, limited duration (seven years in ancient Middle East) or more a form of adoption (bringing a new member into the household). Only Europeans made it large-scale, systematic torture, rape, and murder. And that one atrocity went on for two hundred years. Four hundred in South America.

I doubt I need give another litany of our crimes, nor do I believe guilt bears much healing. But it is important to grasp our place in human history, of what we as a society have been like in relation to others, how others see us and why. And when something like Waco, Texas occurs – the murder of

---

[21](...continued)
we each have our own sanctuary. But what also changes is what is considered normal social behaviour. Last decade's breakdown is this one's norm. Given that our physiology (which includes the brain) was forged to a hunter-gatherer context, there has been much breakdown. We might be more conscious of what might better accommodate us in all aspects of our lives.

[22] Certainly once humans covered the earth, maybe twenty thousand years ago, all areas have experienced the shoves of human movements. These shoves have become more traumatic as human herds increased in size. But only the bottleneck of the Middle East, between Africa and Asia, comes close to the human vise the Atlantic made of Europe. (The funnel from North to South America held promise to assume the same character.)

Note, then, the significance of the similarity between European and Middle Eastern experience. It explains our affinity. The affinity is commonly called "Judeo-Christian tradition," as though a continuum. Culturally, there is no continuum. Any society steals whatever conveniences it from others with which it has contact. Middle Eastern mythology was sufficiently similar (pessimistic) for much to be easily adopted and adapted when, not simply Jews, but Rome and Christianity (a Middle East based religion) came to Northern Europe.

twenty-one children and fifty-five adults by U.S. federal agents – and is whitewashed by the authorities, our capacity for mindless atrocity seems well intact.

More to the point, I propose that in the migrations lies the root of our sense of constant threat, which haunts us to this day. It is still quickly evoked, driving us to social extremes and ongoing shifts of brutality toward each other as one "oppressed" group oppresses the next in our never-ending social policies merry-go-round. We point with pride to how quickly we change, while not really changing at all.

What are other lasting results of ten thousand years in a sink? What motifs are characteristic of, even unique to, North European-rooted society?

1. Competitive Instinct
2. Survival of the Fittest: The Doctrine of Superiority
3. Different is Bad: conformance
4. Self-Hatred: shame and guilt
5. Disassociation (of which Reductionism is an example)

Given the context of European migrations, it is easy to see from where many of these aggressive, even predatory perceptions come. These are fundamental beliefs about social man, deeply ingrained in North European experience. Very understandably so. Once a perception is felt so generally and deeply, it passes itself from generation to generation in even subtle ways. The original stimulus may disappear, but the perception finds its own justifications, creating its own life. More often than we realize, they form the premises of our social policies: how we treat ourselves. This is how we perpetuate them.

1. Competitive Instinct

Even our own psychologists have identified competition as a learned motive, not instinctive nor even natural. But when you're trying to survive in a war zone, everything is threat, and everything a competition. There are those still living by this: "To get to the top, eliminate the competition."

Many see others only as competition, or simply feel ruthless and seek an outlet.

On the other hand, some anthropologists have said that the most powerful instinct is not sex, but learning. They are referring to the nature of all life to strive, explore, discover. Curiosity. All life exhibits this striving; it is basic to survival: for finding food, space, a nest, or mate, even finding a new form (generation of species). It is reaching out. It is not explosive like the strong nuclear force or the overwhelming sex drive. It is powerful like gravity: subtle, slow, but constant and unyielding. It is so subtle and yet so strong that we are rarely conscious of it, but cannot resist its effects. It is what gives us life, often called the Life Energy.

In Europe's confines, this energy imploded into competition: a struggle for survival with everyone and everything around us. Whereas, given a more common or normal context, the truth about any biological society seems to be totally the opposite: Cooperation is the most fundamental response to others, to the extent that *cooperation* could almost be called instinctive. Indeed, nobody gets "to the top," or anywhere, without others' help. In other words, the natural striving by individuals in a society most commonly and naturally manifests in cooperative behaviour: You need me and I need you; what can we do for each other?

This turns out to be true for any society, including our own, or it would not exist. What do you suppose a herd or a flock or a school is? They don't form because they *like* each other. They often don't.

(*Chapter 7*, Social Equality, *will take a closer look at this.*)

2. Survival of the Fittest: The Doctrine of Superiority

We owe the phrase "survival of the fittest" to the British philosopher Herbert Spencer (1820 – 1903), not Charles Darwin. Yet its fame and endurance is a tribute to its representing fundamental perceptions of life for Euro-rooted people. That is, its significance is not in its having been said or by whom, but in its prominence and resilience. Clearly it resonates with common North European experience from well before its pronouncement, and the Euro-psyche well since. Especially for the non-biology public, it continues as the rule governing all nature, and the most basic guiding principle for all things.

It proclaimed superiority as the driving force of nature: the force behind raw survival and the generation of new species. Only the "best" of a species pass on their genes. Only the "most suited" of a group will carry on that group, that community increasingly defined only by a single definition of "best." Evolution became synonymous with progress and superiority. It is *inevitable* that only the fittest could survive, thrive, and continue a species. Wasn't that what Darwin and science were saying?

So we have a definition for "superior": whoever survives. Or whoever thrives or comes to dominate, the means irrelevant.

Replacing "the hand of God," or even Fate, with superiority (or best, or fittest) as the driving force of nature, automatically establishes four things:

2.   The Doctrine of Superiority.

Only some in society (a very few), matter. Only a few (the best ones) are important; they must define the species (or society) and pass that on. All others can be discarded.

There are many unimportant people who are irrelevant to destiny and posterity. It only takes a few for the species to survive, surely you want that to be the best. So all must strive for the betterment of the few, recognizing their subordination.

3.   The Assumption of Merit.

If you survive, or find yourself more powerful than others, obviously it is because you are the Best. You are one of the chosen few. You wouldn't dominate unless you were superior, would you? So whatever it is you have (or think or do, etc), defines superiority, defines what is most desirable. The Devine Right of Kings (being powerful as divinely ordained rather than an accident of time-space) found justification in science. This is why science suddenly became so popular, though never for the masses.

By the same token, it becomes safe to assume that the unimportant are undeserving. If God (or Nature) wanted them to have food and clothing, they would have it. There is no right to expect from others, no "fair share." It is a matter of things being ordained, now by Nature instead of God (whatever that distinction is supposed to be).

4. Godliness; personal knowledge of absolutes.

   Replacing "the hand of God" with Superiority as nature's driving force, makes us Nature's instrument. It puts natures's course in our hands; we *are* its course. The Doctrine of Superiority is the platform upon which to be God.

   If we turn out to dominate others, we are *obligated* to do so. We are the Best, so must thrive to improve the species (or society). All others may, even should, be destroyed, existing only to feed our strivings. We are destiny. We helped ourselves to God's throne.

   Notice that Darwin-cum-Spencer coincided with the peek of North Europe expansionism (late 1800s). One has to wonder whether, when the Japanese or someone else comes to dominate, we will change our evolutionary tune.

5. Uniformity.

   If only a certain (now easily definable) few are Best, obviously whatever they are like is the only way to be. Everyone must try to be that way, or justifiably perish. It's for the betterment of mankind, you understand.

Darwin (-cum-Spencer) was cited by Lenin to justify the Bolshevik Revolution, Hitler to justify Naziism, and American industrialists to justify *laissez-faire* capitalism. (Darwin subscribed to none.)

In the early part of this century, when men wanted to justify what was increasingly a financial and political subordination of women, they claimed superiority: a "natural" entitlement to what they found they already had. Today, you find feminists trying to show *female* superiority. There are women calling themselves cultural anthropologists (even sporting degrees), who look at some of the societies about which we know the least, or at the cave drawings in France, and manage to see evidence of female dominant societies. The gender wars are the same old one-upmanship. If there are two or more of anything, one must be better: the Doctrine of Superiority.

The Ronald Reagan administration's economic policy was explicitly to give the greatest economic benefit to the few important people or entities of society. The ones who "drove" it, who were in a position to influence it;

the few that mattered. That benefit, the theory went, would "trickle down" to all others in "naturally" fair proportion.

"Primary caretaker," and all the above, are examples of our Superiority Cult. Some matter more than others; there is always a better or worse or most desirable; whoever comes out on top, should. This is seen as natural and inevitable. It takes many forms, but it's all the same. Reagan and everyone else simply saw themselves using "natural" laws.

However unpopular we think win-loose themes have become, there is still a pervasive, "I can only gain at someone else's expense." I can only have pride or power or strength or wealth by taking it from another. This is an echo of, "I can only *survive* at someone else's expense." Someone else's loss is my gain. As though there is only a finite amount of life, power, wealth, self-esteem, or anything.

Does any of this evolution mythology have merit? Or is it simply what Europeans found life like for themselves? Dog-eat-dog and survival of the fittest may only be an accurate description of an aberrant situation, not one typical or even common, certainly a context long since gone for us. Is it the way we want our society to be: the values we wish to drive it?

Be careful about what we are discussing. A *contest* can certainly be fun and satisfying. Always has been, always will. A test of skills, knowledge, even strength can and should be entertaining, strengthening, and help growth; it makes limits clear. Win-loose *games* are hardly horrible or shameful, but imputing *superiority* or personal worth into their results is open to question. Not so much to moralize whether good-bad things are themselves good or bad. It is awareness of where we are insidiously imputing such assumptions without realizing it so we can assess their validity.

We should, indeed, look to Nature for what most naturally drives us. But if we let Nature speak instead of projecting ourselves onto it, we may be surprised.

What is the reality of biological existence? Be warned that the superiority cult inevitably projected back into biology. Whether scientist or tradesman, you still see through your culture's eyes. At this time, however, the superiority theme and its biological justifications are increasingly considered dogmatic, Victorian evolutionism. Steven Jay Gould, for instance, part of the team that worked on the reinterpretation of the Burgess Shale of British Columbia, wrote many books, each displaying increasing frustration at getting his new perspective across to the public mind. He was up against the exact same thing as those seeking equality of parenthood: deep cultural biases.[23]

Even Euro-rooted scientists are realizing there is no such thing as evolution as in "progression". There is adaptation, and it is as chaotic as that to which life must adapt. There is no "natural selection," as though inevitable or predictable, as though there were any measure for better or worse, or for who will or deserves to thrive. There is no selection. Who survives is as chaotic as life's environment.

The new evolutionists are declaring two forces to biology: context (that to which life must adapt, its importance to all life the reason for its emphasis in Chapter 1), and chance (random events). None of which, I might in all honesty point out, rules out any "hand of God." For all science or any human can ever tell, both are evidence of exactly such a hand. Perhaps it's good to finally put such things back into His hands, not ours.

For science, life is a chaotic system. The fossil evidence is showing that species do not simply undergo constant, gradual change. New species do not appear at a steady, slow pace, any more than all in one day. Rather, they will remain stable for hundreds of thousands of years, showing only minor changes. Suddenly, there is a large die-out. Just as suddenly (within a few thousand, even hundred years), many new species appear as though from nowhere, far too quickly to be explained by gradual mutation.

The environment (earth) constantly changes. Randomly. Sometimes slowly, sometimes a lot at once. Who survives? It depends on whether you were a shoal creature when the oceans rose, or a day creature when the skies darkened. Who survives is as chaotic as the "order" of the universe. A solar flare, an impacting comet, a melting iceberg, a colliding continent. These things determine survival or "success." It has nothing to do with "superior" hooves, bigger teeth, beating out your neighbour, or saying your

---

[23]Disclaimer: In what follows I do not presume to speak on behalf of Steven Jay Gould or any of the other many scientists working in this area. What follows may not fully or most accurately reflect their exact thinking. The idea is to, as briefly as possible, give a flavour, to stimulate self-awareness and a critical eye. I encourage the reader to spend a little time in the library discovering what was kept from him in high school biology.

prayers at night. There is nothing inevitable or predictable. God is dispassionate about who flourishes or withers, whether individuals or species. Just that life strives. The whole.

Consider individuals within a species. Were you born during a season of plenty, or drought? Hardly matters what comprised your gene pool, does it? Does the drought winnow out the weak, or does it winnow indiscriminately? It is increasingly apparent that *chance* has a great deal more to do with thriving or surviving or carrying on, than any criteria for "better." This is as true for individuals as whole species.

Saying the drought only, or even mostly, eliminates the weak or those somehow less fit, is the same as saying when a nation sends a generation of its men to war, only the lousy ones are killed, the good ones return. Or the best warriors return. Or that the gene pool is improved or even meaningfully altered. Anyone who has been to war can tell you that bullets are as indiscriminate about which "good" people (or soldiers) they hit as "bad" ones spared. Good and bad, by whatever measure, return in equal proportion as left.

If a nuclear warhead falls on your city, will it kill only the weak? Then why would the draught, famine, or fire be in any way selective?

A few years ago, an attractive young Florida woman was infected with AIDS by her dentist. There was an outcry. How could this happen to such a bright, innocent thing? Just before dying, she testified before Congress. "I did nothing wrong, yet I got AIDS," she complained. Implicitly, homosexuals *deserve* AIDS. It's proof they are Bad.

The belief only Bad people get cancer or multiple sclerosis or AIDS, and Good people are healthy and rich – or survive wars, droughts, and famines – is still deeply part of us. "Survival of the fittest" is exactly this superstition: God, or Nature, favours The Best. Just the assumption there is such a thing as a "best" is clearly trying to read into nature what we want to be the case. There is absolutely no evidence to support it, any "reason" for survival is assumed, can only be projection.[24]

---

[24]This superstition is also the reason the dangers of smoking make it, not simply a risk, but tobacco and everything to do with it, Evil. So in true European form, we seek conspiracies from thirty years ago, a context in which even national

(continued...)

Today's princes are called billionaires and still held in high esteem. Bill Gates is one. Is he one because of some innate gift or superhuman effort for which he deserves great reward, or because of an accident of time-space? Yet many hold him in awe, assuming the former (the assumption of merit). There are many geniuses who are not billionaires, and many billionaires who are not particularly meritorious. Blessings and curses land on whoever is there at that place and time. We do not control all things.

There are many things in life we do control. There are many we do not. In trying to discriminate between them, we have a strong cultural bias toward the arrogant.[25]

What does happen in nature is some form of adaptation. When the context changes, so does life in accordance with it. Life is self-perpetuating. Indeed, that is its exceptional nature: the only system that does not display entropy.[26]

Okay, so what are the "rules" for adaptation, for generating new species? Isn't it the same "natural selection" based on the same best or fittest or most suited criteria? It does not appear so, but we move that discussion to the next section.

---

[24](...continued)
addiction research centres were declaring tobacco non-addictive.

[25]This trait is classically called "determinism": a belief in absolute Right, absolute Justice, absolute control. Interestingly, Heisenberg's Uncertainty Principle coincided exactly with the fall of the Russian Czars, Ottoman Empire, and Hapsburg Empire: the crumbling of absolute rule in Europe. This has not meant instant democracy. But the slow process is showing, and all absolutism, waning. We live in a universe of *degrees* of things – like success or truth or goodness or control – not absolutes. We are not gods.

[26] Life is special, different from all other systems of the universe. Any other system dissipates over time. It breaks down, seeking chaos. Consider life a single system covering the earth, within this chaos. It does not dissipate. Even given a varying environment, it has proven it will continue forever (barring sudden, extreme, change like falling into the sun, eliminating its environment). It does not consume (destroy, use up) its fuel or the forces sustaining it. The total mass of the earth has remained constant, more gaining slightly from outside. Rather, life may alter it, then itself adjust to the altered fodder. It constantly creates and re-creates itself, in whatever needed form. Self-perpetuation.

We Europeans have long seen progress. The horse exists today, its many relatives do not, therefore its single hoof must be "superior," and its relatives were ancestors on the way to the One True Horse. We are the only one of the *homo* genus to exist today, so the others must have been inferior. They *had* to die out. They are our *predecessors*, leading to us. This perspective is still taught in schools today. A bit self-serving, don't you think?

Bad news. There was never anything inevitable or superior about the horse or us. We just happen to be here now, at this one point in time. Simply part of the body of life that has no one "true" form, having no purpose we can discern other than simple continuation, continuation in *whatever* form it must be for its context. Our current existence is chance, and transient, same as for any species.

> It is only in appearance that time is a river. It is rather a vast landscape and it is the eye of the beholder that moves.
>   — *Thornton Wilder*

While we call dinosaurs and many others "unsuccessful" for not being around at this point in time, they existed for 100 million years. *Homo sapien sapiens* have existed perhaps 200,000. Tell me how successful or inevitable we are in another 20 million.

James Burke did a delightful series called *Connections* for the BBC. He traced the series of accidents and coincidences it took within our society to produce almost everything with which we are familiar today: the telephone, plastic, radio, jet propulsion, photography, the internal combustion engine. All the things presented to him in school as though one naturally led to the next turned out to be the result of totally independent events and pure chance. There was no well-defined linear connection from any one part of the development, say, of photography, to any other. Photography did not "develop," so much as come to exist. Chance meetings, errors pursuing something else, random events. Had other accidents occurred, other things would occupy our lives. It brought home how chaos is the most basic law of the universe.

Studies are finally being done to see what happens when there are too many of one species of a bird for an area to support, or too many males to females or visa versa. Do they fight it out to the death, only the strongest surviving, as Europeans see themselves always doing? No. Those who don't get nesting sites or mates this year simply don't mate that season. They hang around in the trees until their chance comes. Maybe it will come this year, maybe spares this year, major participants the next. The population stabilises without murder.[27]

Who thrives or passes on their genes is random. It has nothing to do with merit, or special skills, or beating others up. Rather, one's time comes, or it does not. When a resource becomes scarce relative to the population, new strategies for food, defence, and procreation develop, eventually resulting in a new species.

Progression? The dung beetle did not exist before mammalian dung. Is it an advancement from mammals, or an adaptation to? Viruses, often called a pre-life form as they are less than a cell, could not have existed until cells did, so cannot literally be a *pre*-life form. They only become active and multiply within a cell. Since they could only have come into existence after cells, are they an "advance"?

Life spreads in all directions, simply filling every nook. Which direction is "up" is mere opinion.

Intra-species strife is short-lived. Instead, some find a new way of living. The body adapts to the new demands of a changing context. (In this case, now crowded.) The new ones are different, whether they are better is a value judgement too easily self-serving.

What of strength? I watched a nature show the other day about polar bears. While watching cubs venture from their snowy den, the dramatic voice-over said, "This is an environment where only the strong survive." But if a tooth goes bad or you step on a thorn, all the strength in the world won't help. There are hundreds of skills. Physical strength is only one, and meaningless in many species. There is also luck. Yet North Europeans see only brute strength.

The feminists who insist women have always been oppressed by men, purely on the basis of men's greater physical strength (so obviously women have always only done what men forced them to), are just as guilty of

---

[27] One reference: Edited by Ian Newton, *Lifetime Reproduction in Birds* (London: Academic Press, 1989), especially see pp. 452 – 453.

valuing only physical strength and thinking only in its terms, not the myriad of other skills and talents available to them and any human, which are critical for a society to thrive.

Social Darwinians (in the United States, often called Republicans) have always amused me: Why go to all the bother of building a civilization, only to make of it a jungle?

And what of that uniformity pillar: Everyone should be like whoever seems most successful? It turns out that over-specialization (every member of a species being the same) is a one-way ticket to extinction. The Panda feeds on only one species of bamboo. When that bamboo experiences its cyclical die-out, the Panda's existence hangs in the balance. On the Hawaiian Islands are numerous specialized finches. Some eat only one kind of berry, others only nest in a certain tree formation. Any change to their environment, and they're gone.

Variety is most desirable. Because you never know to what changes you will have to adapt. What is "best" or most desirable today, will kill you tomorrow. Other things can suddenly become more needed.

There are now very few hunter-gatherer human societies. In two or three more generations, they will be gone, industrialization having overtaken the world. It will mean all humans are dependent on a single lifestyle. If we then have that Armageddon nuclear war, who of our species is equipped to carry on?

To see what Nature thinks of uniformity versus variety, look only to dogs, cats, or people. Are all individuals the same within each species, or are there even sub-groups?

Many years ago, when my younger brother was doing his post-graduate studies, he confessed that geneticists are saying that our improved medical care is harming mankind. Today, diabetics, hemophiliacs, people with cystic fibrosis, and others are living long enough to pass on their ("inferior") genes. The total gene pool is being degraded by defeating natural (read "superiority") selection. (Which, of course, assumes that we and what we do are not natural.) The purpose of much genetic research seems to be to prevent such people form being born. Both are expressions of the Doctrine of Superiority.

Perhaps increasing the variety of our "gene pool" is strengthening. Perhaps we are assuring ourselves greater versatility. Maybe we are wrong to regard these things only as defects. Are the people who have them, or their children, saying, "You should not have let me exist?" Are they saying, "Don't let anyone else like this be born," or only those inconvenienced by them? If our environment suddenly and radically changes, and some of these so-called defective people turn out the only ones who can cope, who is the defect?

The effect on our social policies of the dominance and uniformity themes is the perception: If I'm not dominating, I'm oppressed. Unless I'm on top and the only thing that is, I'm underneath. Indeed, much of feminist rhetoric seems so predicated. "If we don't get everything all our way, if our needs are not the only thing considered, you're oppressing us."

More Alternate Evolution: New Species

Classical European evolution theory asserts that adaptation is extremely slow and follows predictable, or at least identifiable, patterns of random genetic mutation. So if it is not trying to make the adaptation processes into a matter of superiority, it is trying to make it into a mechanical and chaotic one, robbing Life of its life. This assumes life's cont*ent* is random, not simply its cont*ext*, which helps us continue to rob life of its miracle.

Yet there is considerable evidence, not only of species springing up far more rapidly than genetic science can handle, but of purpose and intelligence to that springing. Not an external, moving-hand purpose, nor a mechanical formula. But a purpose from within the creatures themselves. Their own personal striving. The body knows it must adapt, and does so rapidly and to a specific goal.

It is easy to pick apart any of the evolutionary dogma. For instance, were the "laws" of selection true, there would be no women with small breasts nor men with small penises. They'd have been bred out of existence a hundred thousand years ago as less desirable. If sparrows are brown because it is a superior colour, bright colours attracting predators so only dull sparrows survive, and that's why they are brown, why are there brightly coloured parrots and budgies? If two eyes are superior to one, where are the species with four?

You can selectively breed dogs, as has been done for centuries, until you produce a new breed of dog. But it will still be a dog. Recognizably and unequivocally. You will not produce a goat, a camel or a fish. If even purposeful selection can't produce a new species, how can superiority selection, or even random selection? How can there be "selection"?

So from where do new species come? Surely there is more to this adaptation than any form of selection, if selection (which requires some form of superiority) there is at all.

A cell mutates, and does so randomly. Not a whole body all at once, not according to any scientific measure of mutation. But to develop a new feature like a bill, surely all the cells of an organ must undergo the identical change at the same time. Not to mention finding others of the species with whom to mate who are experiencing the same "chance" mutation, so it carries on or builds. How "chance" is any of this? What are the odds? And do the occurrences of new species support that rate? (No. They happen rapidly and in bunches.)

While plants existed on land for over two thousand million years, flowers only appeared 65 million years ago. They quickly appeared in seemingly unrelated species. Explain that. And if plants produce fruit so animals will carry their seeds by eating the fruit, didn't the plant have to "know" there were animals to produce it, not to mention what they would eat? Did plants bear fruit before there were animals to eat it? The evidence says no: only once there were. And if these features are mere chance mutations, where are the plants and animals with odd features having no purpose, but neither causing extinction?

Compose your own. It only takes slightly more imagination than the average scientist. It is difficult to say there is *no* purpose: no "intelligence" of some sort at work. It is just as difficult to assert that adaptation is pure, predictable mechanics.

Perhaps adaptation is not a matter of selection at all. Perhaps it is not a matter of what randomly comes into existence, then who dies and who thrives. Perhaps, instead, the body as a whole responds to new demands and opportunities in its environment. Perhaps adaptation is not some law of the universe like the law of gravity, mindlessly obeyed as an external force. Perhaps it is internally experienced by the being.

North Europeans saw superiority, hence, inevitability and progress. We did not stop there. We have also tried to impute mechanics and inevitability into adaptation, as though it was like building a clock. As though Life were just some set of formulas automatically (and hence, inevitably) obeyed. Life cannot be seen to have a will or existence of its own. We want ourselves to have been inevitable, as it would assure us eternity.

But the Egyptians, for instance, spoke of body wisdom. We often refer thinly to "instinct," but the former infers an intelligence (an awareness of need; desire) and will (striving; intent) by the body, not just by what we use as consciousness. Will and intelligence: life. After all, any biological entity is a living thing. All of it is alive, not just its mental consciousness. All the cells may want and strive as does a one-cell entity. The body "knows" and responds. It devises and effects strategy. Will and intelligence: the whole body responding at once to its environment.

Did the duck-billed platypus get its sensitive leather bill by some accidental, gradual mutation? The fossil evidence shows that it developed within only a few generations, and has not changed for several million years since. Possibly a group of one kind of creature started finding it could live on what they (as a group, whereas mutations occur to individuals, even only individual cells) could find on the pebbly bottom of an Australian stream. So, the body accommodated very readily. Not with the stroke of one sudden mutation, nor with hundreds of millennia of selective breading, nor with gradual, random mutation. Body wisdom. The body (the whole being) "knew" or sensed new demands or opportunities, and responded.

The point here is that the world is neither as hostile nor as cold as we imagine it, and therefore continue to make it. Rather, we are surrounded by wonders, mysteries, and miracles, yet came to carry ourselves with arrogance as though knowing all the secrets. There is nothing left to surprise us.

One begets the other, though, doesn't it? Fear of the world necessitates an insulating arrogance so we can be unaffected and pretend we are not afraid. Europeans lived for thousands of years in an unusually high state of fear. Our schools do not teach wonder, but that we have all the answers (and here they are, so learn them by rote), there is nothing for you to fear, nor discover. Pity, for there is much at which to wonder.

3. Different is Bad

Different was clearly a threat in Europe from at least 5,000 B.C to 1800 A.D. Anyone coming along who did not talk, act, or dress like "us" is a portent of strife, eyed with suspicion and alarm.

This is not common. Although any animal (including humans) will exercise caution on encountering the unfamiliar, there is as much curiosity (the strongest instinct: learning or exploring). To develop a reflex-like response of fear, threat, and need to destroy takes generations of negative experience. Further, in such a circumstance, anything reinforcing the comfort of sameness assumes greater significance.

Conformance is loyalty and safety. Difference is threat and is feared. It must be eliminated.

Up to the late 1800s, left-handed people in Europe were sometimes executed or simply mob-murdered. The word "sinister" means left-handed. I know left-handed people who were educated in Catholic schools in the 1960s. The nuns would rap their knuckles if they tried to write with their left hand. To this day they write right-handed, do everything else left-handed.

Most societies regard transvestites as something magical and promote them to priest or shaman. In our culture, we have long tried to kill them off. Many see them as a threat to family. That is, a threat to our assumption of and total conformance to our one model of family. A threat, simply by being different from our model of normalcy. Or perhaps, just a threat to a code of strict conformance to it.

The hatred North Euro-rooted peoples seem able to automatically muster for anything different is unparalleled. If you still think it's only right-wing people, consider the intolerance of the left. In Eastern Canada, in the 1990s, a man called Zundle wrote a small, silly booklet declaring the Holocaust a hoax: It never happened. This is like insisting the world is flat. He was, of course, one of those neo-Nazis. Though he'd committed no crime, wounded neither person nor property but only spoke his opinion, he was hounded and charged with crimes, frankly to the point of becoming a folk hero. This is violence and intolerance, not to mention self-defeating.

In the 1870s, Mary Lincoln, wife of the former U.S. president, was committed to a mental institution because she had "funny" habits like attending seances and keeping her money sewn to her petticoat. It had become the fashion to institutionalize anyone with unusual habits. We have long spent much effort to make our society one-dimensional, political correctness and feminism simply this year's example.

As a child of the 1970s with its Black Pride and Afro hairstyles, it is now disheartening to go to the northern U.S. and see not a single African American woman with natural hair. Everyone has it straightened or wears a European-style wig.

Different is bad; conformance, the only safety, the only acceptance.

Our problems with "different" infect our struggles with "equality." In the male-female debates of the early 1900s, were men saying women were inferior (unequal), or simply different, with their own "turf." Were they simply saying that women were separate from men though just as important? The word inferior was used, though not nearly as often as is represented today. Was the meaning "different"? Would anyone know today? Certainly both genders have always been guilty of considering themselves better than the other. Much of that is normal self-pride, not a wish to dominate.

And who is saying what today? Recall the "uni-sex" of the 1970s: Equality is sameness. When some of today's young women try to emulate men and maleness – seeing maleness as the ideal, seeing no intrinsic value to and contribution from femaleness in either their own or other's times, even seeking male power rather than female power – does that not make *them* the "male chauvinist?" Are they not the ones making it a male society? Have men ever really said women were without value to society, or have only some women?

Consider the opposite extreme (as all we have is extremes). In the U.S., as in South Africa, racial segregation was a formal *recognition* of differences. It was also, however, opportunity for mass oppression. Opportunity and public funding of social programs such as schooling could be withheld from one well-defined group to fatten the other. Different was made to mean inferior; injustice, justified.

Yet does integration mean denying differences, insisting everyone act, talk, and look the same? Should it be cultural genocide? All along, "American melting pot" has too often meant "everyone conform to an average norm." It suggests that only sameness is equal, or good, or valued.

Have we progressed? How good are we about people being different from ourselves? How good are we about ourselves being different from others?

That may be the real question: Do we accept ourselves as individual – different – and still see our connectedness to others? If not in ourselves, how in others?

4. Self-hatred: Shame and Guilt

You do not brutalize others unless you feel brutalized yourself. And hating others is only an extension of hating oneself. We are a shame-based culture.

Before founding the Lutheran church, Martin Luther was riddled with guilt. He couldn't sleep at night, almost always wore a hair shirt, and subjected himself to other common European self-torments for purification. (Suffering is good and purifies; pleasure a sin. Jolly lot, aren't we?) An inspiration, appropriately called a religious revelation, relieved this guilt, convincing him to pursue this vision to the point of excommunication from Rome. Salvation assumed new meaning: an immediacy. It could be realized on earth. Well, this sold like hot cakes.

The point is his initial state of constant guilt and shame. In this he was typical of Europeans, or his inspiration would have found little following. He was able to offer relief from a common European state. Europeans had long coined the term "original sin" and biblically justified it to describe this innate sense of unworthiness. The popularity of the original sin motif stands as testament to it as a part of normal European experience.

After all, if you live in constant fear – if you experience no "salvation," no relief from threat – after a while you just kind of figure you must deserve this horrid fate. Just as much as the king figures he deserves his. So this was the universal European experience of life: unworthiness. It is the sense of always being trampled and shoved aside, of not mattering. You can go to Scotland and see the remains of a stone-walled church where the tenant farmers were clustered with their families after being driven from their land during the Highland Clearances (1800s). There is graffiti from those people, "Glencalvie people, the wicked generation . . ." They handily blamed themselves for their misery.

Small wonder such a people would treat Arabs and Africans and Indians the same way: innately deserving of only ill treatment. So treated others assures that they are as undeserving as ourselves. It shares the shame.

We have a long history of shame. What follows is a more recent example of the Euro self-image:

> But common men are not, in any particular group, at any particular time, given as a whole to nobility of thought or of deed. Common men spend the majority of their free time and most of their excess energy in small, unpleasant activities which, in the aggregate, stay the advance of common man himself. Common men are greedy and superstitious, self-seeking and without trust – because they are not especially trustworthy themselves. They are clannish, narrow-minded anthropoids, hating work, hating novelty – but hating monotony also – backbiting, mean, cruel, grasping, insolent where they dare to be, and sullen, if not craven, in the presence of that which impresses them. The vast and vomitous outpouring of their vulgarity appalls and nauseates even themselves, at times, and hardly any common man is able to live with the others, even for a few hours, without some violent complaint, criticism, or reproach of his associates. The world of common men is worse than a monkey-world, because common men know better than what they do, to their consequent endless, bitter guiltiness.[28]
>
> — Philip Wylie, *Generation of Vipers*, 1942.

Irrespective of the platitudes of politicians seeking public favour, the above still represents the typical view of "other people" in our culture. It is held by almost everyone who comprises it. You see it in the women at coffee break cackling over some awful neighbourhood event, making it sound like everyone is to be feared. You see it in the men sneering at some other group, be that group defined by profession, company, income, or race. It is the reason the right-wing insist on leaving the "weak" (or unlucky) by the side of the road to perish; equally the reason the left-wing insist everyone

---

[28]Philip Wylie, *Generation of Vipers* (Dalkey Archive Press), p. 101. ISBN 1-56478-146-1.

needs their enlightened guidance, needs them to run their lives and kindly explain right from wrong. We still think very little of ourselves, commonly displayed in our view of others.

The above passage is strikingly reminiscent of how we, just a generation or two ago, described Africans, Arabs, or Indians ("monkey-world"), or any other people we brutalized.

It is our *self*-image. It is our self-hatred, projected onto others. Wylie's description ". . . backbiting, mean, cruel . . . insolent where they dare to be, and sullen . . ." describes his own tirade. The book is called *Generation of Vipers*, is he not a prime example? This man hates himself, turning it to others.

> You never hate your brother for his sins, but only for your own. Whatever form his sins appear to take, it but obscures the fact that you believe them to be yours, and therefore meriting a "just" attack.[29]
>
> — *A Course in Miracles*

Corollary: The more free of sin (or guilt or worthlessness) am I, the less I see in others. The more worth I see in myself, the more appears in others. It's a miracle. What needs healing is our own self-image. Not other people.

We have only started being magnanimous towards other cultures in the last one or two generations, even taking a genuine interest in Native American cultures, Oriental religions, and so forth. This only came once we created a sense of security, which, for us, only came with world domination.

Victorian morals, and its daughter political correctness, use social shaming to rule. That means they are effective on us. We kowtow easily. Witness the growing number of men actually ashamed of being male, even apologizing for it. That's power. I heard a television hostess elude to "the infamous testosterone," as though taken for granted that maleness is innately evil. And men buy this. Nobody challenged her.

Social workers are trained in the art of using guilt and shame to bully their clients, to impose their own values (or their carrying of society's).

---

[29] *A Course in Miracles* (Viking Press,1996), p. 651. ISBN 0-670-86975-9.

They call it "confronting." The shame-blame-righteousness syndrome is a multi-billion-dollar-a-year industry: Fleet Street in Britain, television "magazines" from *60 Minutes* to *Sally Jessy Raphael* in the U.S. It is insidious.

In 1562, three Brazilian natives were taken to France and exhibited to the boy king Charles IX:

> The King talked with them for some time; they were shown our way of living, our magnificence, and the sights of a fine city. [I] asked them what they thought about all this, and what they had found most remarkable. [They said] they had noticed among us some men gorged to the full with things of every sort while their other halves were beggars at the doors, emaciated with hunger and poverty. They found it strange that these poverty-stricken halves should suffer such injustice, and that they did not take the others by the throat or set fire to their houses.
> — Montaigne. Essay, *On Cannibals*

Europeans have long, not simply accepted, but died defending systems which oppress them. (Well, it's *our* abuse and we'll protect it like any good tribalist!)

The remarkable thing about Custody-Access-Support, is how little rebellion or outcry there is against it. Depending on jurisdiction and what is considered compliance, between 63 to 84 percent of men subjected to it actually go along with it. This is a society of wimps. Or, more accurately, a society of men conditioned to resignation, conditioned to not mattering, to being kicked around.

Healing self-hatred is needed. A little structural reinforcement would go along way. Even just stop the bullying.

Being patronizing is no help. That only diminishes, being an expression of the same low regard.

5. Disassociation

Disassociation is a symptom of trauma.

If our society has a mythology, it is disassociation. We see ourselves separate from nature, never part of it. We speak of animals as distinct from humans as though separate forms of life. (We are as animal as they, and the sooner we embrace this the more readily we may deal with, even enjoy, ourselves.) We think of nature as something separate from us. But we and all we do is as much part of it as is anything else. Those careless toward nature and those who insist no animal should be in a zoo are equally displaying the same disassociation. Why not extend to such fellow creatures as we can what benefits to our civilization may exist, such as regular meals, medical care, and freedom from attack?

We are the only culture to have separated religion and science. Not merely separate: at odds. Physical world separate from spiritual, in different universes.

Work and home are separate lives, independent of each other. Even for us, it was not long ago that work and home were indistinguishable. True for a tenant farmer and a tradesman. We send our children to institutions, are not involved in their learning, and do little to impart our own knowledge. Learning is separate from home and family, as is religion, and separate again, philosophy or outlook. These all used to be indistinguishable. The disconnections have been escalating exponentially.

Why do we watch movies? Because at least ninety percent of our self, our psyche, experiences it as real – as really happening. Otherwise we wouldn't watch. So when the entertainment industry parades studies and expert opinion that children (not just adults) "know" that all that television violence is not real and are not affected by it, it is outright denial. As is all disassociation. Yet we accept it.

We have one body of law for crimes against society (criminal law), and a separate one for crimes against an individual (torts, or civil law). How can you say society is the victim of a theft, but an individual is the only victim of cheating? What's the difference? How can you say society is the victim of a physical assault, but only the individual a victim of character assault? Sometimes a crime is not a crime, and sometimes it is both.

We think the Holy Trinity (God the Father, Son, and Holy Ghost: the mind, body, and spirit) is something external, not that it is a description of our own self. We try to deal with pregnancy independent of sex, as though they have nothing to do with each another. We distinguish things that are indistinguishable (like means and ends), yet enmesh things not necessarily related (like marriage and parenthood). We claim to separate church and state to not require one religion, yet cannot distinguish a person's private, personal life from their performance of public office, and impose a single morality (religion) to which we do not ourselves adhere. (The Royal Family, Bill Clinton).

If our society were an individual within itself, it would be committed.

John Romer, archeologist – and as often the case with archeologists, one of the best cultural anthropologists around – traces the earliest signs of our disassociations to the roots of the Renaissance in the early 1300s. This is when we started to move from a profound world to a profane one. We started to move from a sense of sacredness toward everything around us, from participation with God, to all things being objects of study. The mind alone, no soul or body. The lost Trinity. He uses the Bible to show our general loss of oneness with nature:

> Just as the modern secular world has separated abstract beauty from its images, so the Bible has lost the golden covers that it wore for a thousand years and changed into paperback: the Bible has become a book. And piety cannot replace the golden covers once again, as some Victorians would try to do; that [the flux of new religions from the 1600s to the 1840s, but equally applies to today's New Wave — KC] was a work of reaction and imitation and was not born in simplicity and innocence. The terrible threat of this loss of innocence had hung over Europe for several centuries and people fought and died around the issue. The new vision had begun to grow inside Europe in the late Middle Ages. Indeed, the Bible's slide from sacred to profane may be said to have been started, though inadvertently, by that most gentle Tuscan scholar, the poet Petrarch. For Petrarch popularized the awareness and the love of style, a fascination with form, with the abstract beauty of words and of nature. In many ways, this was the birth of modern man.[30]

He is describing the beginning of loving beauty for beauty's sake, divorced from its connection to, and involvement with, daily life. It is the beginning

---

[30] John Romer, *Testament. The Bible and History* (Michael O'Mara Books Ltd., 1988), p. 289. ISBN 1-85479-005-6.

of, instead of singing, having specialists sing, who we watch. Instead of joking with friends, watching a comedian. It is the beginning of what this book is doing: not participating in life, but examining it. It is disassociation from living life, from active participation with God.

Our Industrial Revolution began in the late 1700s and is now in the technology and services leg. It is likely not yet over, though slowing, and is the latest manifestation of this aberrant disassociation. Distance from nature makes it infinitely more possible to study and manipulate. This has brought us tremendous material wealth. More than anyone could ever have imagined could exist.

It has come at great cost. Great ecological cost, social cost, and spiritual cost. We used to have stability. We all used to know that we definitely belonged to a larger scheme, and exactly where. We knew our contribution.

Note the implication. Industrialization is aberrant, not natural or inevitable. It is a product of much of what troubles us, a symptom of why the Native American is (or was) serene and noble, we, ill at ease and fidgety. It is our separation, further from the Garden of Eden than any human imagined. We do not see ourselves as part of the universe, but the universe as something to put in a beaker or under a microscope. The detachment might have started with beauty, but it continued to all of nature, becoming science. We now seek relatives on distant planets and imagine settlements on Mars, rather than seeing ourselves as the product of our own planet, our relatives around us.

Don't get me wrong. Now that I have airconditioning, I'm certainly not giving it up. And industrialization is likely the only reason we no longer have slavery. But to what lengths are we taking the underlying disassociations, and to what purpose? Has anything other than the material quality of life improved? Not that that is without meaning. But alone, it may be.

Everyone today seems so pre-occupied with speculations about life on other planets, one has to ask: What if we're all there is? What if there really is no life on other planets? Has anyone considered that? What if, in the end, our planet turns out to be the only one in the universe that has ever, or will ever on its own, produce Life? What if we're it?

Scary, isn't it? Why is it scary, because it faces us with our uniqueness and preciousness?

If we still saw the universe limited to this *terra firma* and contained by the sky, if we had no notion of other planets but still believed ours was the entire universe, would we return to regarding it as sacred? Would we recapture our close connection? Perhaps our speculation about other life is merely another capitulation of our responsibilities, another extreme in disassociation.

Rome

Here we are in Central and North Europe in 150 B.C., wild tribes whose idea of battle is to paint ourselves and whoop in chaotic charge, and living in trees. When in march thousands of Romans. Legions, dressed the same, marching in unison, glittering. Tens of thousands at once in perfect, orderly lines, followed by still greater opulence. Machines never heard of. Writing. Money to facilitate trade. Stone buildings. So many foreign practices, and so powerful. Imagine the impact, the awe. It was overwhelming.[31]

The impact of Rome on Europe (us, the barbarians) was similar to that of Europeans on African and American Natives some 1,700 years later. The newcomers were so different, powerful, and confident, our gods were destroyed. Everything we'd known about the universe before was gone and made meaningless in one day. What we have and are is no good. "Good"

---

[31] One of the great Euro-chauvinisms, well represented by J. Bronowski's 1974 book and miniseries, *The Ascent of Man*, is considering civilization a continuum. Egypt to Greece to Rome to (ta da) us. (Note the implication of progress and merit in "Ascent." Whether we are better than any before us, rather than simply here at this time, is a value judgment some may dispute.) We would rather identify with the lineage of previous civilizations than our more humble origins, see ourselves the new, improved guardian of all that has ever been noble, not to mention omitting all the other great civilizations of other continents. Evolution/progress.

While any society steals what conveniences it from others with which it has contact, it has its own roots and life. A more useful view of societies is flat in both time and place, considered side by side. We Europeans were the barbarians who overran Rome. We are not the Romans. Every so often a society assumes a degree of complexity that may be called a civilization. This is a random event having more to do with reaching a critical population density than any "awakening," and each civilization is unique, bred of its own context. North Europe society (including its many transplants) is simply the most recent to become a civilization (maybe three hundred years). Typical of most such, it has been full of itself ever since.

– or at least power, all things desirable – is someone else's. It is external and foreign. The best we can do is imitate.

Like African countries trying to copy a European notion of nationhood and government not native to themselves, Rome remains our image of civilization to this day. (As does Greece, only because Rome emulated it.) Civilization and all that is good or powerful is something foreign, not us ourselves.

Most still speak of the Roman Empire as though it was admirable, the definitive civilization, our measure of greatness. Still today, when we wish to coin a new official term in biology, medicine, or law, we turn to Latin or Greek. They are the ultimate well from which to draw validity and authority. Not our own, limited background. (Or does it only seem limited the more it is forgotten, replaced with someone else's?)

Latin was a required course in most high schools until the 1950s. Latin! Unused for fifteen hundred years; never the native tongue of England, Germany, or Scandinavia. *Czar* is Russian for Caesar. The Hapsburg empire, and any other that dominated Europe until the 1920s, used the eagle as their emblem. It is the symbol of Imperial Rome. The implication was explicitly to adopt Rome's authority. Enter a Euro-Christian church with its vaulted ceiling and stained-glass windows, you have entered a Roman palace. We even retain Rome's view of Attila the Hun as a demented barbarian. He fought Rome on behalf of North European tribes.

From Roman occupation (circa 100 B.C.) to late in the Industrial Revolution, when Europeans wanted to make themselves noble, they emulated their idealized image of Romans. It is from here we get the North European image of a father as cool and detached from his children. While this was attempted by maybe 0.2 percent of Europeans until recently, since it was the nobles, it became the ideal to which all would strive.

Such is Rome's lasting impact. It is the source of all that is valid, of all authority, even our image of God. It is our adopted lineage.

Rome was an extortion culture. It is said that Julius Caesar rose to prominence by owning Rome's only fire department. A wealthy house would catch fire and he'd arrive to dicker over its price before extinguishing it. ("It won't be worth that for long.") Rome commonly took over countries (Greece, for one) by threatening annihilation, simultaneously holding out the option of peaceful but total subjugation.

Rome was also an absorption culture. They invented nothing, adopting all they could from the civilizations they conquered. (At one stage they conquered as much out of envy as fear.) "Roman arches" are Etruscan. "Roman togas" are Greek, whom they admired most. Japan today is a similar culture in this regard: copying all they can from others and utilizing it to the fullest.

The Romans did have their ingeniousness, but creativity and innovation were not among them. Individual selfhood was not among them. They excelled at what one might call "organization". Brilliant administrators. Order. It was ruthlessly enforced, but infinitely clear. The Germanic peoples took to this like ducks to water. To the free-spirited Celts, however, this imposed, externally devised "perfect order" was anathema. (The Celts are the people of the Holy Grail myths: Each individual seeking their own ultimate answer, their own personal source of life.)

What Rome was good at and admired for would today be called fascism. The lineage is unmistakable: austere straight lines, raw power, militarism, unquestioned obedience, firm rule. Some still consider Rome admirable.

Then Rome became The Church. It trans-muted, remaining the one and only great authority of Europe for all time, long after the material empire was dismantled. Europe still needed a Rome, couldn't live without it. Or didn't want to live without an ultimate, higher authority.

It was a reverse takeover. Rome took over Christianity, not so much Christianity, Rome. Rome assumed the mantle of Christianity, and in this form assured itself eternal life. As soon as Rome declared itself Christian, all other religions were repressed with greater vigour than Christianity had ever endured. Rome did not so much become Christian as Christianity became Roman, an expression of and vehicle for it.

Rome's place in our mythology was assured by the "darkness" that followed its leaving.[32] By 500 A.D., Rome was gone. By the 700s, the Arab

---

[32] Another great Euro-chauvinism: "The *world* in darkness" is used to describe the years from classical Rome to the Italian Renaissance. Europe may, today, consider this a period of "darkness" for itself, though even that is debatable. But these centuries were when India and China, already thousands of years old and also part of *the world*, continued to thrive; the Arab world became expansionist and rivalled the size and grandeur of Rome; Mesoamerica became very sophisticated in

(continued...)

Empire started to expand into Europe. Who was to stop them? They also took over the legendary cities of the Bible. In 1066, England was invaded yet again and taken by the Normans. The migrations returned; the law was whatever anyone was strong enough to enforce, no longer one steady, predictable force, however narrow. In 1241, Batu Khan (the Mongolians) took Budapest. Everyone knew they were next, but all they could do was flock to the churches in terror and tremble. There had been six hundred years of order and stability: *Pax Romana*. Now it was back to inferior little anybody's booty. Those nice, peaceful days of stability under Rome were looked back upon with increasing nostalgia. Rome was ultimate anything and everything. Anyone attempting order or protection – or simply seeking power – would have to carry its banner.

What did Rome leave us?

- Reinforced inferiority
- Externalization of authority
- Mind control

The first can also be seen coming from the migrations; the two experiences reinforced each other. But the last two are distinctly from Rome and its occupation.

1. Inferiority

Rome reinforced the lessons of the migrations. When Shakespeare wrote a play that was not for the flattery of the current Tudor monarch, its locale was either modern Italy or ancient Rome. No place north of that. Anything worthwhile was regarded to be elsewhere, not within ourselves. We were nothing.

---

[32](...continued)

agriculture and astronomy, wealthy enough to build cities whose size and complexity dwarfed anything in Europe until the 1800s. Europeans, however, returned to the trees.

Not until the 1800s did anyone in Northern Europe see Northern Europe itself worthy of attention.[33] That is, only once we entered our own expansionist phase and found we could treat others the way we saw ourselves as having been treated. Only conquest made us valid in our own minds. After all, that was what made Rome. We still study only kings and wars as history, only give credence to other expansionist societies and conquering peoples.

2. Externalization of Authority

There is only one authority for all things. It is external, imposed, and absolute. Two thousand years later, that motif retains its stranglehold.

There being external authority (however much it originates from human beings) is not the problem. There has and always will be some, that being what a society is. The problem is exclusivity: The notion that *all* legitimacy and authority is external, and that only *one* such authority exists for all things.   This was simply Rome itself, imposing central control. We internalized this (Rome, after all, was father-everything) and have lived by it in different forms ever since. These forms might be a religion, a country ("god and king"), or The Law. In all cases, there is one and only one authority, it is external to humans, is absolute, and the only source of validity.

To understand what is being described, realize that Jews argue with God. One on one. Rabbinical councils have been known to decide, "God is wrong." Can you imagine Euro-Christians ever thinking this? In our world, authority is absolute, unquestionable, and external. It is unquestionable exactly because it is external. We can't touch it.

What is the difference between Jews and North Europeans? I call it the lost Trinity. The Trinity (God as Father, Son, and Holy Ghost) is seen as existing outside ourselves, not as a representation of ourselves. (Father: wisdom and knowledge, the mind. Son: the flesh. Holy Ghost: spirituality;

---

[33]The birth of Holland can be seen as the start of a truly independent North Europe Civilization.

the ineffable qualities of existence.) Whereas for most peoples, God is not external. He is personal, inner experience.

Our architecture has always emphasised vertical lines. From church steeples to skyscrapers, all dominant lines reach up. Contrast this to Chinese architecture, the Forbidden City an example. The dominant lines are horizontal. These are a people who have arrived. They are comfortable with who and where they are.

All authority being external relies on and reinforces inferiority.

1. Anything right or valid is external, not from within. God is high up, far beyond our reach (our churches' steeples), all powerful, not questioned. Authority on anything is not personal; only "others" know.

2. We (the barbarians) are unworthy (by nature, uncivilized); not a valid measure of anything. We need the external to tell us when and whether we are any good. This is the lack of validity to own's own self, to our own, personal experiencing of life, and our own judgment.

Note that the lost Trinity is a very potent disassociation. Disassociations have been building for a long time.

Sigmund Freud described three layers to the human psyche: the animal id (animal in the bad sense), the individual ego, and the civilized super-ego, which was the internalized "voice" of society (external authority) and kept the others social. This was not a new view. Indeed, psychiatry and psychology have always simply studied their own culture, not humanity.

Shortly after World War II, William Golding wrote *Lord of the Flies*. In it, a group of children are shipwrecked on a deserted island (a favourite British theme). Without adults to "discipline" them – without external authority to keep order and civility – they degenerate into gratuitous violence, as though human nature to do so when left to itself. It was a very popular book. It was one of our homages to "law and order." Because goodness knows, you can't trust human nature. We are innately evil (id).

Our culture carries a basic belief that our inner, most personal, and deepest selves are not simply invalid, but to be feared. Bad. The devil's throne. This is the opposite assumption of Eastern religions and almost every other people. Most *seek* their inner voice. We fear and hide from it.

In any case, has anyone wondered from where those externally imposed civilizing constraints come? People write laws and devise convention. But if people create laws, what happened to evil human nature when doing that? There would seem a contradiction. Perhaps only a few people are Good. The ones God put at the top with that "if I'm king it's pre-ordained" thing.

So we see the roots of some common European motifs. Only the chosen few have a private line to God and know how things ought to be. The majority ("other people") must be forced into civilized behaviour. Only an external authority (whether the law, Divine Right, or political correctness; same thing) maintains human decency. We know what's best for you. Etc., etc. All the usual European excuses for slavery or running other people's lives and otherwise abusing them. Because we do not love ourselves; commonly hold ourselves and hence others in contempt and suspicion.

Yet we call ourselves a democracy. I have seen kingdoms where the people are more free, because they are respected for being as human as the king, not assumed to be dogs. (Not everyone equates king with god.[34])

Today, the common North European right-wing stance is still that the only effective motivator is a whip, or jail, or threat of starvation, because people, especially faced with benevolence, just wouldn't do anything, certainly not the Right Thing (what we want). The common left-wing perception is that people have been misled or somehow "need our guidance," leading them to imposing *their* values. The same low esteem of people. Not much to choose.

Is your God inner experience or external authority? Which is to say, is He inner or external authority? Which do you most honour?[35]

---

[34] In the Arab world, for instance, Ross Perot would be a king. He's simply the guy with all the money and thousands of people working for him. A state is more akin to a corporation. Not everyone imputes divinity into their rulers and governments and statehood as Europeans are still inclined to, from Divine Right to the "sacredness" of The Office of the President. Projecting our own cultural habits onto others is a good way to fool ourselves into inappropriate action.

[35] Possibly the best answer is, "Give unto Caesar that which is Caesar's."

3. Mind Control

If you come from a Euro-Christian background and begin studying other religions, after a while, one thing leaps out at you. Almost all other formal religions deal with behaviour. Only European Christianity deals in beliefs: what is in the head. When European writers describe other religions they start with beliefs. But this is because of us, not the people about which they write. What we call systems of belief, are systems of practice.

(A qualifier. Eastern religions – far less formally definable, such as Taoism, Hinduism, and Buddhism – deal with personal experience and wisdom. The more formal Middle Eastern religions like Judaism and Islam, are mostly codes of conduct. Still, neither set deals with beliefs as does European Christianity.)

The Hebrews go from the Ten Commandments to the price and treatment of a slave, to a daughter's marriage, to the treatment of a cataract. Jewish law deals with how man behaves toward others: social behaviour. In increasing detail. There is nothing about how to think, nothing on what to believe. Only behaviour. For it is your behaviour toward others that makes you rightful. What is in the heart or mind touches no one directly, so is irrelevant. You can believe and openly argue anything (even with God), and still be a good Jew, so long as your behaviour is respectful of others.[36]

Islam emphasises the "straight path:" rightful behaviour. The five pillars include not simply "thou shalt pray," but exactly when (five specific times a day), what is said, and how. Not simply charity as a principal, but exactly how much, to whom, and how often. Social behaviour. Not beliefs, not mental images. The beliefs are: "I believe in Allah and Mohammed is his prophet." That's it. Nothing more nor less; that makes you a Muslim. From then on, it's conduct toward others.

But Euro-Christianity's very premise is the Nicene Creed, devised for Constantine's 325 A.D. ecumenical council. "I *believe* in God the Father

---

[36]There is another interesting contrast between European Christianity and Judaism: Other people decide whether you are a Christian. Others decide whether you are baptised, may take communion, have last rights, or are buried in holy ground. Others may excommunicate you. This is a powerful dependency.

If you are a Jew, God can't take that away. That is The Covenant.

Almighty . . . " and in this and in that, etcetera. What is in the mind. Nothing about how to behave toward people. (Which, among other things, means European Christians can *do* just about anything and still be a Christian. Which all too often has been the case.)

Initially, Rome was a secular state. They had their traditional gods, but, as an absorption culture, were as interested in others'. Foreign customs and beliefs were originally interesting and welcomed. They had no interest in imposing their own customs, enjoying the variety pulled within their frontiers. Their only interest – Rome's concept of empire – was simply tax collecting. Tribute. That, and the richness of others' learning, was what was "in it" for them.

There are many stories of centurions being disciplined, even crucified, for offending local customs. Local customs were to be respected, even honoured. It made tax collecting easier. Why would they complicate that?[37]

Religious and cultural intolerance did start to rise around Julius Caesar's time (the time of Jesus), when there became more "them" than "us". Rome's size and dominance was already becoming a little tiresome, even to the Romans. Having learned all they cared to from others, the sense of threat from things non-Roman (which, by then, was mostly Greek anyway), grew. So by about the first century A.D., there was some official suppression of what were regarded as fringe religions, Christianity among them. Rome started to fear or be concerned about what people had in their heads, and would welcome a way to control it.

Then Rome assumed a religion. And persecution of all other religions took on a ferocity never before seen. Religious intolerance was instantly part of Christianity, for some increasingly important political reasons.

It was a shift in Roman administrative approach. Rome, built on the unquestioning loyalty of its own people, was losing control of its far-flung empire, there being proportionately fewer of its "own" people, especially in its army. On what could Rome rely? After several hundred years, a deteriorating confidence in loyalty is hardly surprising. (It is said the real

---

[37] Here, Rome and European fascism (never restricted to Germany, Spain, Italy, nor the 1930s) definitely diverge. Rome was, if anything, benevolent. While they certainly saw themselves superior, this did not mean they saw their guests (conquered peoples) as subhuman, worthy of contempt. Contempt – the extreme hatred of "lesser peoples" – is distinctly European.

historical question of the decline and fall of Rome is not why or how, but what took it so long?)

Suddenly, a secular state assumes an official religion, repressing all others. Rome had discovered a new way to unite and control its empire, something with which it had hitherto not concerned itself as it had never had to: beliefs. What it had always received from its subjects was total personal commitment. Not just behaviour, but behaviour rooted in the inner person. They found a way to express that expectation from those not born to Rome. Constantine, already a god-king, converted to Christianity to unite with a god that had no ethnic identity, but was growing in popularity throughout his diverse empire. He united that belief with obedience to Rome, tying it to earthly authority. Divine Right was born: Constantine relinquished his own divinity to be God's representative. So what people had in their heads and hearts became the business of the state: the business of society.

In this unification of empire and religion, behaviour is secondary to a person's internals (perceptions, beliefs, and thinking). During the Inquisition, you were not dragged off the street and tortured for your behaviour. There were criminal laws and sheriffs for that. It was your beliefs they were after: how and what you thought. After all, when the beliefs are there, the desired behaviour follows. And the only behaviour in which we have interest is obedience, not respecting others, which may or may not suit our purposes.

Society's business now lay beyond behaviour, into a person's mind and soul. This for central control, not social order. For Europeans, this was the unification of church and state. Protestantism fought against it some fifteen hundred years later, and thought they'd won. They only won in appearance: the mechanics of church and state. The precedent that society's business extends to what its members think, remains.

Today, when you hear, "We have to change peoples' attitude," you are hearing that continued presumption. We used to call it propaganda, now we have politely "public awareness campaigns." It isn't enough for people to behave respectfully toward others, people must think the right way. And just as true today, this is to serve central control, not social order, already governed by its own rules as we shall see later.

Consider how afraid we are of someone "poisoning our minds" or those of others, especially our children's. This is saying we do not expect people to think for themselves, fearing in others what we treasure for ourselves. While professing a conviction for free thought on one hand, we try to control it on the other.

I found the following inscription on the wall of a grade one classroom. It comes from a children's cartoon series:

> The I-Care Rules
> 1) We listen to each other.
> 2) Hands are for helping, not hurting.
> 3) We use I-Care-Language.
> 4) We care about each other's feelings.
> 5) We are responsible for what we say and do.

Lovely, isn't it? It's what every parent wants their child to learn. There is only one problem. The only thing those children are learning are the words, not the behaviour. Because it hardly matters how much propaganda we apply, our children will only learn to treat others the way they are treated by us. Behaviour. And it won't be many years before they realize their parents' hypocrisy, just as my generation did over the Viet Nam war, and other things.[38]

Another effect of focussing on thinking is that behaviour is as often ignored or excused. "He had good intentions." Well, Adolf Hitler had the best of intentions. He strove for what he thought would most benefit his people. What more could you ask of a leader? Yet what he did was abominable. Do a person's intentions or thoughts matter to society, or behaviour? If someone murders your daughter, does it matter whether he was in love with her or a serial killer? If we make it clear what behaviour

---

[38] There is a glaring omission of socialization skills in these "I-Care Rules:" assertion; speaking up for one's self. If someone *does not* listen to you, what do you do? If someone uses hands (not to mention words) for hurting instead of helping, what do you do? These are the real socialization issues.

So what are those promoting this trying to say, that "caring" is only about others, not oneself? That they want a society of people concerning themselves only with others' needs and never their own? Are we simply teaching the old Euro inferiority complex: Others matter more than me?

is acceptable, people can think and believe what they will. What is in the heart and head is one's own business, not society's. Only behaviour is social.

Given these traditions of not trusting ourselves nor having confidence in others; of disassociations; of intolerance of differences, even thinking differently; given the terrors of the migrations and authoritarianism of Rome and their lasting effects, we can turn to the specific mythologies currently supporting the structure our society imposes on those so foolish as to divorce.

3) Myth 1 – Women Have Children

The first of the five myths blocking a presumption of joint parenting addresses the general father-elimination from family (what I call de-patrification) that has been a strong trend in our culture for many generations. While not unique to our culture, we have taken it to great extremes.

This subject leads us into the middle of our on-going gender wars, as feminists fight to keep children and family to themselves. Dealing with that, however, is largely relegated to footnotes, because these wars are a symptom, not an underlying cause.

Our belief that only women have children is also supported by a fixation on the mechanics of everything.

The Magic of Mother

It is common only to long-time warrior-expansionist societies – like the Greeks and Romans – to separate patriarchy from family. It serves making men into permanent warriors who go great distances for long periods, possibly to never return. Although it is rare for a society to "pop-off" into expansionism and become that militaristic, they are the only ones we study, the only ones we consider worthy of our attention and to which we compare ourselves. Which says something about us. China, for instance, with all its power and wealth, which could easily have conquered all Asia and Europe had it inclination, stayed within her own frontiers. China always courted minimal contact with others, even trade often discouraged. When you read European historians recounting this you find them baffled, as though there must be something wrong with these people. Everyone is *supposed* to be expansionist. People satisfied with where and what they are confuse us. We call them complacent; something's wrong with them.[39]

Our degree of militarism is rare in human social history. Just a full-time professional army is extremely rare among all societies that have ever existed. And warrior is a narrow perception and use of maleness. The energy "maleness" certainly has to do with sanctuary definition and maintenance. Aggression, just by its narrowness, is a perversion. And men do not do this, but a society. (Of which women have always comprised at least one-half, last I looked.)

Nothing promotes such narrow expression of maleness to prominence like fear. Warrior dominance is rare because of the amount of fear required to effect it over long periods. Examine your favourite warrior society and look for the intense fear base. In Sparta, two-thirds of the population were slaves; waring cities. In Shogun Japan, centuries of warlords on a crowded island. In Rome, a large slave population, and conquer or be conquered by others (population press, Etruria and Cartage only among the factions).

Contrast these fear-based societies to, say, early Mesoamerican societies (Incan, Mayan, etc.) and their emphasis on equal balance between maleness and femaleness. There was equal significance for diverse natures; the sun and moon were equally honoured. This is by far the more common motif among societies. (Despite feminist mythology of endless oppression.)

---

[39] The plot of numerous early *Star Trek* episodes involved coming upon an idyllic society where all enjoyed contentment, and finding ways to disrupt it so they, too, could "progress." Add our "evolution" and inevitability themes and everyone "by nature" must become what we have. Industrialization is inevitable, and if it doesn't happen, there's something wrong with you.

The other day I watched a PBS show of an American travelling in Africa. Despairing of the material poverty of one country he said, "If the West stood still for a thousand years, this country would still not catch up." We do not see ourselves as different, but advanced. Superior. Our only evidence is material wealth.

Those people have been successfully living "that way" for tens of thousands of years. We, less than a hundred. Should we last so long, we might be entitled to some pride. We are materially wealthier than any could have imagined, capable of supporting a population of billions.. Are we ever satisfied? Content?

In another segment, the same tourist pointed out that those people were able to make a party and have a very good time with each other out of a long train delay which drove him batty. Have others as much wealth as we, simply in different forms?

If that African nation stood still for a thousand years, we may never catch up.

3) Myth 1 – Women Have Children 71

There has never been a "male-dominant" society, whatever that means, men having never comprised more than half of any population or it would have trouble surviving. There have certainly been male*ness*-dominant societies, and which, to repeat, a society as a whole does, always initially out of defence: a response to fear. There have also likely been femaleness-dominant societies, though the evidence is less clear. Minoa, the Mohawks, and Etruria are possible candidates, though more likely examples of balanced ones. (We're getting into matters of opinion and relativity. Warrior societies, however, are unmistakable.)

One would have to regard either as equally unhealthy. They are responses to unusual circumstances, and their occurrence rare in the annals of human societies when stacked against the totality of those that have existed.[40]

---

[40] For the academic at heart, I will be more detailed. It is certainly true that when Europeans came upon the tribes of New Guinea and the Amazon, we found societies in a constant state of conflict with neighbours. (Exactly as the Scots and Slavs and European tribal societies.) Indeed, for Amazonians, battle is second only to snakebite as the most common cause of death to those surviving infancy. What does this tell us about natural societies, war, and warrior societies? First, two observations.

a) War, for us, involves a specific enemy and goals. It is constant, total fighting until those goals are met, or both sides tire. For a tribal society (the Scots, *et al.*) there is rather a persistent state of rivalry. While most of any individual's time is spent on the normal pursuit of family survival (food and shelter), every so often a group goes off on a raiding party. It relieves boredom. So one could say all members of the society are always warriors, or one could say that these "parties" are exactly that: the occasional, infrequent (two to three a year), fling. Still, ongoing conflict would seem a part of the so-called natural life, but not all-out war.

b) The Inuit of Northern Canada, however, present a striking contrast. There is no word for war. There is no war, no rivalries. (And were Europeans baffled! It became the cultural anthropology joke of the early 1900s that a typical Eskimo family consisted of five people: a mother, father, two children, and a researcher.)

In the first case, we have environments having attained the maximum population the lifestyle can sustain. In the second, Northern Canada's natives are the most recent pre-European immigrants to the Americas in a still sparsely populated, harsh environment where everyone very much needs and relies on everyone else for survival. All this establishes is that, once a population of a species reaches a fixed level, any animal defends its territory. Period.

But there is a quantum leap from defending one's territory (what constitutes any one group's territory always subject to argument), or even from maintaining a fixed population, to taking over, not just a neighbour's territory, but that of people you've barely heard of. This is distinctly human, and even among humans its rarity cannot be overemphasized. The unusual society suddenly becomes expansionist,

(continued...)

When one examines the most common societies to have existed – hunter-gatherer and agrarian – family itself is an integral community. Patriarchy and matriarchy are in equal balance, with equal involvement with children (having and rearing them), and in economic and social life. The children, too, are part of all aspects of the life of the family or tribe or society.[41] One might conclude this the more natural state for humans: equal balance of patriarchy and matriarchy, and equality of parenthood.

In our case, it was not just expansionism. The Industrial Revolution sealed patriarchy's elimination from family, working much like constant war. Prior to it, work and household were indistinguishable. All members of a family were involved in the economic and social life of the family, economic and social life being undistinguishable.

Then came industrialization, and the disconnections escalated. For men to spend six, twelve-hour days a week in a factory or mine where brawn was in demand, it was necessary to build a mythology about how special mothers are to children so it's okay for there to be no daddy. Disappearing dads reinforced the idea that mothers are special to children, and mothers being all that children needed reinforced the disappearance of fathers, until it all appeared perfectly natural. This also separated women from society's economic life.[42] And don't forget that up until then, it was only nobles who

---

[40](...continued)

bullying everyone they can find. You have to have experienced a great deal of pressure to suddenly go popping off trying to ensure you'll never have another rival anywhere, ever. But we can readily name most societies as though they were the only ones that existed besides ourselves, or the only ones that matter: the Bantu of Africa, Incas of South America, Rome, Macedonia (Alexander the "Great"), Arabia, etc. And we call them "great." They are exceptional, and whether to be admired or anything about them emulated, debatable.

[41] The best one hears said about children in our culture is, "They are our future." This may be exactly the problem, our systemic abuse of them: They exist in some other time, not now. Children are part of society NOW. They are not so regarded nor treated, have no legally recognized rights, are without immediate existence.

[42] Increased specialization is a principal distinction of civilizations from other structures (agrarian, hunter-gatherer). In itself, it does not cause inequality. However, should one area then diminish in importance to the whole, those who have

(continued...)

were able to emulate the lingering image of Rome and their separation of fathers from family for purposes of conquest. For working people to have this indulgence was considered a treat, though not necessarily by the working people.

All the following are circa the early Industrial Revolution:

> The future destiny of the child is always the work of the mother.
> — Napoleon Bonaparte.

> For the hand that rocks the cradle
> Is the hand that rules the world.
> — Wm Ross Wallace, *Ruler of the World.* 1865

> Men are what their mothers made them.
> — Emerson, *Conduct of Life.* 1860

> A mother is a mother still,
> The holiest thing alive.
> — S. T. Coleridge, *The Three Graves.* c. 1796

---

[42](...continued)

lost significance do indeed become unequal to the others. Some feminists try to portray women one hundred years ago as insignificant in society because they had no role in what are *today's* few power structures: government, industry, and media. Today, we have a greatly reduced set of power structures. One hundred years ago, church, household, and community were each far more important than any of the current ones, and running a household was nothing trivial, as it has become, unless you consider food, clothing, and a warm, clean home of no value. Government, by comparison, had almost no meaning to the mass of society. It was not involved in anything near the community level, and had the significance of today's Super Bowl game. It was sport. So, separating into male and female roles forged by industrialization did not in itself mean women had no, or even diminished, significance to society as a whole, and believing it did is an excellent example of our difficulties with different versus equal, not to mention projecting the present into the past. But when industrialization trivialized running a household, and mobility and mass communications dismembered community, and science replaced or became our religion, now it would be unfair for women to not participate equally in what few social power structures remain. However, then trying to keep family all to themselves is a bit suspect.

There is none,
In all this cold and hollow world, no fount
Of deep, strong, deathless love, save that within
A mother's heart.
> — Felicia Hemans, *The Seige of Valencia*. c. 1830

Mother is the name for God in the lips and hearts of little children.
> — Thackeray, *Vanity Fair*. 1848.

Thou, while thy babies around thee cling,
Shalt show us how devine a thing
A woman may be made.
> — Wordsworth: c. 1848

The bearing and the training of a child
Is woman's wisdom
> — Tennyson, *The Princess*. c. 1845

So for the mother's sake the child was dear,
And dearer was the mother for the child.
> — S. T. Coleridge sonnet: c. 1798

We seem to have imputed considerable magic into the female parent. Clearly only a woman can raise a child; only a woman really cares. Men don't matter the least, couldn't enter into consideration.

There is a duality: Not satisfied with telling children that only their mothers matter to them, we conversely decided that men don't really care much about children and want little to do with them. We made fathers disposable to family, being needed elsewhere. Loving children is no longer human, it is female.

This found expression in Freud declaring men not biologically predisposed to parenting (women not biologically predisposed to anything but), describing only his immediate, Victorian culture. It was called "momism" by Philip Wylie in 1942, and later, the "motherhood mystique" by Richard Warshak. Our legal system proclaimed it as The Tender Years Doctrine ("a mother is the *natural custodian* of tender years"), and this myth continues to expresses itself today when, if a man cares for his children, it is "role reversal" or "getting in touch with his female side." Because everyone "knows" caring for children is only a "woman thing."

This biology-is-destiny notion is championed by the National Organization for Woman (an American feminist umbrella group), children having long been women's power base.[43] Well, when society creates a structure uniting women and children as one, it can hardly be surprised when women fight to keep it.

On one side of the coin is the "male provider." A man's only worth (to his family, to society) is in how much money he can make and how high he can climb on the corporate ladder. Obsessing over this, his only value, leads to workaholism to the neglect of his family.

In non-industrial societies it is hard to distinguish "provider" by gender. Even were it true that only men get raw food and only women prepare it (which is not true but a common projection from us), is not each equally

---

[43] The only persistent opponent to a presumption of joint parenting is feminist organizations. Reference: National Organization for Women (NOW) *Acton Alert on 'Fathers' Rights'*, 1996. Also examine the hearings of any legislature when they have considered presumed co-custody. Also see Appendix III.

While some feminists have decried this mystique, most defend its presumptions and results. As this is written, the U.S. House of Representatives is considering an amendment to the Violence Against Women Act, which is itself a testament to women's use of male chivalry to gain special treatment, not equality, and instead of calling such chivalry sexist. The amendment, Section 241, asks the states to "have a presumption that children shall have their main physical residence with their primary caretaker parent unless that parent is unfit," effectively abolishing joint parenting. This has nothing to do with violence to anyone, much less to women. It is women trying to eliminate fathers, a violation of children.

providing?[44] It would seem the myth "male provider" is our own invention, to satisfy other agendas.

At least in Victorian times, when other conventions made divorce rare, a man could count on his family to always be there; a man could choose the extent he would be part of his family. When divorce became rampant, that choice was removed. A few, disproportionately powerful women's groups, cling to this removal, as though it had to do with women's independence. It has to do with women's power.

So Custody-Access-Support is natural. To us, now, due to our context: industrialization.

Our degree of father elimination from family has probably never been achieved by any other society. By now we've done a remarkably fine job. Family as a matriarchy consisting only of mother and child (with someone lurking about thoughtfully paying for everything), is well ingrained in North Euro-rooted perception. It is not surprising to find it institutionalized in many ways. In the early 1800s in the U.S., when a benevolent slave owner had to sell some of his slaves, he would try to sell a women and her children together. Not the father. "You can get another one in Georgia," one man was told when he asked to see his wife and children before being carted off. This is a projection of our values, not what any other society sees as a family, certainly not what the Africans believed, judging from the desperation in the letters of separated families.

---

[44] Another favourite projection of our culture onto others is, "Men hunt, women gather." When the young men climb a tree to collect the honey from a hive, are they gathering or hunting? When the women go to the field and dig around for particular roots, are they hunting or gathering? When the men build a dam in the river to trap the fish and the women grab them with nets, is one hunting and the other gathering? Or are we simply calling anything we think of as male, "hunting," and what we think women mostly do, "gathering"?

There certainly are hunter-gatherer cultures, but I have yet to hear a meaningful distinction *between* hunting and gathering. It is a single term describing an economic system comprised of many, many activities. You'd be surprised how many and how much effort goes into being able to eat. There are also certainly differences between men and women, but I have yet to find such differences in "providing," be it the physical or non-physical necessities. Rather, maleness and femaleness seem equal parts of the same whole, both human first, male or female second. Even in Europe, the notion that men only provide all physical things and women only all psycho-emotional is only found starting from Victorian (mid-Industrialization) times.

In the 1960s, social workers coined the terms "nuclear family" and "extended family." This is more European reductionism, and helped facilitate moving a member from one division to the other. In 1969, another social worker invented "bonding." (Every generation also thinks it invented sex.) It was mostly used to re-enforce "primary caretaker:" There is and can only be one person who provides all nurturing, a child seen as "bonding" to only one person. (Uni-paradigm-ism – this "one only" theme – is dealt with next). Normally, this is the mother. "Normally," only because we had eliminated Dad, needed for industrial wealth.

The other side of the coin is a system in which women expect to raise *their* children at someone *else's* expense. This is their natural right, our image of what motherhood is. Women's use today of children as their power base may be their greatest single abuse of children, family, and men. The abuse is claiming a monopoly, denying fathers and children each other.

By now we lack any motif of male nurturing, any notion that maleness nurtures as much as femaleness, however much in its own way. Indeed, male nurturing is considered an oxymoron. The only examples in our media of men caring for children are as jokes: movies such as *Big Daddy* and *Three Men and a Baby*. Even Eric Fromm, great Jungian psychiatrist of the 1960s and '70s, called approval-disapproval "father love," and unconditional, all-accepting love, "mother love." Not because it is true or accurately represents humanity, but because it is true and accurately described his Germanic culture to see patriarchy only in terms of discipline, and matriarchy exclusively as warmth and comfort.

In my family, my father was the source of quiet, sure, unconditional love, my mother was approval-disapproval. She was a classic "churchlady" and approval was rare. Just the existence of approval-disapproval as any kind of parental love is culture bound (is very North European), who is supposed to be its source, even more so.

Maleness is not even seen as life-giving, life-creating. That is strictly female. This is a bit obviously a defiance of sheer biology. We seem to have wandered rather far off the old nature trail, haven't we? How did we get this far off without noticing? What horrible forces have compelled us? Well, that was the point of covering them in the second chapter, "Background".

We do not believe in parental equality: that both parents are of equal significance to a child, that both equally love unconditionally and totally and should be given equal consideration, that both are equally important to the child, each in their own way, for possibly slightly different reasons, or that the child has a natural right to both parents, or even needs more than one parent. We certainly do not institutionalize it. Not because it is untrue. Not because the vast majority of people do not intuitively believe this. Because of the structures we found ourselves in, and for which we now find rationalizations.

Are these the presumptions of humanness we wish to institutionalize, perpetuate? Is this the society in which we wish to live?

> It is not that man must be in sync with or adapt to his culture, but that cultures grow out of sync with man. When this happens, people go crazy and they don't know it.[45]
>
> — Edward T. Hall, 1977

Most people of either gender intuitively recognize the equal significance to a child of each parent, especially those new with child. They intuitively know it is equally the child of both. But none of our laws or conventions reinforce this. Quite the opposite. So the problem is not people, it is officialdom. Our formal culture doesn't fit us.

Man is not infinitely malleable or there would be no revolutions. We cannot form ourselves to whatever structures without bearing a cost. Better to form our social structures (our context) more closely to what man is like. Unfortunately, that runs up against that awful image of what man (ourselves) is like, which is why such attempts are resisted. We still do not use what is natural to ourselves as our guide for our institutions because we retain that lingering fear of our nature; that what is natural to humans is to be resisted, even punished.

Instead of treating fathers like criminals, thus making them such, we might consider treating them with the same dignity accorded mothers: Treat all parents as parents. If our society has a gender issue at all, surely it is

---

[45] Edward T. Hall, *Beyond Culture* (Anchor/Doubleday, 1976), p. 282. ISBN 0-385-12474-0.

mother/father versus parent. And changing the semantics won't change the fact. The real treatment must change: the structures.

We have a system in which women commonly expect to raise *their* children at someone *else's* expense, expecting to be the only parent. A system in which money is men's only function, not any spiritual or emotional nurturing. (Or, what fathers do is not considered nurturing.) This is seen as the natural order of the universe.

And who put this system in place? Men? Women? Well, maybe it was us: society. And what produced it was situational: context. So let's stop finger-pointing and blaming and worrying about who did what to whom. Let's assume some responsibility and simply address "what do we want our society to be like now?" That means all of us together, not gender-divided any more than race- or religion-divided.

Admittedly, this section presumes that fathers (or at least patriarchy) are very important to children and their growth. It presumes that they are as important as matriarchy and for much the same reasons: Both parents are humans, after all, similarities between the genders far exceeding subtle differences. This section does not try to *establish* this perception, but presumes it.

For me, exposure to other, especially more basic cultures, and personal experience, are sufficient proof. For those needing "scientific evidence" that even contemporary American suburban men "bond" as readily and deeply to their offspring as women, that they as biologically respond with nurturing, that they play, however slightly different, just as vital a part of any child's development as do mothers, or for those who need to know *what* makes fathers important, not otherwise satisfied *that* they are, I recommend:

> *Throwaway Dads. The Myths and Barriers That Keep Men from Being the Fathers They Want to Be*, by Ross Parke and Armin Brot. Houghton Mifflin Company, 1999. ISBN 0-395-86041-5.

Ross Parke has spent his career studying fatherhood, and has written many important books on it.

Also dealing with the contemporary North Europe-rooted "urban myths" in this area, half being Victorian leftovers, half feminist scapegoating that feeds our fears and righteousness:

> *Divorced Dads. Shattering the Myths*, by Sanford Braver with Diane O'Connell. Tarcher Putnam, 1998. ISBN 0-87477-862-x

But as declared in the introduction, mine is not to duplicate the work of others. Rather, it is to chronicle cultural patterns so we may make better informed choices about what we want our society to be like, so that we structure our society less by accident or minority agenda.

The pattern of de-patrification of family in our culture, of which today's urban myths are but today's expression, can, I believe, be traced not simply to our own warrior-hood, but more to our imitation of militarist Rome. It was consolidated by industrialization, and saw its zenith with the Victorian cult. It is a tremendous schism with reality, whether you take your reality from personal experience, or the material in Ross Parke's, *Throwaway Dads*.

Still, when I say, "exposure to other cultures" has convinced me fathers matter as much to children as mothers, the reader may legitimately wonder to what exactly I refer. It is not easily quantified, not without committing the European sin of reductionism. Family is a whole, and what is performed by adult males in one group may be done by young females in another. But male nurturing is the Tupian father helping his son make his first arrows. It is the European father teaching his daughter to milk the cow. It is the Baka father getting the children to help build the night's shelter. It is the elders of the village around the fire at night telling the ancient tales, everyone joining in to act them out. It is as natural as breathing and repeats in every culture in all their ways, including the suburban American father playing ball with his son. It occurs in every society, except those few that erect barriers like endless wars or industry.

Nurturing is as male as it is female, male nurturing much the same, both being as much human, both equally parents. If there are differences, male nurturing is more in doing than talking. It is in playing – physical socializing – and encouraging independence (something matriarchy often abhors). Like breathing, it simply is. To go further is to tempt discussions about maleness versus femaleness, overly covered by too many to the neglect of our vast commonalities. I take it for granted, as most do intuitively, even in this culture, that any healthy society or family is an equal balance of matriarchy and patriarchy, proof simply being equal numbers of men and women. How else is a child to learn robust living? What proof is needed? One may as well ask what makes mothers important.

Men do not need to be told this, nor do most women. "Officialdom" does.

Euro-Anthropology on Male Nurturing

I attended a lecture by a prominent cultural anthropologist where he presented the not uncommon thesis that women are physically smaller and less muscular than men, retain the higher-pitched child's voice and have other features (like less inset eyes to appear larger), to appeal to men as needing care, as with children.

I normally warn against back-rationalizations (taking something that exists today and making up reasons) as hot-beds for projecting existing assumptions. But there may be something to this. Consider our culture's archetypes of female sensuality: Betty Boop, Marilyn Monroe, the Spice Girls. They talk like babies and act like children. When a woman wants something, especially from a man, she will commonly use "charm": She becomes sweet, coy, coquettish, and oh so dependent that only you can save her universe. She reverts to childhood. Helplessness or childishness are common female seductions in any culture, not only ours.

And it works! It works incredibly well. Almost every time, unless you come up against an "unfeeling" man. Mature women get steamed with how well it works, until they discover themselves pulling it when facing a traffic ticket.[46]

---

[46] This is, and always has been, men's slavery / woman's power. For instance, a female victim evokes instant and strong response in men. But a male victim is a turn*off* to women. Some who point to our society's laws of over a century ago delight in showing that, taken literally, they indicate female

(continued...)

But not two paragraphs later the same anthropologist proclaimed that men are not biologically predisposed to nurturing children. Margaret Mead voiced the same opinion.

Am I the only one seeing the contradiction here? One of these premises has to be false, or the other doesn't work.[47] Either human males are at least

---

[46](...continued)
subservience to men. They conveniently overlook two facts:
1) Property then, was not as it has become. Now, it is transient and disposable. Then, it was not simply permanent as in lifelong; property was one's posterity. It was the expression of and conduit for strong family ties, to the past, present, and future.
2) *Therefore*, these laws were written from a presumptions of *male* subservience to *property*. (Ergo, " woman on a pedestal.") Men were expected to die for it, its meaning well beyond their mortal lives. Until the late 1800s, if a woman committed a crime, her husband was punished.
    Anyone can tell you Eve's biblical curse. Few can tell you Adam's: to *toil all your days* (in service to your community, your women).
    Men and women have always been each other's slaves, "slave" an odd reference for interdependence, but the one most popular today. Women often complain of men not understanding them. Are women any better at understanding men and maleness? (Are even men?)
    Consider the universal hero archetype. It is quintessential maleness. (Archetypical strength for men is in overcoming. For women, it is endurance. Notice the interdependence, that we are equal parts of the same whole. One cannot exist without the other and only exists for the other.) But what is The Hero? Is it one who goes about beating up others? Or is it the one who *accepts responsibility for the protection – the nurturing, the well-being –* of his community, and therefore, acts. Maleness is responsibility. And women have long played on this, relying on it in many ways, feminism a fine example. (As do men rely on female-ness, also making use of the interplay in different ways. Since we are all "prisoners" of the same dynamics, one would think it grounds for mutual understanding, not exploitation.)
    Many female writers, like Cathy Young, wonder to what lengths men will continue to accommodate what are often extreme and irrational demands from the women's movement, as though it completely represented this society's women. But women (or, really, community) has always been men's slavery. We are demanded of by it, die in trenches by the droves at its behest. Women have always known this, and use it. Sometimes not very nicely. The "not always nicely" is a cultural problem, not a gender one.
    For more on men's powerlessness, see Warren Farrell, *The Myth of Male Power* (Simon and Schuster, 1993). ISBN 0-671-79349-7.

[47] This is actually another example of Euro-disassociations. It is very common for a Euro-rooted scientists to learn something in their professional life, even become famous promoting it, only to leave it there. They do not apply it to

(continued...)

as predisposed to nurturing children as are women, or why do they hang around women and children at all in any human society that has ever existed, not to mention easily conned (excuse me, charmed) by childlikeness? They may express their nurturing in different ways. This hardly makes them any less prone to or capable of it, nor less important to their children.

Mechanics Fixation

". . . from woman's body."

A principal quirk to European thinking that strongly reinforces the idea that only the mother has children, and commonly used to this end, is mechanics fixation. Indeed, the Industrial Revolution was bred of it, mechanics already our cult.

Europeans invented the clock in the 1000s. We were so proud of it that every visitor to China took a few as gifts. The emperor had an attic full, but the Chinese were hardly impressed. We thought we'd defined time and expected everyone to be amazed. We even love mechanics that don't *do* anything.

We believe if we know *how* something happens or works, we totally understand it, have captured its essence, know it completely. As though how something works is the thing itself.

In 1953, a couple of researches at the University of Chicago placed water, ammonia, methane, oxygen, nitrogen, and hydrogen in a flask, applied an electric charge (theoretically simulating lightning or ultra-violet light), and a few weeks later found amino acids (a combination of H, C, O, and N). Amino acids may combine to form complex proteins; proteins are the building block of cells. A far cry from creating life in a flask, wouldn't you say? However . . .

The media all but claimed they had created life in a flask. Euro-religious organizations (churches) were shaken. This was playing with being God:

---

[47](...continued)
their personal lives and beliefs, their politics, or anything else.

the *mechanics* of the creation of Life. No more miracles, only science. European religion was threatened by science, again.

See that uniquely European rivalry between religion and science? It is over *how* things happen. That *how* became and is still disproportionately important. Knowing or explaining *how*s makes you chief priest. (Superstitious, aren't we?) In this case, we had seemingly captured (an extremely small part of) the *mechanics* of life coming into existence, so God was threatened.

What if someone really did discover how life began? Would that change the miracle of its existence?

Look, if you were God, don't you supposed you would have an infinite number of *ways* to do anything? *Hows?* What does it matter which You chose? The miracle is *that* it exists. Not how. *How* is irrelevant. It could be by any number of hows. Who cares? It may be useful to know to mimic for our own purposes, but hardly of religious significance. Which is the level to which we have long promoted mechanics. We worship technology; use it to prove ourselves advanced. When the Church had a monopoly on how, we worshipped it.

That trees and lakes and mountains and planets exist. *That* Life exists and strives. *What* these things are; this is awesome. Truly miraculous. Astonishing, irrespective of the hows. It could have been any of a thousand ways how. Who cares how?

Well, we care. We care, one might say, to an ungodly degree. We debase everything, eliminating awe and wonder, by attending only to *how* they came to be, or work, or do whatever they do. Mechanics, not *what* they are or the miracle that they exist at all. Mechanics fixation to the point of blindness to *what* things may actually be, to their significance to their context, to the very context of which they are expression.

Homosexuality naturally occurs in roughly ten to fifteen percent of any population. Always has, always will. And every society makes something different of this, telling us a great deal about that society (its level of tolerance of differences and ability to utilize). Most call such people enchanted; we, a threat. But for our society to accept homosexuality's existence at all, our scientists had to discover enzymes in the womb that may affect gender, and all this kind of nonsense. A *how* it (may) occur. We cannot just accept *that*, and does so naturally.

The egg is fertilized within the female parent, and gestates there. Given we are mammals, it must gestate in someone's body, and someone must produce the milk. This is the *mechanics* of human procreation.

But we have imputed considerable significance, even magic, to an arbitrary choice of nature: into the *mechanics* of pregnancy, birth, and having children, rather than *what* it is. Since the child gestates in and ushers from a woman's body, we all the more readily believe that women have children, not men.

What if men carried the child? Would women suddenly have no stake in the matter? Would it no longer be as much the female parent's? Would they care less for their children? Is this why some women feel threatened by the idea of men bearing children, because given our mechanics fixation, they would no longer have any?

Does how a child comes into the world matter more than what it is?

An Alternate View

I humbly submit a non-mechanics, non-industrial view. Women don't have children any more than men do. Couples have children.

Couples have sex (I think it still takes two); couples get pregnant. A couple conceives, bears, and raises children, not any one person. And both love as much and unconditionally, however much expressed in male or female ways. Both equally and unconditionally love and take the same pride for exactly the same reason: that new life is their bonding. It is their mutual extension, equality if ever there was any.

But this would require thinking holistically. Systemically. And that there is more than one parent.

What is a child? Not how.

A child is, biologically and behaviourally – assuming consent – equally the product of two people. Equally the expression of two people's will, decisions, behaviour, and biology. It is an expression and extension of both, equally. Unless someone dramatically changed the laws of biology since I went to school, not to mention those of human behaviour. Did every pregnancy suddenly come only of rape? It's been years since I heard anyone suggest only men desire or initiate sex. Both genders desire and seek sex for exactly the same reason: it is the body's yearning for eternity.

(It is still sex that produces them, isn't it? There also seems a puritanical denial of the connection, or another of our disassociations: a desire for sex with nothing to do with natural consequences. But I believe pregnancy is still usually the result of two people's own mutual (mutual!) decisions and behaviour, isn't it? Over which both might equally accept some responsibility? Pregnancy may be random. Accident it is not. It is *supposed* to happen when you do that. It's why we crave it. Being prisoners of the same context, you'd think we'd want to deal with it together.)

There would seem a little real life, day-to-day equality in this Miracle of Life thing. Many seem disinclined to acknowledge it, possibly for some political agenda. It might upset the status quo were it formally acknowledged and institutionalized in our laws: that *what* a child is, is equally an extension, expression and product of two people: their decisions and behaviour, however naive it may have been, and of their biologies. (At least two people. In all other cultures, a child is considered to have two *or more* parents. Never one. Most common is one mother and any number of fathers. For the Australian Aborigines, "siblings" include what we call cousins: your bothers and sisters are all those of the tribe of your generation. In typical North European reductionism, we are the only culture to have reduced children to the fewest possible, while still having any.)

What to do about the consequences of consensual sex? Two people were equally involved, both must equally face that question, both having equal say. Accountability is to each other. Not to anything external. They were the ones who decided to get into bed with each other. Does one suddenly not want it to be a partnership anymore, want exclusive say over the consequences? Would seem a bit late. Rather a trying-to-wriggle-out-after-the-fact. Not very responsible.

Most *men* consider women too frail and delicate to be held accountable for their decisions. Only men should be. Male chivalry: let women decide everything. Or male slavery, depending on how it is used. Some *women* consider this patronizing. Other women, however, use it as a shield from adulthood.

For here is where social accountability naturally lies: to each other. Not to some external authority. Each individual, to each other, one on one.

Always has, always ultimately will, however masked. You have to live with your neighbour and he with you. Same for lovers. So we would do well to more clearly embrace and reinforce, rather than corrupt it. Leave it up to both, equally. This applies to the result of consensual sex, irrespective of the stage of its development (five days or fifteen years).

At the moment, only a woman decides whether a child is even born. As though it only happened to her, she the only one involved, her "accident," only her pregnancy. And if she decides it lives, the father must pay at least half the costs forever. For a decision in which he had no say! Feminist equality.

You can't butter your bread on both sides. You'll get your hand dirty. Which we have, but which is so far only taken as opportunity for indignation toward those who can't quite grasp the irrationalities and inequities and what is done to them, and refuse to go along, not as reason to correct the system producing such "problem people." Either only women have children, so leave us men out of it all together (don't expect anything from me when I'm told it's not mine nor my decision), or a couple, equally. This holds as true for post-divorce child care as for pre-birth consideration. The *pregnancy* (the child, at whatever stage) is equally that of both. So in consensual sex pregnancies, both must have equal say on abortion, and thereafter, the care and raising of the child. (As for as abortion, surely we can at least give the child this protection: the choice of both its parents.[48]) Because *what* any child is, is the equal product of both parent's biology and behaviour, irrespective of the mechanics of birth.

---

[48] "A woman's body, a woman's choice" was a popular feminist slogan-argument to justify only women deciding about abortion. (Not to suggest for a moment that feminism is only interested in power, not equality.) Note the mechanics fixation required: The embryo gestates in my body, therefore *is* my body; I should enjoy the same dominion over it.

What is an embryo? A woman's body, or just a guest, a visitor, and equally the "body" of both parents, or possibly even its own? "A woman's body a woman's choice" is one very unimpressive argument. Yet what speaks volumes about our culture is the weight it has carried. People actually think it makes sense, and society as a whole adopted the attitude that abortion is only a woman's choice, having children having nothing to do with men.

Surprisingly, since then, some men have gone on woman-killing rampages. And we are aghast. Male oppression!

Perhaps we think we can disassociate the issues of abortion and child care. It seems to me we are seeking the fundamental assumptions of parenthood: its model, its description, *what* it is. So it would seem that any law passed, institution established, or convention declared must at least be predicated on a consistent vision. Principles are the first thing on which to agree before getting into the *mechanics* of implementation. What are our assumptions about parenthood and family: equality, or only women have children? Otherwise, we may be using different premises for each law to only cater to whichever group cries the loudest on that issue. If we do that, we can hardly wonder why these structures produce "problem people," even murderers.

For social policies with respect to family and children, a premise of equality of parenthood hold promise to work best for all parties. A presumption that patriarchy and matriarchy are of equal significance to any child at any stage; that family is most naturally an equal balance of patriarchy and matriarchy; that a child is, from conception, equally a product of both's choices, behaviour, and genes; that it is equally treasured; and that this is society's duty to enshrine and protect. Not that some are more equal than others by virtue of some superstition we created about mothers being special, nor by the power-grabbing of the few.

Enforcing this equality is the only business society as a whole has in these matters: not making decisions themselves, not robbing people of their own parenthood by presuming it themselves, not imposing this week's most popular social views. Simply ensuring balance between the two parents. Structure, not content.

But our culture does not seek balance and symmetry. It thinks in conflict and dominance. This was evidenced years ago when men saw themselves as "head" of the household and master of it, however untrue it ever was operationally. (Women used to be kind enough to humour us.) This is just as evidenced today by feminists taking the same myth even more literally to claim women were ever any more subservient than men then or women now. The conflict-dominance view is evidenced when feminists insist only women should decide about abortion and men have nothing to do with children, or women would be oppressed. It is in our society insisting post-divorce children have only one effective parent, implementing sole custody, which effectively eliminates the other parent.

This is the belief that conflict is avoided only by outside authority or dominance of some form, not in balance, not in a level playing field, not in equal capacity and accountability only to each other. Such is our cultural history.

4) Myth 2 – Uni-paradigm-ism

The second myth supporting Custody-Access-Support is likely the most potent, superceding even our gender myths. I call it uni-paradigm-ism: the belief there can only be one ultimate authority for all things. Addressing it forces us to first identify and deal with enmeshment.

Many people's initial reaction to a proposal of co-parenting (what goes on in a marriage, after all) is, "The child would find it confusing." Which is to say, they, as North Euro-rooted adults, would find two authorities confusing. The same goes for two households: Obviously there can be only one. Sometimes it is conceded, "It could only work if there is an extremely high degree of cooperation (read sameness) between the two." A need for one-mindedness is assumed: one thought process, one being, one parent.

Implicit to this is regarding a married couple as one literal being; that a child has always had but one parent. Not that they are two separate people with a *spiritual* binding, but literally one. Only when they divorce do they return to being two; while married they are a single entity with a single mind. This is our enmeshment concept of intimate relations. While marriage represents a spiritual union between two people, we see it as (and try to make it into) a literal and total union.

In most North Euro-jurisdictions, no one is required to testify against their spouse; it is testifying against oneself. More troublesome, it is still generally considered that one partner signs contracts and commits to obligations for the other. Either one is the other. This is why, upon divorce, whatever has been acquired by one during the marriage is considered acquired by both, however untrue this may be. We don't care; the whole point of social convention is to turn unreality into reality.

So when a couple (one entity) separates and suddenly becomes two, obviously only one can be that one parent and have all authority over all aspects of the children's lives. There always has been one parent. Uni-paradigm-ism: one ultimate authority for all things.

This was likely never the case while married, or if it was, probably the cause of the divorce.

I submit that a child, like all of us, needs stability. This does not mean uniformity or sameness nor only one of everything. Two stable, permanent households – two stable, permanent parents – are as stable as one. And retaining the same parents in the same way while gaining a second household would seem considerably less loss and greater consistency than what is imposed today. I also submit: the more parents the better. Not the fewer. This is an opposite view from those who object to a child having even two. I submit that this is the way almost all societies have operated, few drawing such thick lines between related households. But "nuclear family" versus "extended" makes it easy to move members from one to the other.

Enter an Eskimo village or any native village in North America, and you see the children going from house to house. Children are communally raised; everyone takes responsibility for them. Multiple households; multiple authorities. Or, the entire village is one household. When you walk into an African village, a European sees a set of huts as separate households. It is more accurate to view this as one household with separate bedrooms. They do not have nuclear and extended families. They have families.

Think back to your own childhood. In a healthy neighbourhood, the community was a continuum. You were at home in many of your friends' houses. Children do not make the same separations European adults consider definitive.

So why do so many automatically believe co-parenting, and a child equally part of two households, is unhealthy, difficult, confusing, or whatever? As though children in the past, even in our culture, never had multiple households like grandparents', and uncles', and, yes, separated parents', and didn't know where to go for what. Surely "home" can and often does consist of two or more households. Many in our own culture have summer homes: They have two households which are home. Is not any child's home where at least one parent is? Does the building make a home, or the people in it?

One can identify two related blockages: enmeshment and uni-paradigm-ism. Clinging to the first is partly a function of the second.

Enmeshment

Narcissism is the inability to distinguish where I end and someone else begins. People who study this identify over 120 forms. It can be as simple and common as continuing a conversion with someone that you started with yourself, oblivious to the fact he has no idea what you're talking about. Or it can be as sinister as what Eric Fromm delineated as "malignant narcissism": the un-submitted will, as experienced by Adolf Hitler, Joseph Stalin, and Saddam Hussein. (A lack of "higher authority" beyond their own will, like a morality or a god. Just whatever they want.) We are all subject to some forms of narcissism as it would take a saint's awareness to never fall prey to it.

Authoritarianism is narcissistic: a failure to distinguish between me and someone else at the physical level. Another way of putting it is that authoritarianism takes a spiritual truth (you and I are one) and insists it be literally or physically the case: no literal or apparent differences – no distinctions of any kind – "you must be an extension of my will and desires." If one is ever angered by defiance, this is one's authoritarianism. It denies others' will or selfhood, their having their own ego and judgment, their own physical manifestations.

I am calling this failure to distinguish enmeshment when it is mutual between two people, as often happens in close personal relationships in our culture. In this case it is a lost or merged identity, and many think this is what being in love is. One's personal ego identity is "us," no longer "me." This is an occasional part of intimacy. As a constant state it is an illness, an unwillingness to be different. You can tell an enmeshed couple by how boring they are: neither will do or decide anything without the other; both insist on doing everything together and thinking the same, they overtly try to be literally one being. It would be an act of aggression to be individual.

Contrast this to the most beautiful expression of human intimacy I have heard: "I am the keeper of your solitude." Meaning, I, more than anyone, know and honour your differences and privacies, even from me. (I wish I could find the author to give proper credit.)

Now take parenting. My children are, indeed, an extension of me. They are a continuation of my life, spiritually. This is why they are so unspeakably important to me. This is something to reinforce, not undermine.[49]

---

[49] In attempting to deal with authoritarianism in Euro-rooted families, social work suffers another confusion with predictably threatening results. The best they say against custody is, "nobody owns children." This attacks the wrong thing. They may mean to target exclusivity of one parent or authoritarian so-called possessiveness, but falling into this word trap assaults the sense of "ownership" (belonging) inherent to family. It attacks the very heart and soul of family, the physical-spiritual attachment, as though seeking parental authority for themselves, too often the case. ("You don't own them; we do.")

The sense of "my children" – of this human "ownership" or attachment – is vital to nurturing. They are "my" children. You do not expend so much for someone else's. It is also the source of natural protection, so not to be trifled with, but leveraged.

One reason for the confusion over the personal sense of "ownership" is semantic: our property-related vocabulary. The second, more basic problem, is what Edward Hall calls "extension rebound." First, "possessiveness" is a misleading term. As described above, what is meant is requiring or expecting someone else to literally *be* me: a physical extension of my will, denying the alternate ownership of thoughts, feelings, and action. This does not even describe possession of property, property having limited soul or behaviour. So attacking possessiveness *per se*, or ownership in general, is too easily an assault on the wrong thing. Possessiveness is not the problem, but the wrong word. Insisting something be a literal extension of self, is.

Now the heart of it: the extension rebound with property. Which came first, property or family? I suspect there was always family, property a more recent invention, having meaning only to affluent societies. So property is an extension of family. Not the reverse. We do not confuse children or spouses with property and never have, however popular a myth. We confuse property for being family. We extended that sense of "mine" (belonging; ownership; personal identity) from family to inanimate things like land and tools. (This is the "extension." The "rebound" is thinking the reverse has occurred, as though property were the dominant human concern, which then makes it "bad" to be so-called possessive and protective of one's family.)

That strong sense of attachment – of "mine," of personal identity – is terribly important and fundamental to parenting It is a natural and "good thing", to be fostered, not attacked. It is not authoritarian. People do "own" their children. Their children "belong" to them, not you. Nor is extending that attachment to inanimate objects inherently bad: Being possessive of "my stuff" is protection. The "bad" is something entirely different: denying who is the real owner of specific feelings and behaviour. Narcissism.

In fact, the *authoritarian* possessiveness of projecting feelings, thoughts, and beliefs onto others may not be so much a denying of someone else's selfhood, as not accepting one's own. It is failure to say "these are *my* feelings" and being an individual, but copping out of ownership of them (seeking escape from the isolation

(continued...)

If I want my children able to continue that life on their own, I need to make sure their life – their will and mind – are their own, not a copy of mine. I need to be sure they explore and experience things for themselves, with me there to discuss their choices, not making them. For, especially once I'm gone, they will have their own experiences – see and be exposed to things I never can – and must be capable of their own reactions. This requires I ensure they have their own will and know their own thinking, come to their own terms with their own existence. Their physical and mental independence is important so that they can be that spiritual continuation of the life I also have only borrowed for a time.

Do you see where the confusion (and authoritarianism) lies? It is in any attempt to make a spiritual connection a literal one, to insist anyone else think or act exactly as I instead of on their own, instead of being different. It is the failure to distinguish spiritual from physical. Note also the many sources of intolerance of difference. Enmeshed with someone else, any difference is a personal violation. This is what "defiance" is.

We have long tended to take the Bible literally, too, instead of representationally as it was written. So when it fails to live up to historical fact, it's obviously all lies. It was never written as history, as a European-style historical account. It is a representation of spiritual experiences. Both the fundamental Christians who take it literally and the cynics who pick apart "fact" are making the same Euro-centric mistake. (Same structure, different content.) Failure to distinguish between spiritual and physical reality.

So we do this with marriage. A spiritual connection is treated as a literal, physical union. They are not two unique beings, but one. For everything, on every level. On the one hand we disassociate spirit and body, only to regard them one and the same physically, exactly because "spirit" has disappeared from formal acknowledgment.

---

[49](...continued)
of selfhood) by generalizing them as though they come from heaven and must be experienced by all. This is another result of a poor self-image, of not feeling entitled to one's own opinions, or that they would not matter.

Granted, the authoritarian self-extension ("possessiveness") and family belonging often get interchanged. That is no excuse for social workers or other professionals to confuse them.

The enmeshment view of love and marriage may well be one of the factors behind the soaring divorce rate. While the national average for the U.S. is 50 percent (the highest in North Europe-rooted civilization), demographers are currently estimating the divorce rate for new marriages at 60 to 65 percent. After less than two years, they may suddenly discover differences between them, even fundamental ones. That's pretty disillusioning when you thought everything was supposed to be the same, that you must both want all the same things at all times.

Our enmeshment concept of a married couple, a form of narcissism, certainly makes us believe the children of a married couple have only one parent to begin with: a single authority source. As though married people never disagree or children never know of it (echoes of a Victorian fantasy world), or as though children haven't always related differently to each parent, probably the reason God gave us two. But where God created two, man saw one. North Europeans peoples do not accept people's separateness, certainly not if they're married.

Uni-paradigm-ism

This is the underlying problem: we believe in one God.

The problem is not believing there is only one God as in seeing the underlying unity of the universe. The problem is the way we have externalized and generalized this until we are monotheistic about everything. There is, must be, and can only be, one and only one ultimate authority for all things at all times and all places. Not just in heaven, but on earth. (Failure to distinguish physical from spiritual.) It must be the *same* ultimate authority for all things and times and places (the uni- in uni-paradigm). There is but one response to a type of event, irrespective of context. There is one Rule, one measure, one Right, and everything else is Wrong. This produces absolutes, and conflict: Right and Wrong; Good and Bad. Extremes. Two things cannot be simultaneous right.

This is not God. Being external, there is not much spiritual about it. This is Rome, the One Ultimate Authority for All Things. But it largely became our image of God; it became the European God, and the European way.

We think it would be confusing for a child to have anything other than one authority for all things. He might see inconsistencies and contradictions. Rather than taking that as evidence that there are differences and learning to adjust to them – learning the versatility of dealing with different contexts – the child might decide he can't believe anything. It is as though we believe that without absolutes, there is nothing (one extreme to the other). So especially a child must have One Ultimate Authority for All Things – we must maximize his absolutes – or it would be unhealthy. God forbid a child would see differences in the authorities around him, as though he doesn't already have teachers at school to provide that, and as though married couples are never inconsistent, each from minute to minute, never mind between themselves.

Some of us think absolutes unhealthy, not to mention unrealistic.

One expression of our uni-paradigm-ism has certainly been classical determinism – one absolute Truth or Right, absolute control, etc.– but that is not all.

Was *Tyrannosaurus rex* a hunter or a scavenger? He must have been only one or the other.

For the first hundred years of European geology, the One Theory was catastrophism: Any geological formation was the result of a single, catastrophic event. This was overthrown in the late 1800s by uniformatarianism, and for the next hundred years, the single theory was slow, even, continuous geological formation for everything. Might the truth be both depending on what formation and what part of it?

Should students, or children, or employees be treated gently or firmly? You can only have one policy or the other. God forbid you would be "inconsistent," yielding to circumstance. You must have a predetermined response. (As distinct from: There are times to be firm and times to be gentle, and only your judgment can distinguish them, there is no formula.)

Is reality internal or external? We will accept all one, or all the other, not both equally, not a balance between them.

European psychology spent decades arguing nurture versus nature. That is, arguing whether personality was the result of genetics *or* environment, not how the two combine.

In the United States, free market principles and capitalism worked wonders for the nation's material wealth. So they are used to run public services (the post office brags of turning a profit while it cannot deliver a letter in two weeks), health care (how many dollars you have is the worth of your life and the lives of your children), and the so-called public air-waves (where making a profit is the only measure of worth, not community well being or service). Anything to do with community and the country has one set of principles: pay your way materially, or die as worthless. There is only one standard for all things.

Nuclear physics drove itself crazy for decades seeking the Grand Unification Theory: one model to explain all energies and matter. One Law of physics.

All are examples of context elimination: reductionism. All sacrifice attention to context for the sake of attaining One God. For instance, at the stellar level, Einstein and relativity are appropriate; at the human-to-solar level, Newton; at the subatomic, quantum mechanics works. Enormous leaps in scale produce entirely different contexts – entirely different universes – with entirely different laws. Euro-scientists are hard-pressed to accept this. Everything must obey One Law, and we'll *make* that the case.

Some religions, including some ancient Christian sects, say God is simultaneously goodness and evil. Such embracing of the dualities of life is very confusing to most Euro-origin people.

So we have the primary caretaker, who is not simply primary, but exclusive: Only one person gives all care and is all authorities. Our divorce customs simply institutionalize an existing cultural motif. How could any man take exception to occasional visits and paying for everything? That's all he's ever done (supposed to have been doing according to the official myth); all being a father is. Fathers only make clumsy attempts at nurturing if there is no mother, because ONLY WOMEN (there can only be one) NURTURE! Women do one thing, men, another; all one and all another. Our formal minds do not think in pluralities or balances, only ones and ultimates.

Tobacco suddenly became a deadly poison that causes instant death on contact, an opposite but equal extreme to denying its dangers. It is either good or bad, and if bad, it's all bad and must be totally eliminated.

Richard Nixon organized the "plumbers" to commit illegal break-ins at the psychiatrist's office of a political enemy, at the Democratic Party's national office, and possibly other places, and perform other "dirty tricks."

He also used the IRS and other federal agencies to attack political enemies and used the CIA to stop an investigation into the plumbers, both also illegal. Bill Clinton committed a sexual indiscretion and had the decency to lie about it under oath (because it's nobody's business) rather than kiss and tell. Both broke the law; both must be treated identically. One Law, one way of doing or reacting to all things, behaviour stripped of context.

Since anything is created only by its context and only exists by that grace, one would think the insanity to this, self evident.

Uni-paradigm-ism is similar to authoritarianism as it takes a spiritual reality – our oneness with the universe – and tries to create a physical, literal unity. This is a level at which such unity quite specifically does not exist. That's the difference between the two: spiritual oneness and physical separation.

Uni-paradigm-ism is largely a yearning for the good old days of innocence, for the profound world we left where we naturally lived the underlying unity. Unfortunately, from where we are now, until we acknowledge and embrace the physical level separation (our differences) and respect it for what it is, we are not likely to regain any underlying unity.

I postulate that our disassociation from our spiritual selves buttresses this. That disassociation makes it the more urgent to cling to any unity we can find, especially in the only world we have left, the material.

Uni-paradigm-ism is not authoritarianism *per se*, as it does not seek control. It is the result of acceptance of or resignation to authoritarianism. It is a benign, though terribly narrow, mind-set: insisting on one rule. Its danger is its narrowness.

It is why we insist on the enmeshment view of couples, insist on seeing a couple as one entity: We cannot live with duality. Just doesn't fit that mental structure we carry.

Contrast to Uni-Paradigm-ism

As suggested, this One Absolute God is more Rome than God. For instance, the "nothing" we fear existing without absolutes is the fear of the chaos and lawlessness without Rome.

This has little to do with how nature, life, and the universe actually seem to be structured, though certainly the way Rome convinced all Europe to see the universe for their own purposes: as a unified, hierarchical flowing down of power from a single source. The perfect order for the administration of a large empire.

This is fine for central control. It is irrelevant to civility, as we will see in Chapter 7. More to the point, it has little to do with non-government affairs like family life, community, and family structures.

The reality of day-to-day living is that when you go home, there is one authority structure, at work, there's another. At the Elks Club, you're the boss, at the Lions Club, the junior inductee. Walk into court, you find yourself in yet another structure, yet another position for you, another set of rules. Drive on the highway, another set of laws applies, another set of conventions to which to answer, different people having the right of way under different specific circumstances.

The world seems ruled by multiple deities. In day-to-day living, which authority is obeyed – who is in charge, what god worshipped, which paradigm operational or set of values most appropriate – is situational. Which, for one thing, suggests we each take our turn at leadership in a society or group. When our turn arrives is dictated by what is going on. If one thing is happening, I defer to the person responsible or most expert in that area. If something of my jurisdiction or expertise comes up, I take the lead. That is my job as one in a society: to sometimes follow, sometimes lead. Which time is which is dictated by the context.

But ours is an extreme-to-extreme culture, only one extreme at a time, and all of it. Smoking is all good, then all bad. Abortion is all bad, then all good. Contrast this to the Chinese who say, "All things, in moderation," which could be paraphrased as, "All things have their time and place." You probably think murderers should be eliminated. But when a war comes, we want everyone to be one. They are heroes.

I remember feeling smug as a child when the teacher would explain "but such-and-such a people believed in one God." One of the few like us. Nice to see there were others as advanced in their thinking. Well, we "knew" there was one God, and we were the best society. Therefore, one God there obviously was.

I now have a far higher regard for multi-deity ("polytheistic") cultures as having a firmer grasp of reality. I believe their psycho-spiritual orientation is closer to the way the universe is actually structured. The god of celebration is worshipped at its time, the god of war under other circumstances, the god of fellowship at yet another. All gods are important and exist simultaneously, it is for us to tune in to the circumstance and to which is taking precedent. Which is demanding our attention, or we will suffer for missing it, for not properly honouring the right thing at the right time.

But that's my personal vision. Perhaps we can at least come to terms with the fact that, in a family, as in any group, there are many demands with which to contend, many roles or authorities to be had, whether you call them gods or not. Enough for every member to keep fully occupied. There cannot be one authority for all things, it's not practical. No one can be good at everything or simply do everything. There is a need for economy, there is a need for fun. There is need for cleanliness, and need for rambunctiousness. Which god is honoured depends on what is most needed at the time. One way or another we all find roles to play and their time to be played.

Or, if we retain the one god motif, at least acknowledge His many forms on earth, in day-to-day life, in the physical world. Not just one, uniform super-being having one essence, but all the different essences of earthly existence.

So, while our culture-formed minds carry one structural image for everything – which is a wonderful and practical-sounding theory and a perfect replication of the structuring of the universe under Rome – the reality of existence does not match it. And few bother to notice. So far. But you can notice that most societies have felt more comfortable with multiple deities (multiple life authorities), and only societies dependent on tight control have a single god, or a highly dominant one like a god-king. In which type would you like to live?

> It is not that man must be in sync with or adapt to his culture, but
> that cultures grow out of sync with man. When this happens,
> people go crazy and they don't know it.[50]
>
> — Edward T. Hall, 1977

That Contrast, In Marriage

As another expression of our culture, few studies have been done of healthy families. We only study sick ones. (Whatever we think we'll to learn from that, and who decided who the sick ones are without a model for healthy?) The few studies that have been done[51] show that a healthy family organizes itself (much to the surprise of the researchers) so that each parent has prime areas of responsibility. He may be in charge of house maintenance, she of meals and kitchen. He of putting the children to bed, she of keeping the bathrooms clean. He drives the kids to school, she takes them to the doctor and dentist.

After learning each other's preferences, rarely does one discuss their jurisdiction's issues with the other unless something extraordinary arises, in which case the other's counsel is sought. But responsibility for the final decision is still clear: the one who has to carry it out. The parents basically leave it to each other to take care of things: specialization. As each child comes of age, they also acquire their own duties – their own role – or never feel part of the whole.

This might make a useful template for divorce arrangements; a way to ensure both parents have equal operational involvement in the children's lives. You take care of clothing; I, of health care. You take care of schooling; I of after-school community activities. This is also a way to divvy expenses without transfer payments. It may even overcome the problems that lead to the divorce: make divorce a safe haven to which to

---

[50] Edward T Hall, *Beyond Culture* (Anchor / Doubleday, 1976), p. 138. ISBN 0-385-12474-0.

[51] Edited by Froma Walsh, *Normal Family Processes* (The Guilford Press, 1987).

retreat from an imbalanced situation, instead of a hell. You know: community support for each parent's role and vitality in the family unit. This is the reason Chinese and Indian and everybody else's marriages last: community support.

(But don't tell the Divorce Industry this could lead to fewer divorces, or they'll never go along with it!)

"Let's take the garbage out together. That's something we haven't done yet as a couple." I don't think enmeshment is a real healthy template. But it's the one we currently use.

I believe this is how groups function: each member with specific, vital roles. Not everyone doing the same thing together, or one person doing everything. Someone correct me if I'm wrong. (Later sections look at this in more detail.) One thing is for sure: Custody-Access-Support naturally occurs absolutely nowhere. So imposing such a structure on any group just because there is conflict between two of its members, rather than resolving that conflict with *functional* separation, is not just asking for trouble, it displays a determination to destroy the whole group.

Separation

We can look more closely at how division of responsibility (overcoming our enmeshment bias) may be vital to making divorce far less sordid and traumatic.

Anyone divorcing is intent on removing the other from their personal life, with varying degrees of determination. Divorce is about separation. Therefore, any attempt to perpetuate marriage, to require the couple to continue to deal with each other as though still married in any form, will needlessly create abandoned children. Because those who want to divorce, will, one way or another. Should we be compelling them to the greatest extreme?

Right now, under CAS, we use the one household model – paid for by both parents even though one is not a part of it – to try to perpetuate marriage. This perpetuates the marriage's physical manifestation when its spiritual reality is gone. (Supposedly, so the children won't realize anything is different. God forbid the children's material world should be disrupted;

better to make mincemeat of their social-emotional-spiritual life to preserve it.) Not only does this eliminate the non-custodial parent from his children's daily lives and upbringing, but there occasionally arises some resentment when he thought he'd left the marriage, only to be required to continue paying for something in which he has, and wishes no further, part. Given his lack of involvement now with either the children or that household, we can hardly be surprised at the problems that arise.

If we just add to this or even replace it with, "both make all decisions together with respect to the children," a common definition of joint custody, although we return to a two-parent structure, we are also forcing them to deal with each other more than they did when they were married. It is another attempt to perpetuate the marriage.

Someone determined to divorce, will, just as is happening now. Presto: still more abandoned children. Didn't solved anything, did we?

The intention of divorce is to reduce conflict in one's life, not perpetuate or worsen it. I, for one, would not want to live my life constantly looking over my shoulder wondering from where will come the next attack on what I'm doing. This is why I prefer the term co-parenting rather than shared parenting, as the first implies separation (by division of responsibilities), while the later ("sharing") rings of enmeshment, like doing or deciding everything together. That's not even done by happily married couples so where the heck does that come from? ("Share" is unspecific. It usually really does mean one of "split" or "divide" or "rotate". But too often it will mean some form of enmeshment.)

The reason to emphasise this is that our social workers are usually only trained as marriage counsellors. "Let's get these two together." Their orientation is often towards enmeshment, and in managing others' relationships, rather than defining the structures within which people manage their own. This makes anyone determined to divorce, bolt in the opposite direction.

Divorce is about separation, not more or different forms of enmeshment, or different forms of continuing the marriage. Few seem to understand or be prepared to accommodate, much less ensure, separation. If divorce is separation at the human or spiritual level, shouldn't our social and physical structures reflect this?

Two things need protecting upon divorce:

1. The separation of the adults.
2. The roles and relationships between children and each parent.

We will often not attain the second without the first – without each parent being secure in their separation from the other.

Another, equally important point is, sometimes ensuring the roles and relationships means defining them. This is true in cases where an equitable role never existed, which will either be a cause, or a symptom of the causes, of the divorce. It is also true for out-of-wedlock births. In the former case it is even more imperative to first ensure the parents' separation.

Why would we want to dishonour the wishes of the one desiring the marriage to end, especially when it is not needed to preserve the rest of the family? If the couple does get along so well they're happy to "share" all decision making, great. (Though one would wonder why the divorce.) But if joint decision-making is made a requirement of continuing to be a parent, we have solved nothing. We have returned to not allowing divorce, or there will still be divorce, however unrecognized and un-accommodated, even punished. Because we cannot make people's personal decisions for them, like with whom will they relate how closely. There is no reason this should mean children have only one parent.

Division of responsibility naturally occurs in any group, including any family. Use it. It accomplishes both separation and meaningful involvement with the children for each. Given this level playing field, when cooperation is required, it happens naturally, on its own, simply because each is secure in their role, the structure *allowing* cooperation, both parents having equal strength and independence.

5) Myth 3 – Linear Thinking and Classic Materialism

The third myth blocking equality of parenthood comes from our love affair with Aristotelean linear thinking. Used exclusively, it led to a purely physical view of the world. When linear thinking is applied to family, it creates an unrealistically narrow definition of it (men care for women who care for children). Along with other abuses this creates, it still drives much of left- and right-wing agenda with respect to family.

Upon entering a Moorish city in Spain some time in the 1400s, a Crusader, instead of burning all the books, read some. Europe discovered the Greek philosophers and intellectual stimulation. Another three hundred years passed and, combined with other forces, what we now call the Enlightenment happened. We started becoming our own civilization.

Of all Greek and Roman philosophers, Aristotle received the most attention. He was made our "Father of Science." Aristotle emphasised linear thinking: logic. If A and B, then C. Cause and effect; one thing follows another. For Europeans at that time (1400 to 1800), it was a revelation, as we had been worshipping entirely different gods. Reason was driving nothing; fear ruled all.

Cause and effect has since become the only accepted method of thinking, all others discredited as being all the same irrationality. We can only have one of anything, including one way of thinking, so all others have been lost to us.

Linear thinking is important for checking the rationality of our notions, and it accords a structure by which to ensure reasoning is complete. But it is not all there is to reasoning. There is also systemic thinking: taking things as a whole and simultaneously considering the inter-related parts.[52] Humans usually do this intuitively, as it cannot by its nature be made into a formula.

Linear thinking is well suited to dealing with the physical world. It falls apart with seemingly chaotic systems like internal human experience and inter-human relations. Linear versus systemic thinking is similar to the difference between Newtonian science or Euclidean math, and quantum mechanics, the science of chaos, and non-Euclidean geometry. Each has their use and place. (The three most important things: context, context, and context.)

But we are uni-paradigm-istic. There is only one way of doing all things: one god, one answer, and only one way of reasoning. We were in awe of the master of reason, Aristotle and his cause-and-effect formula, all things since have been forced to fit it. All other reasoning has been discredited as superstition or otherwise invalid when not provable by linear formula. Therefore, "men take care of women and women take care of children" makes sense. How else would it be?

The last battle was in the late 1800s. It was really the replacing of the Church and aristocracy by the middle class, and accomplishing this required a new paradigm: new terms of reference. To overthrow the old, you need something new. The intellectual battlefield was the philosophical war over materialism.

At that time, materialism did not simply mean preoccupation with money – its acquisition and disposal – as it does today. It meant a physical world fixation: only the material world has existence. It is measurable, so the only thing you can be sure exists. Therefore, only the material world could be considered real. Nothing else was reliably "there," so had to be dismissed. Physical science to the exclusion of spirit and emotion, which are "irrational," non-linear, and cannot be "proven" by cause-and-effect formula, not to mention, cannot be predicted or controlled. Proof came to mean a formula that always holds true irrespective of context, supporting the elimination of context. This made reductionism one of the new gods.

---

[52] Some anthropologists maintain there are three modes of thinking: linear, systemic, and representational. I suggest representational a means of expression, not thinking. That said, I remain receptive to other suggestions.

Understand that passions were increasingly seen as betraying humanity, or at least Europeans. They were our barbarism we were anxious to live down, or from which to free ourselves. Fears and superstitions were either used by the Church to control (and the middle classes now wanted that), or expressed themselves in the atrocities like slavery of which we were increasingly ashamed. They were the source of our hypocrisies and, to the new "enlightened" middle classes or sub-nobles, needed to be eliminated. Pure (linear) reason was seen as the saviour. It could make us as noble as we saw the Greeks and Romans. It could make everyone noble, so was democratic. Free Masonry perfectly expressed this new religious belief in rationality as providing fairness, democracy and nobility. A new, enlightened society.

One compromise was the separation of church and state. "Let's eliminate this church thing (as much an overthrowing of Rome) to get on with our new secular life." Distinguishing spiritual from secular is unknown to any other society. It freed the *nouveau* nobles to concentrate on making the wealth that would give *them* nobility. Rationalism also took the common European theme of denial of the flesh, and pushed it to prominence, hence exclusivity.

All this produced a society with a mind, but neither body nor soul. We deny our flesh and mortality, trying to hide from the fact we will die. We try to avoid death as long as possible, to the point of denying many of life's pleasures and other forms of puritanical punishment. Other peoples have long looked for ways to make their inevitable death a proud and noble an event. We do all we can to avoid it. We deny our fears, preferring to parade an arrogant assumption of control over everything or knowledge of everything, until the inevitable unknown and unknowables of death finally takes us. Which is why we fear it so much: It represents all our fears.

Our fears continue to show by the subterfuge of the witch hunts and conspiracy theories that have long characterised us, now simply masked with scientific proof, not to mention aided by an efficient electronic media. The werewolf scare of the 1600s, causing the torturing to death of thousands in France and Germany, are today's PCBs, breast implants, tobacco, child molesters, UFOs and government conspiracies. Our rationality is as irrational as ever.

Materialism also became European society's ultimate determinism. Determinism says there is one absolute Truth, Right, or Answer to everything. We soon came up with absolute Laws for even nature, promising absolute control. It only gave control over physical things, increasing our obsession with them, and all nature was reduced to only physical nature.

One needs the other: linear thinking, most suitable for the physical realm, and the physical-only view of Reality.

Whatever is not physical was removed from official consideration. Judgement and wisdom were replaced by fact and measure. But we are still human. So we have a society of people struggling to make their way and find personal satisfaction in a physical-only society. This is very hard. Adolescence is particularly difficult: all the things called childish and shamed, natural interests and wants to ignore. Adulthood does not look attractive to many of our young.

Of course, we simply replaced one religion with others ("King and country," "my country right or wrong," capitalism, and communism) to justify the same atrocities previously done in "the Name of the Lord," and science quickly became as dogmatic as the Church had ever been. (Same structures, different content and players.) We didn't change a bit, other than making our world more narrow.

Even that absolute control over the physical realm is not turning out quite as nicely as it was supposed to. We still can't control earthquakes and hurricanes, and that unsinkable *Titanic* thing was an embarrassment. Then Heisenberg discovered uncertainly! We may yet learn to be human.

What did change, however, was the acceptance of the materialist assertion that only what the five physical senses detect actually exists (constitutes reality). Its zenith was in the 1950s when B. F. Skinner said, "If it can't be measured [it doesn't exist]." He really said, "If it can't be measured, *forget it*," allowing there might be something but science certainly cannot be bothered with it, but ". . . it doesn't exist" is what was heard. We forgot all the rest. It can be neither controlled nor predicted, so what use?

Urban Myths: Evil Men

- Men and women are equally the initiator of physical domestic violence. Half the total violence is reciprocal (and equal parts initiated by each gender), the other half is evenly split between, only committed by the female, and only by the male. (Source: 1975 US National Family Violence Survey. *Change in Spouse Assault Rates from 1975 to 1992: A Comparison of Three National Surveys in the United States*, Murray Straus and Glenda Kaufman Kantor, presented at the 13th World Congress of Sociology, Bielefeld, Germany, July 1994, and many other sources. All countries show consistent figures.)
- In the U.S. in 1994, husband on wife severe assault had an occurrence rate of 2.0 percent. Severe husband assault of the sort promoted happens in only 1 of 50 households. (Source: 13th World Congress of Sociology, Bielefeld, Germany, July 1994.)
- In the U.S. in 1994, wife on husband severe assault had an occurrence rate of 4.6 percent. (Ibid.)

The next two figures are clearly only because women have the majority of custody. Equal incidents of physical child abuse are committed by the male and female parent in two-parent households. The data skews to the female only when single-parent households are included, almost 90 percent of which are female-headed.

- 55 percent of parents who kill their children are mothers. (Ref: *Murder in Families*, U.S. Dept of Justice, Bureau of Justice Statistics, July, 1994, pg 5-6.)
- Women commit the majority of all child abuse. (Ref: *Child Maltreatment 1996: Reports from the States to the National Child Abuse and Neglect Data System*, U.S. Government Printing Office, 1998, plus other sources.)

Equally true, however, is the convention that a woman who commits a crime deserves our sympathy, a man is a monster.

- "Every year, 3 million cases of child abuse are reported in the United States," is commonly cited, men commonly imagined behind most. But two-thirds of these reports turn out to be false, leaving one million cases. Of those, 50 percent involve neglect (passive abuse) and 25 percent are physical abuse (over half of each kind committed by women, not men). 12.5 percent are sexual abuse (approximately 70 percent indeed committed by men, the rest by women). That's 0.3 percent of children in the U.S. suffer substantiated sexual abuse. This is very bad. But possibly as bad: have you ever heard *that* figure reported? To account for non-reported case, a common rule-of-thumb is to multiply by 3, not 75. That would yield 0.9 percent of all children. Child abuse of any sort is a horrible crime. But is it so rampant as to throw all society into a panic, much less suspect every male? (Ref: *Throwaway Dads*, Ross D. Parke & Armin A. Brott, Houghton Mifflin Company, 1999, pg 36 - 37.)

Urban Myths: Evil Men (. . . continued)

- In 1984, Diana Russell claimed 54 percent of women had been the victim of incest (by a male relative) or sexual abuse (by male non-family member). This forces a conclusion that an equal proportion of men are paedophiles and rapists. When only incidents of physical contact were included from her study group, the number dropped to 38 percent. This still included attempted hand-holding, fumbled or attempted or unwelcomed or inappropriate kisses, however non-sexual, brushed legs, etc. Any contact they simply didn't like or found uncomfortable. This stretches any definition of sexual assault. Yet since then, a frequent claim of "authorities" in child abuse is "1 girl in 3 (or 4) will be sexually *molested* (a term usually reserved for fondled genitalia or rape) by the end of high school." Which implies a lot of evil men. Compare this to the 0.3 percent of substantiated cases of real sexual abuse cited above. Even were you to assume the 0.9 percent projection (to include non-reported cases), and that a *different* 0.9 percent of children were molested every year, and that *all* victims were female, maybe 1 in *6* girls would be molested before leaving high school. And you'd have done a lot of stretching. On the other hand, as the military has long known, you can get a lot of public sympathy, not to mention government money, with inflated figures. Possibly as evil as sexual abuse is persecution of the innocent. They are the same corruption of innocence. (Ref: *Throwaway Dads*, Ross D. Parke & Armin A. Brott, Houghton Mifflin Company, 1999, pg 37 - 38.)

- John Walsh is a U.S. television personality whose six-year-old son had been abducted and murdered. He caused a sensation when he testified before Congress, citing NISMART (National Incidence Studies of Missing, Abducted, Runaway and Throwaway Children) figures that 1.5 million children go missing every year, "This country is littered with mutilated, decapitated, raped, and strangled children." Except that almost all of them get found perfectly well. 450,700 are runaways; 438,200 are lost, injured or otherwise briefly missing and show up (73% within 24 hours); 345,100 were "abducted" by family members (only 2% being classic "child-snatching," none where the child was in danger, 83% of the time the reporter of the "missing" child knew were he or she was , only 10% lasting more than a month, the vast majority simply late, and note that a mother frustrating a father's visits is not likewise considered to have kidnapped). That leaves only 3% of the referenced number (3,200 to 4,600) as abductions for harmful intent of the sort every parent most fears. Terrible though this is, it is not 1.5 million decapitated bodies. (Ref: NISMART, Washington, D.C.)

What Have We Lost?

The triumph of materialism takes "validity is only external" and extends it to "*reality* is only external." We ourselves are not valid, not a legitimate measure of anything, and what we experience is not even real. This can create a lot of confusion for a human being, reinforcing the European inferiority complex.

Amputees have all long spoken of the ghost limb: They can feel and control the missing limb, even experience chronic pain in it. For years Euro-scientists pooh-poohed this, treating it as a psychological problem: "Not gotten over the loss. Denial. All in their head. Not real." Until a few years ago when a researcher in California discovered brain cells whose job is to mimic (be) each part of the body. When a body has had a limb through at least age two, the brain has formed physical patterns to control it. When the limb is removed, these remain. As far as the brain is concerned, it's still there. It took physical evidence to stop "professionals" from ignoring the word of those actually experiencing the ghost limb. *We* tried to tell *them* what they "really" experienced, based only on the (limited) physical evidence we could touch, see, or feel, and assumed it complete. If no physical evidence is seen, it doesn't exist, not that we haven't discovered it yet.

Anthropology and archaeology play the same game. Europeans have only seen physical evidence of Chinese or Indian civilization that can be verified as 5,000 years old, therefore we assert that they are that old, even though the Chinese and Indians know their history goes back many more thousands of years, and tell us so. We call their evidence folklore, as though invalid, and discard it, preserving "our" civilizations (Egypt, Mesopotamia, which somehow became ours) as the oldest.

We have probably eliminated eighty percent of reality – of total human experience – from formal recognition. We are the most narrow society to have existed. This is classical materialism. It has been our cult for over a hundred years. For whatever historical reasons, the triumph of classic materialism and exclusive linear thinking was Euro-culture's ultimate, formal denial of the legitimacy of personal experience, human judgement, systemic thinking, and all that is ineffable about human existence.[53]

The effects are wonderfully illustrated by Dr. Richard D. McCall in his book, *The Way of The Warrior Trader*. Dr. McCall has a Ph.D. in psychology, is a clinical psychologist, a Zen Master, a *samurai* warrior, and holds a black belt (fifth degree). By birth, he is Euro-American. At this point in the book he is trying to convey to a Euro-rooted reader the difference between Western and Oriental thinking:

> . . . [we] discuss what motivation appears to be. Funk & Wagnall's dictionary defines it as "a conscious need, drive or objective that incites a person to some action or behavior." This typically conventional definition tends to explain why so many people suffer from a lack of fulfilling and lasting motivation, and why so many of today's books, tapes and so-called motivational seminars fall short of their objective. In essence, they generally tend to preach that all that is necessary for motivation to exist is a reasonably desirable "dangling carrot" to pursue. Experience has taught me that nothing could be farther from the truth.
>
> In order to help you understand motivation from the warrior's point of view, at least initially, let me offer the expanded definition that would likely have come from a *samurai*. His definition of motivation would probably have been "the end result of holding within your heart a balanced blend of passion, life purpose, a meaningful mission or target, *and a genuine recognition of the fact that* now *may be the only chance to fulfill all three!*" As you can see, there is a great deal more implied in this definition than in Funk & Wagnall's, once again highlighting the difference between Eastern and Western philosophy and thought. The dictionary simply recognizes the importance of some external target or objective, whereas three of the four

---

[53] A lot of other traditional European institutions saw their end at the same time: alchemy, Dionysian practices, Gnosticism, etc. Even religion became more narrow. A loss of balance: science to the exclusion of all else; a techno-science-cult. Knowledge is a commodity; understanding, wisdom and skills not measurable so without value or even definition. Without definition, they are never mentioned, as though not existing.

requisite conditions in the *samurai*'s version are internal, and
even metaphysical in nature.[54]

One can see how much of reality we have lost; how much of our selves.
Few discover their life purpose because it would mean looking within for
one's own, which presuppose anything valid there. Looking within is as
often considered antisocial or psychotically religious.

If you look at a phallic symbol and say, "It represents an erect penis,"
you are European. If you look at it and say it represents *the energy of male
life creation*, you are a human being.

There is a Santa Claus. He is real and exists. Unless you believe the
spirit of warmth and closeness and giving (of which he is the
personification) is unreal, does not exist. (I might add, he is our only
remaining male motif of nurturing.) But our mythology says, "There is no
Santa Claus." We feel obliged to explain this to our children and fear their
thinking otherwise.

Ask my father if he is hungry, he looks at his watch. Is it time to be
hungry? My brother shivers on the sofa of his house. He gets up, looks at
the thermostat, sees it is set to 21°C like it "should be," so sits back down,
wrapping himself in his blanket and continues to shiver. Neither uses
himself as a gauge for even the most rudimentary functions. Only externals
– only physical measurements – tell us anything, are valid or reliable.

While much of what is called "New Wave" is certainly a return to
superstition, and a lot of the embracing of other religions is imitation, not
genuine, their popularity makes two very powerful statements.

1. Human spirituality is real, and cannot be ignored. It will find
   expression.
2. Our culture does *not* satisfy this basic human reality. It doesn't come
   close, doing more to undermine than embrace and support it.

---

[54] Reproduced with permission of The McGraw-Hill Companies. Richard D.
McCall, *The Way of the Warrior Trader* (McGraw-Hill, 1997). ISBN 0-7863-
1163-0, p.12

Our treatment of blood ties is a prime example of that hostility toward natural humanness. Family is our *biological* tie to our past and future. You can't get more fundamental than that; not just fundamental to humanness, but to life. Yet look how we regard it and treat it. Look at our divorce and adoption customs.

Our material-only focus, facilitated by exclusive linear thinking, which omits what it cannot control or predict, has done wonders for our material wealth. We have far greater material wealth than any society imagined possible. Because there's nothing like linear thinking for dealing with the purely physical.

It has come at great cost.

One example of the damage to our social processes is our view of assault. Even though meddling and bullying are as much personal violations,[55] and a being (the psyche) cannot distinguish violations from different sources – whether verbal or physical, they feel the same – our laws only recognize physical violence as assault. Our conventions say that only physical violence is bad, and do not recognize anything else as violence. This legitimizes non-physical violations of people, which we do systemically. Indeed, meddling and bullying are not simply acceptable, but multi-billion-dollar-a-year industries. Our media has us believing they can and should penetrate the most private areas of anybody's life on any pretext, as though they have a right, even an obligation, to do so. Violating people remains a large part of our culture, meddling often taking the guise of "helping."[56]

Victims of our society's systemic violence experience a profound confusion about what gets treated as right and wrong – who is treated as

---

[55] Meddling as assault, for instance, has a simple definition that is not apparently much understood. If I ask you to do something and you do it, that is helping. If nobody asks you and you "help," that is meddling. At the least it takes matters that are mine out of my hands; at worst, and very commonly, it does damage to things with which I am trying to deal, from which I cannot recover, and which affect you not at all. It is as much a personal violation (violence) as anything physical.

[56] The structural solution, of course, is simple. Define legal assault as assault. Any assault, not just physical. This will also have the advantage of eliminating most tort lawyers as it promotes so-called personal wrongs to social crimes. Whether you call it liable, it is still assault.

victim and villain – while trying to be part of what is actually an insane society. We call it alienation.

Sanity's Return?

Then, in the 1960s, a biologist invented ecology: the interrelated nature of the biological world. The "biosphere." It is multi-dimensional, each part effecting all others simultaneously in different ways, not linear. This got into the social sciences as General Systems Theory. General Systems Theory says that all things are cause, all effect, instead of a linear one cause to one effect. It is used to understand the intricate interrelationships that constitute a family (or any group), where you cannot affect one member without equally affecting all others, each is simultaneously affected by and affects all others. There is also, now, holistic medicine. And economists (good ones) must grasp that they, too, are dealing with a system (the economy) that defies linear formulas. One event causes many reactions in seemingly unrelated areas and ways.

North Europe-rooted civilization is rediscovering systemic thinking. You sometimes even catch people thinking holistically.

Lingering Conflicts

An excellent current example of the conflict between linear and systemic thinking – indeed, of the harm of linear thinking – is presented by the recent ad campaign launched by feminist interests against *male* violence to *wives*. The ads are certainly not anti-domestic violence or anti-spousal violence. They characterize the man as evil for physically violating his wife, and singles him out. There is one "bad thing" (the man) and one totally innocent victim, the only thing needed is to stop him. One cause and one effect. This is very like the old cowboy movies where they wore either a black hat or a white hat.

The truth of domestic violence is that it is systemic. Taking just couples, even North Europe-rooted social scientists talk today of co-dependence. To put it parochially, both are being equally violent to each other and themselves, although possibly in different ways. Isolating on only physical violence or the violence of only one party (context-elimination) blinds us to our own violence. You cannot "treat" one party without treating both as a system. All parts need each other to exist, and if each finds a different partner, they will find someone where the same things happen.

This systemic view assumes that violence is culture-centric, not gender-centric, and not just physical. It assumes each gender equally violent, however much in their own way. This clearly does not suit the agenda of the ads' sponsors. So they are not anti-domestic-violence ads. Indeed, particularly when one learns that women are equally guilty of initiating mutual physical violence and of being the only physical attacker, one has to wonder what the sponsor's agenda is. The ads look likely to do more harm than good – provoke violence in volatile situations rather than reduce it – exactly because they isolate on one member. What are the sponsors hoping to accomplish? A monopoly on public sympathy? Special treatment? Are they as guilt of bullying?

Mere anti-maleness campaigns simply commit the same abuse about which is complained. Righteousness is not an agent of change, it is an agent of oppression. This society has long been brutal to its members, it simply finds new content (targets). To try to put our brutality in gender terms is, to say the least, sexist, and commits the very victimizing of the innocent used as the instrument.

Exclusively linear thinking is at work both in stringing a family out into one-pays-the-next who nurtures-the-next (Custody-Access-Support) and in the equally sinister anti-maleness campaigns currently popular. Both also deny men all that is good and right and life-affirming about maleness. Maleness is narrowly and thereby perversely represented, more so now by feminists than by any so-called male society, and more narrowly than women ever were. Where is the social progress? Both Custody-Access-Support and male bashing are expressions of this society's perverse myths and sense of morality; gender myths only increasing in perversity, and simplistic notions of right and wrong not even worthy of a Hollywood fairy tale.

Is it on this we wish to base our laws and conventions, our formal culture, our social structures?

Conclusions

In Custody-Access-Support we have a social system based on a linear concept of family, when family is a system requiring systemic treatment as much as an economy, the biosphere, or any other. It also treats a spiritual entity, family, as a material one. Dealing exclusively with the physical is itself a degradation and commits gross unfairness. Trying to pretend the non-material eighty percent doesn't exist because "I don't know how to deal with it" is not just a cop-out, but means real issues are not just ignored, but exacerbated. This is an horrendous abuse we inflict on ourselves. It is not any form of "them." It is ourselves.

Notice the implication of that last statement. Feminists are not the problem now, any more than men were in the past. They are just its new expression. How can we expect feminists to behave, given our cultural context? How have they and all the rest of us been taught to behave toward any violation, except with their own?

Notice how culture-bound this reaction is. African Americans have long simply wanted to be part of America, left to lead normal, quiet, simple lives like everyone else. They are not rubbing slavery or black-white issues in everyone's face. (Far more whites do that.) They have shown little interest in bullying white America back, or any form of dominance of their own, though having far, far greater complaint about their systemic treatment than any European American woman.

The abuses of linear thinking and a physical-only reality, whoever commits them, is part of the legacy of the victory of classic materialism in North Europe-rooted civilization. It may be time to address the whole, and restore some balance.

6) Myth 4 – Divorce is a Sin

T he fourth of the five myths supporting CAS as "natural" involves lingering perceptions about marriage. It has to do with what is at stake upon divorce versus what should be, and whether we still even allow divorce. Our divorce laws are a confusion of old and new values, often conflicting. The previous discussion on having become a physical-only society comes into play.

What the state (or society) thinks it is doing defining whether anyone is married or not is a separate issue. The *social* reality is that marriage exists between two people by mutual consent. It is the couple, not the state, who decides this. Divorce, however, is at the discretion of one: It takes only one of a couple to declare a marriage over. Society simply puts games in the way; those determined to divorce are forced to play them. This is the systemic cause.

What are our formal (publicly held) attitudes about divorce? They are still that marriage is a social institution (as distinct from a personal declaration), and should not end. We examine our themes of marriage the institution, marriage's sacredness, protection, and property. Where might there be truth, and where traps?

Marriage the Institution, Divorce the Threat to Society

Most of the public may no longer see divorce as the threat to all society it used to, but much of this view still lingers in our laws (our formal conventions). It is worth reviewing some chronology and issues.

I remember the debate in the 1960s when Canada's divorce laws were "liberalized," as was happening in most jurisdictions. The only change was to add mental cruelty to adultery as the grounds for the state "granting" a divorce. In England they call it "unreasonable behaviour." Even if both wanted to split, you couldn't just say, "We want a divorce and the reason is none of your business." You had to accord blame. It was another twenty years before no-fault divorce was implemented in Canada and most of the United States; by 1999, England and Germany do not even provide this.

At the time, the common resistance to even this liberalization was, "We certainly don't want divorce to be easy."

Why, what is accomplished? What benefit in difficult divorces? What are we protecting?

Urban Myths: Victim Wife

- Women initiate 63 to 67 percent of all divorces in the U.S., Germany, and Australia; men, 25 percent; the balance jointly initiated. (Women seek divorce 2.5 times more frequently than men. Source: Any study ever done. *Surviving the Breakup*, Wallerstein & Kelly, ISBN 0-465-08345-5. *Divorced Dads*, Braver & O'Connell, ISBN 0-87477-862-x, pg 134. *Whose Decision Was It*, Beuhler, Journal of Marriage and the Family 48:587-95, 1987, plus many other sources.)

- Lenore Weitzman's 1985 book *The Divorce Revolution* claimed that women and children average a 73 percent drop in standard of living after divorce; fathers' increase by 42 percent. It was a bombshell whose effect is still being felt driving social perceptions and policies. Except the drop was *to* 73 percent of pre-divorce, not *by*. The numbers had been misreported. There turned out many other problems with the 10-year California study: use of seriously outdated equivalency scales for costs during high inflation times, ignored effect of taxes, and errors in expense allocation. When Dr. Sanford Braver of Arizona State University and a team of researchers, as part of an eight-year study, reassessed the data, it was found that mothers and fathers each commonly experience *no change* in standard of living. (*Divorced Dads*, Sanford L. Braver and Diane O'Connel, Tarcher Putman, 1998, ISBN 0-87477-862-x.)

Urban Myths: Victim Wife (. . . continued)

- Mothers experience a fourfold increase in depression, hospital admissions, and work problems on divorce. Divorced fathers, a ninefold increase. (Ref: *Marital Disruption As a Stressor: A Review and Analysis,* Bloom, Asher and White, Psychological Bulletins 85:867-93, 1978.)

- Three years after divorce, 20 percent of male initiators regretted it, 1 percent of female initiators. Further, 66 percent of *left* woman were now glad of the divorce, only 50 percent of male *initiators* felt as strongly. (*Divorced Dads*, Sanford L. Braver and Diane O'Connel, Tarcher Putman, 1998, ISBN 0-87477-862-x.)

- 42 percent of adult children of divorce report their mother tried to keep them from seeing their father; 20 to 40 percent of mothers confess to this; up to 75 percent of fathers report it. Whoever's statistics you believe, it is a rampant and serious problem, bred of the inequities inherent to CAS. (Ref: *Ceasfire!*, Cathy Young, Free Press, 1999, pg 209. Also see *Surviving the Breakup*, Judith Wallerstein and Joan Kelly, ISBN 0-465-08345-5, whose figure was 50 percent.)

- In divorce-related accusations of child-abuse, women make 95 percent of accusations, at least 75 to 80 percent of which are false. In a large number of cases an obsession has been found with hurting the ex-husband at any cost, including coaching the children and shopping for a therapist to support their claims. (Ref: *Sexual Abuse Allegations in Divorce and Custody Disputes*, Holida Wakefield and Ralph Underwager, Behavioral Sciences and the Law 9, 1990; *Personality Characteristics of Parents Making False Accusations of Sexual Abuse in Custody Cases*, Holida Wakefield and Ralph Underwager, Issues in Child Abuse Accusations 2, 1990.)

They saw themselves protecting "The Institution Of Marriage." They believed the *institution* must be respected and not taken lightly. That is, people exist to serve their social institutions, not the reverse.

This is a society gone insane.[57] If our institutions are not there to serve us – do not fit with and reinforce our humanness, the realities of human existence – we must make them do so. For what species are these institutions intended, cows? If our social institutions are not for human beings and do not serve, express and accommodate that humanness, including the regrettable or tragic things that happen, what are they for, to turn us into some other species? What other creature tries to force itself to be what it is not?

This already makes a personal relationship into a business deal where the original terms must be honoured irrespective of changing circumstance or new personal discoveries.

Human reality is not a business contract. Any relationship is always undergoing constant change, reassessment, and redefinition. They must change and re-form, for that is life, their nature to be organic. They are a living thing so it will happen whether society "allows" it to or not.

This means some end. But part of any ongoing assessment is natural human values such as loyalty and commitment. Trust them. Let them enjoy their own expression. They cannot be forced, for force will make of them a trap rather than a haven. ***If remaining married is not as free a choice as becoming so, you are not freely married.*** The mere existence of divorce lawyers speaks volumes about the inhumanity of our divorce customs. Marriage is personal, not public. Society has no business here.

China and the Arab world are two societies where divorce is extremely easy: just say it is so. Both enjoy divorce rates of less than 7 percent. (It has been increasing in the Arab world with increasing Europeanization. The traditional norm for both cultures is closer to 3 percent.) There are many reasons other cultures' marriages are more stable than our own. Easy or difficult divorces clearly have nothing to do with it. Divorces will happen

---

[57] Another example of extension-transference. The social institution of marriage is an extension (external representation) of inner human realities. Making the institution more important than the human experience (giving it the significance) is the transference. We transferred significance out of ourselves onto something we created. When this happens, we have dogmatism.

or not; divorce customs only determine how traumatic it is for however many will invariably go through it. Some always will; why be cruel? It is a personal tragedy, not a public crime to be punished.

Why do we not strive for naturalness in our social structures, for reflections of ourselves? Because we retain that lingering fear that what is natural to us is horrible and to be fought, not accommodated.

Unholy

Marriage is considered sacred. Nothing wrong with that. The problem is when we think it more sacred than family.

Divorce is seen as tearing asunder the sacred, so already the end of everything important, rather than simply two people discovering different needs, interests, and tolerances than assumed at the start. So we make divorce that: total destruction, the Armageddon of the whole, because the sacred element is gone. *Failing to distinguish between marriage and family.* This has always resulted in society basically punishing children for the divorce of the parents, which *does* make divorce a sin. (Perceive it so; make it so.)

(To put this in terms of the previous multi-deity paradigm: Upon divorce, we are still worshipping the god of marriage, not the god of family. If we care anything about the children, this is the wrong god for this occasion. When divorce comes, the time for worshipping marriage has passed. It failed. Divorce is the time to honour the god of family.)

Since marriage has long been regarded the sacred thing, our divorce customs still revolve around attempting to preserve as much of the previous whole as possible. This is done by, 1) surgically removing one party as the one leaving, 2) keeping everything else in place – children and household – as though they remain in the marriage.

Supposedly, this will minimize the damage to a whole that no longer exists anyway as one or more new ones are forming. We perform a total elimination of one party, rather than allow normal adjustments to changing dynamics by all parties. Or, it is assumed that one party has decided to leave the whole concept of family, not just the spouse, so that's what we turn it into. Whereas all that is happening is a change to only one of the many relationships comprising a family, the old whole assuming new form. In trying to prevent a new whole, seeing it as unholy or less holy, we cause needless emotional-spiritual fragmentation. We try to deny change, attempting finality to alterations, only to create finality to things that should never end and distort naturally occurring changes. We deal with only the physical manifestations, destroying spiritual realities. No wonder it's confusing to those put through it: What are we valuing?

Protection

This brings us to the protection theme in divorce: protect what remains of the previous whole. It remains the rationale for many divorce provisions, certainly for the overall structuring. Our divorce laws are predicated on protecting the one who does not want the marriage to end, assumed to be the female. It is to protect what remains, to make sure her life (now increasingly using the children as surrogates) is as little disrupted as possible, materially. This is fuelled by Victorian images of the callous man abandoning an otherwise helpless female. We may have changed many of the rationales and the nomenclature, but this image still fuels the emotional engine.

That is to say, our laws are not to protect the interests of the children. They are to protect the interests of the wife. Because men are not seen as the protectors and providers of children, women are. So to protect and support the children, you protect and support their mother. A man's responsibility has long been only to his wife in our culture, not directly to his children, and that is the responsibility we are determined he will not shirk, stripping him of any others. He is denied direct responsibility toward the children, only through her (linear).

This is how we do not allow divorce. Support is paid to *her* – not spent directly on the children, nor given to them, nor put in a trust for them – so *she* can continue the pre-divorce household – continue the marriage, the family – on the children's behalf, the father removed.

Feminists take a strong interest in the status quo, anxious that this structure remain, composing justifications.

WHEREAS organizations advocating "father's rights," whose members consist of non-custodial parents, their attorneys and their allies, are a growing force in our country; and WHEREAS the objectives of these groups are to increase restrictions and limits on custodial parents' rights and to decrease child support obligations of non-custodial parents by using the abuse of power in order to control in the same fashion as do batterers; . .

— National Organization for Women
Action Alert on "Fathers' Rights," 1996

Any man interested in parenting is a wife-beater. The connection is obvious.

Although direct gender references are now largely expunged from most laws, and it is debatable whether females have ever been helpless, the female as victim of divorce and male as villain remains behind attempts to preserve any physical status of pre-divorce. It is the old presumption of protecting women from the deprivation of divorce, her only means of survival being guaranteed by the marriage contract. Enforcing that guarantee protects any obligation toward the children, and effectively continues the marriage. We are only interested in enforcing contracts, not that children have the best parenting option, for which lawyers can take considerable credit.

Alimony has mutated into support payments, likewise transferring to children the "divorcing men victimizing the helpless" theme on which all have long loved to play. We wouldn't want to loose a favourite moral theme that has served us for so many generations. One sees it, for instance, in claims of financial disadvantage for divorced women and how readily believed they are, however untrue they turn out to be (*see inset page 122*). Divorced men are evil; divorced women, in need of sympathy. Protect the one being left, if you can distinguish leaving from being driven away. This is an extension of "women are all gentle (helpless) and loving; men tough, mean, and unfeeling."

Which is absolutely true, of course, isn't it? There's never been an abusive, malicious, or despotic woman. That's only men, and all of them.

Gives one a fuzzy feeling knowing our laws are firmly rooted in truth and free of bias.

Despite the fact two thirds of divorces are sought by wives, our divorce customs centre on punishing the husband: his removal from the whole family, not just from his wife, while retaining his life-long (contractual) material obligation to her. They are predicated on the fear or assumption that he is trying to shirk his responsibility to his family, and ensuring against it. This is the image Custody-Access-Support implements: protect what remains of the marriage; minimize *physical* change, prevent divorce (the loss of *his* obligations to *her*).

Also, note how our assumption has always been that she has never had any obligations to him. (One could argue that loyalty has been the wife's obligation, but what obligations remain from *her* to *him* upon divorce, much less are enforced?)We have long formalized marriage as not simply as linear, but one-way. Whereas in truth, any relationship that one-sided does not last. Most women do carry their own weight in a relationship, one way or another. So this is more un-reality in our formal social structures.

Perhaps all women only initiate divorce because they're being beaten, either physically or morally, all men, only out of opportunism.[58] Therefore, women are still entitled to all this special consideration. But at a divorce rate exceeding fifty percent, that is hard to accept. So especially when the divorce isn't his idea but hers, something seems a little wrong with this "protect the woman with the rest of the family" we have institutionalized. It may more often be injustice than protection. Indeed, such a system might present a huge exploitative opportunity for women. One some might defend to the death. This could explain the preponderance of female-initiated divorces, however unthinkable that any women would ever be so . . . what, man-like?

In defining the games people must play to attain a divorce, it is possible to create incentives.

---

[58] These were among the urban myths assessed and dispelled by Dr. Sanford Braver's study, and by a number of others'. *Divorced Dads* (Penguin Putnam, 1998). ISBN 0-87477-862-x.

Besides the obvious irrationalities and inequities, and even if we truly removed the gender biases, even more sinister assumptions lie behind the protection premise.

Property

The whole divorce process turns marriage into a goods-and-services contract. A business deal, not a personal commitment subject to normal human forces. There is property to divide. This is why you can't get a divorce without a lawyer: A marriage is an enterprise which, like any commercial partnership, acquires physical assets. Lawyers want, more than anything, marriage to be a commercial partnership, or there's no role for them.

The property view of marriage is held by almost all cultures, but for much broader reasons. Even for us before the Industrial Revolution, when marriages were family to family, they *were* goods-and-services contracts. This is why they lasted. They were practical arrangements, none of this romantic false expectations nonsense. Each family assumed long-term material obligations to the other. At one level of society, this was survival. At another, politics. (Same thing.) There was nothing personal about it, a marriage of "fortunes," which at the time meant a great deal more than mere property, but certainly included it. At that time, the family assets were not only one's survival, but one's posterity. It was one's existence, from all times past, to all times to come.

We have become more narrow and transient. Now that we define and see all things in only physical form, we deal only with the material property. Property has dramatically changed in meaning. It is now a consumable (as is everything), no longer your family's hereditary survival. Retaining any property motif with such a dramatically changed context can only be dangerous.

Industrialization, and the much maligned but vital welfare state, provide an entirely different context. We have jobs and careers instead of family property. So we claim that marriage is person-to-person, that it is a personal commitment, not a property or business one.

Yet in divorce, we still treat marriage as a deal for property – whether brought in upon the marriage or gained during it – irrespective of what formed and sustained it. In this view, the "injured" (less wealthy) party retains marriage's protection or profits.

This property assumption can hardly be considered healthy in a person-to-person marriage. It supports marrying for all the wrong reasons: reasons of taking advantage of each other. And the idea of anyone "owing" anyone anything is at odds with a couple's normal assumptions upon marriage. (Again, the schism between informal and formal culture.)

Person-to-person marriage is an act of voluntary selflessness, a surrendering to whatever the future may bring, expecting nothing in return, including surrendering to however long it lasts. "You pays your money and takes your chances." This is true of entering any human relationship. Marriage is not a materials contract; the courts have no business here. It is an act of faith. There are risks, and no guarantees; you do it for your own, personal reasons. It could end for any number of reasons, such as death, before you want it to. That is the nature of all relationships, their inherent premise, their inherent risk.

Upon divorce, however, we make marriage an act of selfishness. Given any assumption of either anything "owed" or anything "earned by the marriage," in the bitterness of divorce it becomes a game of "who comes out with the most," however at odds with the original premise of the marriage. Dress people as warriors, they act as ones.

One has to wonder whether this property treatment is *causing* divorces. Is it what, more than anything else, is undermining the spirituality of marriage? Possibly we would return the faith to marriage if we eliminated the property and the ability to "cash in" a marriage.

Many jurisdictions claim they removed much of this when they largely eliminated alimony. I'm afraid the children are simply used as an excuse for its continuance, the principal reason so many cling to sole custody: It is an entitlement. Support turns children into physical assets.

So compounding the inhumanity of the property approach is treating the children as one of the commodities over which exclusive dominion may be awarded. (Ownership; custody.) But what I am saying is, *the problem is not simply treating children as property, but treating divorce as any property division at all.* Right now, we turn divorce into a property scramble, the children simply swept in with everything else. Support payments make children an asset. Why else do lawyers fight for every penny they can? It can't be because, "The more money she has, the better parent she'll be," or anyone who is poor must be a terrible parent whose children must be removed immediately.

(Lawyers, of course, are too clever for that. The rational for paying the mother, not the children, the greatest possible amount of support, is to ensure the children will enjoy whatever benefit they would have had were we not removing their father. This pre-supposes she will spend it all on them, and the father would not, a blatant gender bias irrespective of words used to implement it. This is what I mean by support as a surrogate for alimony and children the asset to assure it. Of course, if the rational for support is to support the household in its pre-divorce form . . . we're back to the same thing: Children are an asset to assure a life-long pension. This is entirely thanks to lawyers, and their insistence that *marriage* acquires property, such as children, as though it were a business entity.)

Who would care for the physical needs of the children after divorce? Well, if both are equally the children's parents, and both equally free to (however differently) run a household for them, obviously, both. On what basis are we assuming otherwise? This would be in a different form than that enjoyed while married. We seem to consider that horrible, as though there were never major changes like moving to a new city or losing a job during the marriage, or as though they have been outlawed for married couples.

Both parents continuing as parents does not require regulation except in extreme cases; extremes some would have us believe the norm, or should govern what is done to everyone.

If marriage is person-to-person, lawyers have no business having anything to do with their termination any more than their creation. They are for personal reasons only, not wealth acquisition or even security acquisition. Few things are more dehumanizing to all than assigning monetary value to anything to do with human relationships, which lawyers insist on doing, for "moral reasons." For "protection." Or to protect their role, as lawyers are only able to deal with property, not humanity.

Upon divorce, each need only take the physical assets with them they brought into the marriage, either upon or during it. Because a person, at the physical level, is a distinct individual, whether married or not. The argument, "Being married freed him to do such and such," could as easily be, "Being married prevented him from accomplishing much more, so she owes him." The argument is meaningless, even self-defeating.

(*Also see Appendix II,* Divorce Fantasy, *for a more detailed examination of why it is dangerous to divide only physical assets, much less use the children as one.*)

There is a clear exception. There is a strong case for a limited alimony under specific circumstances. Should part of the marital agreement be that one partner stays home for the children's formative years, which creates a career disadvantage should it later become necessary to rejoin the workforce, alimony would compensate such clear material sacrifice made for the marriage. It can be for perhaps two to five years after divorce, and may taper off. It should provide an opportunity to return to material self-sufficiency. Indeed, without such a provision, we would be punishing anyone who foregoes career and money to dedicate at least one parent to the children. We would be structurally motivating "money only, and to hell with children," enough our culture as it is.

This is a case for alimony. Don't call it child support. And nothing is preventing a Dependency Agreement being separately made to cover this, removing any presumptions of material dependence or expectancy from marriage.

Some claim another exception. If a couple jointly builds a business, both are entitled to its fruits in proportion to direct contribution. This is not an exception. This is true for any "couple" or group building a physical asset, irrespective of marriage. That *is* a property issue requiring lawyers, not a marriage one. But it should not be generalized beyond all reason. To assume a spouse part of building a business just because he or she was there but without direct material contribution, is the enmeshment concept. Keep marriage and property issues separate.

There would seem an obvious criteria. If a spouse can "cash in" their partnership while *remaining* married, it is rightfully theirs. Otherwise, anything gratuitously given is gratuitously given, part of whatever exchange within whatever relationship, whether it is companionship or other assets, given for the joy of giving, lawyers keep out! Our divorce laws should not be corrupting marriage by making such giving an "expecting something for it later." Something to "cash in."

Protect Whom?

We can now more cleanly return to the theme of protection. The first and most obvious question is: When only the female partner seeks a divorce without evidence of abuse (real abuse), why would we protect her from its financial, or any other, effects? We don't do that for men. Even beyond that, if we can now assume that everyone is equally capable of survival (however much in their own way and level of affluence) – that women do not have to marry and stay married to the same man as their only means of survival, but are as capable on their own as any man, including as capable of remarrying – does anything need protecting?

Maybe there is something. Who among us, male or female, has not had the experience of unwanted attentions? Of breaking or trying to break off a relationship (or not even having had one), only to have the other clinging, trying to keep it going? This can range from nuisance to threat. Do you not have a right to privacy? Do you not have the right to decide who is at what level of intimacy in your life, to end a relationship no longer seen as beneficial?

Perhaps our laws are protecting the wrong person. Perhaps the one leaving is entitled to protection. The one left knew the risks. However regrettable it may be, it entitles them to nothing in particular other than our sympathy that it could and does happen to us all. It does not entitle them to intrude upon the other.

Perhaps we should be seeking ways of protecting or ensuring *separation*.

Conclusions

With or without children, we continue to make divorce as bad as we can, if only by the violation of dragging as many private matters into the public arena as we can, simply to satisfy lawyers. I am seeing nothing productive in this. I am seeing only harm: People already confused, forced into unnatural posturing. Our current divorce laws have nothing to do with marriage, and certainly care nothing for families.

I suggest we need formal images of marriage and family which do not rely on each other, and that preserves as much of family as possible in the face of changing relationships. Changing relationships between the parents is all couple break-up is, it is only we who make it the dissolution of all relationships. Why does divorce – the separating of only two members – mean the annihilation of all the complex interrelationships? We are one of the extremely few societies to turn something as commonplace as changing relationships into something so traumatic and horrible.

Such a new image would have to entail a cleaner view of marriage as personal and voluntary between two individuals. It would not make marriage a business contract that has to be forced to its completion, or which acquires physical assets of its own as though a commercial enterprise, reducing family to a balance sheet and all the dehumanization of today. Property, not just children as property, must be removed. It muddies the waters and invites alternate agendas, especially those of lawyers.

If society as a whole is so interested in a role, two things do need to be protected:

- ▸ The separation of the adults.
- ▸ The relationship between children and *each* parent. Equally.

Indeed, in many cases the second will not be attained without the first. Divorce is almost always initiated by one partner, resisted by the other. For whatever reason, one has decided to reduce or eliminate the other from their personal life. The wishes of that one should be respected. It deserves protecting. That is to say, there are no rights of retention for the one who wants to keep the marriage. No rights of retaining anything between them, including any physical manifestation of what once existed but no longer does.

What needs protecting is the opposite: the right to leave, the right to divorce, the right to end. For if protecting separation is not a cornerstone, many will not feel confident continuing, or trying to enrich, their involvement with their children, being too busy looking over their shoulder.

7) Myth 5 – Social Equality

The final myth we will cover is more the absence of myth. Despite our constant use of the word, can you tell me what we believe to be equality, or how we measure it, or know who has it and who does not? If we cannot answer these questions, the word is open to exploitation. This lack is clearly a block to equality of parenthood. This discussion may be the most important, tying all others together.

"Equal in the eyes of God."

Today one might say, "We all know we're going to die," death the ultimate equalizer. Both express the same thing: our fundamental *spiritual* equality. "Under the skin," we all face the same realities of human existence.

But if you're being beaten by your master, or systematically abused by society, or taken advantage of by your company with no recourse, equal "under the skin" is cold comfort. What about operational, social equality? What about day-to-day activity? How do we attain it, how do we define it, or assure it? What is it? Does it mean that everyone has to have the same amount of money? Does it require that all possess equal charm or good looks? Witness the feminists who insist half the members of a country's legislature be female or there is no equality for them.

Is equality, sameness?

On the other hand, must every sub-group in society (gays, women, Indians) be listed in the Bill of Rights to enjoy any? That alone would say those rights do not apply to all, only those with sufficient clout to gain mention. This alone is *in*equality. Certainly in our society, which uses the law as the ultimate arbiter of everything, equality means applying the same laws to all people in the same way. (Not to all contexts, to all people.) Is that all? Is it enough?

Seeking Equality

In "Myth 2 – Uni-paradigm-ism," we saw the hierarchical image. It is very efficient for uniform action by a large group. But if the same hierarchy is always applied to all things, it is explicitly inequality. The kindest some will be about men having a role in children's lives is to insist it still be subordinate to the mother ("Only if the mother agrees"). This is the one-parent structure and the same explicit denial of equality of parenthood. It is the same as insisting that men are the sole head of the household. Both deny the real, underlying inter-dependence that not only always has and will exist between men and women, but among all members of any society. Inter-dependence is a flat structure.

In "Myth 3 – Linear Thinking," we saw another commonly assumed structure: the straight line. But the narrowness of "one supports the next who nurtures the next" denies the dynamism of a system and the uniqueness of each individual, so can do as much to deny equality as implement it. This model may not be inequality *per se* (at least it's flat), but certainly too narrow to reliably produce it in very many cases.

So what is? What structuring reflects, even produces, equality?

It has always been all around us, probably too obvious to see. I defer to Robert Axelrod's *The Evolution of Cooperation*. He happened upon this natural phenomenon accidentally while performing a kind of social scientist's game. The meat of the book is in its preface, and can be found as Appendix I, here. Take the time to read it.

To Euro-rooted peoples it is a revelation, just because it is rarely *consciously* acknowledged. The book and its findings are largely ignored, too much challenging the way we'd prefer to think about social man. But it is intuitively obvious.

The Evolution of Cooperation shows that "you need me and I need you" is the basis for a society. Cooperation is needed for any society – of amebas, ducks, or people – to form and sustain, and it *naturally occurs* as long as you need me and I need you. It is not required to need each other in the same way, for the same things, or to the same extent. It is not required that each member need all others. You don't even have to like each other. Just that each has something one or more others want, and authority over whether they get it.

This happens because a very, very simple strategy of interaction with those with which one must deal proves most effective, and very readily comes to the fore: cooperate with those who cooperate (and make cooperation your own first move); exploit back to (or withhold cooperation from) those who try to exploit you. It seems it must come to the fore, and can only come to be the basis for any society. This is how a group of living entities, each with self-interest, comes to deal with each other.

What is equality? It is the basis for this happening: equal significance to the whole, by having something needed or wanted by others. *Equality is the ability to reciprocate, the ability to cooperate or not, having something that makes you matter.* That significance (that something you have to offer) may come in any form, be for any number of reasons, and come to prominence at any time. It is not in sameness. It is in uniqueness, in being different.

Apply this to women in our society. By the 1950s, the Industrial Revolution had trivialized running a household. The introduction of the birth control pill is often cited as a watershed, "freeing" women from traditions. It was just another piece of the scenery. Washing machines, refrigerators, preserved foods, easy shopping . . . until running a household held little challenge, hence, little significance, "freeing" women from anything that mattered. Today, even I can run a household while perusing our new god, a career. Women started to realize that society could do without them, and was increasingly doing so. (No one should hold any delusions: social movements are bred of some form of desperation, not simply high ideals. Why do you suppose it is important to some women to flaunt the fact they don't need men?)

So if society did not adjust to welcome women's return to its economic life – the only thing that now mattered to it – women would definitely have been unequal. *It is not that women are more equal than a hundred years ago. It is that the context within which that equality must express itself has dramatically changed.*

Apply the same to men. When we insist, and institutionalize, that fathers are without significance to their families or to society as a whole as men – when we make them insignificant with non-custody – how "powerful" do you think *men* feel?

One would think the driving force behind all social policies of a society calling itself a democracy and committed to equality would be ensuring the equal significance of all its members.

Equality is being equally important, or the ability to make yourself that. It is produced by the ability to cooperate: having something to contribute, something that gives you social merit. This means having something over which you have exclusive dominion that matters to others, something nobody can just take from you without your say-so. It is having something that makes you matter to the group, the community, the tribe, the family. Not necessarily its only source, but an important or handy one. Take that away – remove a person's ability to give something, the ability to cooperate, having something to contribute – and you have removed him from the group. He doesn't matter. Remove either differences (having something unique) or the individual's dominion over it (to whom and when contributed), and you have inequality.

Equality is not necessarily in everyone being as important as everyone else, *all at the same time*. One's importance will almost always be situational, different people (skills, knowledge) required for different things at different times. Everyone is important, but for different reasons, so at different times. The potential for significance, for one's time to come, must be recognizable. The time may never come; that does not mean the skills or presence need not be there.

One's importance will be for reasons which cannot be anticipated by Parliament or imposed by society beforehand. They occur, case by case, on their own. I need you; you need me; each for our own reasons.

Cultural Blockages

Axelrod's work indicates an overwhelming natural tendency to cooperate, not compete. It indicates that self-interest naturally leads to helping, even rooting for each other; that the thing that keeps us "in line" (social, sociable, the basis of any and all cooperation) is accountability to each other; in each having simple day-to-day, operational, even little, needs that can only be satisfied by others. Or whose satisfaction can be withheld. Not the law, altruism, God (the European external one), or subservience to some person's or group's idea of Common Good. Each other.

So this work is not much loved by anyone. It is ignored outside academia and not much attended to within. It undermines our whole way of thinking, would dis-empower a lot of people. The right-wing thinks the self-interest of being physically separate beings leads to greed and competition, and this is Good (or at least natural, and inevitable.). It must therefore form the basis of all social structures.

The left-wing thinks the same thing (self-interest means greed and selfishness), and it is Bad. Their solution is to eliminate separation with, "Everybody has to love each other," and altruistic "caring." Everyone must think and live the same, everything shared: enmeshment, to not be separate. This is a denial of physical reality – our real physical separation – inevitably leading to authoritarian attempts to control others' lives, however much out of "love and caring."

By contrast, Axelrod's work suggests that the self-interest bred of physical separateness naturally leads to *cooperation*. Not greed and selfishness.

That messes with *everybody's* thinking!

Self-interest already makes us care about each other. I am courteous to you because I want, even need you to be courteous to me. I care about the elders of my community because I know I will soon be among them. I care about and help those less advantaged than me, not out of pity, which presumes superiority, but because I know, "There but for the grace of God go I." It could be me next week.

This is not altruism. This is self-interest and *self*-affection. It is good. You, and caring about yourself, are good. It is the origin of all the goodness in life, just as self-hatred is the origin of all evil.

Everyone is already concerning themselves with fairness and balance for their own sake. It is what is happening in everyone's life, almost every moment of every day. But our formal culture sees only evil coming from physical separateness. So we have a culture premised on greed, premised on "people are bad." Right there it's way out of whack with our humanness and the most fundamental laws of nature.

The right-wing sees threat as the only motivator, that only the law or God or some external force keeps everyone "in line" and must be applied to the letter without consideration for circumstance. There is a ready assumption that people are always trying to be bad, and would be were it not for a strong stick. The left-wing (the righteousness fascists) insists society, being somehow otherwise blind or stupid, must be led or coerced to doing the Right Thing, not otherwise caring about their own selves or community. One says, "the law for the sake of the law," not whether it is fair in a particular instance; the other, "conformance so everyone is the same (not separate) or no one will act responsibly." Both imbue themselves with a presumption of power over other's lives instead of attending to their own; both rely on and perpetuate the sense of threat we learned from 10,000 years of it, now blaming our very nature as its source. Both assume the same need for external, central control for the same reason (we are worthless without "them"); both force their values on others; both are equally intolerant of everyone having their own power and dignity and simply leading their own lives.

Whereas Axelrod's work suggests that people being different, and the greatest degree of difference, is critical to a society's existence. It is also critical that everyone be strong (have power) and their own something to contribute, along with knowing they are as important as anyone else. Empowerment of each, and respect for it.

Who's going to listen to that kind of nonsense?

Something to Give

A principal ingredient to social equality asserts something we've been afraid to embrace because we don't know how. Indeed, we have been increasingly undermining it: people having anything all to themselves, having anything over which each enjoys exclusive dominion, access to which each person solely regulates. Something to give.

The main reason for trouble with this – other than jealously – is thinking only in terms of property and equating everything to it (materialism). Whereas one may have skills, interests, or simply a presences. One may have one's maleness or femaleness to give, offer unique patriarchy or matriarchy.

With property, a society may indeed sometimes need to violate an individual's dominion to satisfy communal needs, taxes an obvious example. But property is external, transient, and not a person. By its nature, it flows within any society. (And as Bertrand Russell pointed out anyway, the origin of all ownership of property is theft.) However personally one might relate to property as an external manifestation of oneself, property is not the person.

But we then extend this treatment of property backward into people. We fail to guard against real personal violation. So be it modesty, privacy, personal dignity, or whatever, our culture increasingly feels at liberty to violate its members, do-gooders and the media usually leading the way. We feel we can and should regulate, for instance, parental involvement, even what constitutes a marriage or family, rather than giving the individuals the power of running their own affairs simply by protecting the right of *all* to do so *equally*.

As an example, I have no interest in peering into the pitcher's ear during a baseball or cricket game. I do not see that as great sport. He is there for a larger game in a larger context. The camera likewise has no business in the dugout or sidelines. That is not where the public spectacle – what all these people are working toward – is occurring. Television invented "the close-up," made it its only tool, and has been eliminating context ever since, convincing themselves we like it.

Respect for other's dignity and privacy is at odds with many interests in our society. (Interests that did not get there by conspiracy, by the way. They got there by context. We put them there.) The media asserts, "The public's right to know," a notion never seen in any social equity proclamation and simply a euphemism for "invade anything about anyone that we think will sell." (It sells because it titillates; it titillates because it is violation, like any pornography.)

Personal violations are increasing. They are acceptable. Jerry Springer and Sally Jessy Raphael make it entertainment, but *60 Minutes* had long dignified it as journalism. Do-gooders are "trying to help," which they never wind up doing but exacerbating an already bad situation, and if you resist society's "help," you are particularly suspect. Many forces prefer that no one have anything exclusively theirs, because *they* want it, parental responsibility an example. We think we have to teach parental responsibility, which assumes a monopoly on it.

Acknowledging, much less defending, an individual's authority would undermine the premise of many people. Fathers get regulated out of their children's lives if they don't get along with their wives. We do not defend their role with their children, but meddle to the point of eliminating it. Social workers commonly try to manage a couple's relationships (content), either between the couple or between each parent and the children. They do not define the structures of equality within which people can manage their own (context).

But equality is being equally significant. And one's significance is only in the relevance of what one has to give, and having it at all. If what you have can simply be taken at someone at else's leisure – if it is not for you to give or not give, like your privacy, if you can be violated on someone else's whim – you have nothing to give. You are impotent.

By the same token, if I do not see my self-worth – do not see what it is I have to give and know I have control over it – I will be more concerned with what others have and seek ways to control *that*. Perhaps this society's preoccupation with others' (often imagined) power, and efforts to take it – be it the government's, men "as a class," business's, and so forth and all the paranoia over it – is only a reflection of ignoring our own, of not feeling we have any. Not in not having any. In not knowing we have. Paying too little attention to ourselves, too much to others.

But witness this incredibly complex society. It is comprised of hundreds of thousands, even millions of organizations not directly related to each other. They in turn consist of a myriad of individuals, also not directly related. There are religious organizations, public and private organizations, educational, commercial. There are libraries, manufacturers, transporters, retailers, research groups, communications, social services; the list is endless. Amazing numbers and variety. And this seeming hodgepodge of random organizations works. People successfully lead lives, extremely large numbers of them. It has only been possible because of and to the extent to which we need each other, and are *free to cooperate*. (Have something to contribute, and dominion over when, where, and to whom we contribute it.) This simple structure works to an incredible degree. Nobody could have imagined such complexity and scale, certainly no one person or group could have orchestrated it. It just happened on its own, each piece building on others, natural cooperation, natural interest in what we each can gain from others by our giving.

If we were anything as selfish or evil or competitive as our mythology suggests, we'd have killed ourselves all off a hundred thousand years ago. While we've certainly been guilty of concerted efforts to this end, has anyone noticed that we're still around, even prospering? Is it possible this means there is something inherently good about us? We are so preoccupied with the extremely rare exceptions to cooperation (wars, strikes, crime) we don't seem to see how rare they are; how overwhelmingly cooperation dominates, taking it for granted as nature's most powerful social force. Addicted to a negative self-image, we only see its confirmation.

For instance, given all the people in the world, not to mention all the nations, the wonder isn't that there are wars, but so few. The wonder of our highways isn't the accidents that occur, but the huge numbers that do not. The wonder isn't the crimes committed, but how few; that they are an exception, that the vast majority of people lead quiet, peaceful lives, interested in others' peace because they are interested in their own. None of this is happening by force, and anyone thinking so is fooling themselves. You couldn't force this much cooperation. Cooperation has increased as society's rigidity, decreased.

The Role of Law

This is not to say there must never be intervention. There is not just one social law. There is also a natural tendency for power to accumulate, as in monopolies and dictatorships. But intervention must be structural, not content, to ensure against such accumulation. This is ensuring a level playing field.

I also am not suggesting we can do without laws. Not only is law the means to prevent accumulation of power, it is also handy to have an external structure to turn to on the rare occasions that normal social processes break down. It tends to reduce endless feuds and living in fear.[59] The point about the law is realizing it, too, is human and fallible, not to be mindlessly and arbitrarily applied. It should only be used to ensure a level playing field (the context for cooperation: that each is empowered), not itself meddle (dictate content: personal decisions).

But since those of us who are not lawyers will spend but a fraction of our lives in direct contact with the law, it probably behooves us to understand and better leverage what natural social laws makes so little intervention necessary. It would be wise to make use of those natural forces in whatever social structures we do construct, rather than going by ill-formed superstitions. Superstition can lead to laws that undermine, rather than supplement or extend, natural forces.

Dimensions of Equality

When you see someone striving for something, do you most readily hope he fails so the prize is there for you? Or do you find yourself hoping he gets it, identifying with the process of getting what *you* want? Most automatically root for others, because each of us has our own Holy Grail, it is not the same for everyone. This is diversity of needs and interests, the wonderful thing about being different. The *necessity* of everyone being different.

---

[59] I will say the same thing, more academically. In *The Evolution of Cooperation*, Axelrod identifies the one weakness of tit-for-tat: the endless echo. Tit-for-tat simply reciprocates the other's last move: cooperate, or exploit. So if both are repeating the other's last move, and "exploit" is introduced just once, there is no end. (The Hatfields and McCoys; endless feuds; revenge cultures.) While a society using only tit-for-tat will thrive overall, individuals can fall into eternal damnation. He postulated a randomly introduced new move to break such cycles: forgive. But forgive can take three forms: actual forgiveness (issue a cooperate move to an exploiting player); leave and have noting more to do with that player; an external authority separating you, arbitrating a final move so each goes on to other players. The latter is a legitimate role of the law, and thankful we are for it. Our current divorce laws, however, are extremely primitive, and ill-founded attempts at the third option. They separate by too little on one hand (spouse), and by too much on the other (children).

Cooperation is the most powerful force of social nature. Without it, any society simply does not exist. It automatically occurs and does not need force, given the context of multiple individuals, each with something others want or need, each equally important to the whole. If we are to enforce anything, surely it is this.

The cooperation model can be taken another level. The "cause" of *Metazoa* (multi-celled creatures) was likely simply crowding. The sea filled with so many individual cells that a new strategy was needed. Cells joined into tighter communities, themselves becoming an entity: Cooperation as a survival mechanism. This repeated into specialized tissue, then organs: still tighter, more interdependent communities of cells as an individual entity in a higher level of community.

Consider the cells of your body. Which is more important than the others? This is a natural, thriving community.

Civilizations seem "caused" by (or congeal from) crowding. People crowded along a water source until they found they were specializing as different organs.

There would appear a recurring pattern. Are we seeing an atractor: a simple theme repeating at successive levels; one based on cooperation out of self-interest? Is this the hidden driving force of life?

Post-Divorce Equality

Competition is generated by the *in*security of an *un*-level playing field.

Under today's Custody-Access-Support, what degree of cooperation occurs between the parents, relative to the general populace? How much additional strife, anguish, and tension is experienced by imposing this structure than occurs with the more natural balance in society at large? Does CAS not undermine the basic "each needs the respect of the other" mechanism? We can hardly be surprised when there are problems.

The thesis of this chapter is that social equality is in being equally significant. It is in equal, however different, involvement with the children. So the ability to cooperate (having something to do/give/offer, or to not as one sees fit; having something with which to cooperate) produces equality. If I want her to listen to my concerns in one of her areas, I'd better listen to hers in one of mine, meaning, I need to have some such areas as much as she does. The degree of equality attained can be measured by the ability to tit-for-tat, however crude that may sound. A normal tit-for-tat interplay is the self-regulating mechanism. (Don't forget that tit-for-tat means respond to their *cooperation* with my cooperation. It is not just cheat-for-cheat, which is the alternate reciprocation making the former more desirable.)

We are not seeking a structure where one parent depends on the other to fulfill any parenting role. That is the problem with CAS. Rather, we seek that both are equally dependent on the other to respect and honour each their's *independent* contributions. Not undermine them, lest the other's be equally undermined. Secure *independence* is grounds for cooperation. Cooperation can only *freely* occur, to occur at all. We seek the structure to ensure this security is mutually sustained; that each have interest in the other's independence, to protect their own.

Cooperation comes from the self-interest of separateness, not from the enmeshment of "everyone has to do the same things," and certainly not from all authority here and all responsibility there. And to repeat, a cooperation-generating context does not require either *like* the other. Make sure there is interdependence for securing each other's care of the child, they'll get along all they have to.[60]

Specific tactics are suggested in Chapter 9, "Implementation."

Infinite Wealth

Feminists feel threatened by men's rights groups. There is an organized monitoring of their web sites. It is as though they feel, if men have self-pride or rights, there'd be less for women. It's an either/or situation:

---

[60] Social work is normally preoccupied with people "getting along": marriage counselling, even in the face of divorce. Totally inappropriate, the point of divorce normally being to stop *having* to get along. This is another example of trying to perpetuate marriage and the damage of so trying. Social work focuses on helping others manage their relationships (when they're probably no better at managing their own), rather than defining the structures within which people manage their own. Dealing in content, not context. Structurally, this simply makes the social worker another party to appease, another agenda in the picture with which to deal. Not much help.

competition for the same finite resource. Indeed, the feminist premise is, "Men have all the power . . . so we have to take it from them." Since there is only so much power, for us to have any requires diminishing theirs, not realising our own.

Some men's rights activists claim men make better parents that women, and show studies to "prove" this. They are playing the exact same one-upmanship game as the feminists: Who is better or superior; who has the upper hand; I can only have pride at your *expense*.

It makes you want to knock both their heads together.

The wealthy feel threatened by any suggestion of fairness for the little guy. There is only so much wealth or privilege to go around; anyone else's gain could only be their loss.

In 1801, twelve million people lived in England. It was the time of the economists Malthus and Ricardo. They postulated the Scarcity Model: There are finite resources, so any country can only sustain a fixed population. (You can't get much more European than the Scarcity Model, a clear manifestation of "survival of the fittest." It gives our deepest fears a reasoned face.) Given the "passion of the sexes," war, pestilence and famine are "positive" and inevitable checks on population. A population therefore naturally stabilizes at the level sustainable by a nation's resources. 12 million people would always be England's population.

Except today, England's 60 million plus live more handsomely that the 12 million of two hundred years ago. Consider Japan, a tiny island with no natural resources save rice patties. Japan's wealth defies all Western expectation.

Something seems to have gone wrong with that "obvious" Scarcity Model. It turned out to be like insisting bees can't fly. All the above are the "survival of the fittest" theme: "I can only have pride, wealth, rights, survival, power at someone else's expense." Because "obviously" there is only so much. It naturally gave rise to the Doctrine of Superiority: that there are only some who deserve to thrive (we just have to find the right definition for "deserve"). What is wrong with it?

While physical resources like farmland might be finite, *wealth* is infinite. How? The leverage of cooperation. To the degree I depend on you for things I need, your increased wealth is my increased wealth, pride, chance of survival, and so forth. Someone comes up with a way to increase farm yield. He sells it to a farmer; both profit. There is increased use of, and wealth generated from, the same physical resource. Both must find a bank for their money; the banks profit. The banks lend this to merchants who increase their offerings, hiring more people.

There is no end to this. With finite physical resources, wealth, power, pride, and all the rest are infinite. I am happy for and help work toward your pride or wealth, for I am dependent on it for some of mine. Your increase increases mine, just as you are dependent on me for yours. To the degree we need each other, your *gain* is my *gain*; your loss my loss. This is the wealth multiplier.

Several decades ago, economists identified the money-income multiplier.[61] It forms the basis of government fiscal policy (spending), which is one of the two ways governments today influence the economy. (The other is interest rates and currency value: monetary policy.) If, say, the government spends one dollar, the recipient saves a percentage of it, but spends most on what he needs. The recipients of what he spends do the same. So they come up with a value: Every dollar the government (or you) spends creates 1.7 (or whatever) dollars of spending in the economy. A measurable influence. Except the exact value of the multiplier turned out to vary quite a bit. And, as with any formula, this model's weakness is in what it omits. In this case, it omits invention. For instance, industrialization started with heavy industry like steel and the steam engine. Its success spawned consumer goods. This spawned services (banks, insurance, brokerage, etc.), which generated more wealth, and now has come technology. Cyberspace is increasing the "space" we have in which to live. There may be an end to it (a finiteness), but we haven't seen it yet so there is reason for optimism, so long as we don't mess with the driving force. Which we are likely to do when we don't recognize what that force is, or mis-attribute it.

All this did not come of greedy hoarding. It came of each making use of what others willingly and happily contributed: Everyone leveraging off of each other. Many, many have contributed to any one invention, institution,

---

[61] First formulated in "Determination of the Multiplier," *The Economic Journal* (September, 1938). Colin Clark, based on work by Keynes.

or organization that exists today, however fond we may be of hanging only one name on everything (uni- . . . something-or-other).

What holds for material wealth holds at least as true for non-material wealth: self-esteem, self-direction, pride, and anything else. It multiplies throughout the community as each member gains. But in our minds, we have been applying what we see of physical resources (finiteness) to all things we desire. We have been wrong. But then, in migration-torn Europe, everything seemed finite, especially life.

The mechanism that has created contemporary Western wealth is the natural interdependence of any society (I need you and you need me); the cooperation generated by self-interest. Not "loving each other" and being enmeshed, nor trying to beat anyone out. It has been created by the self-interest from being separate beings, which breeds as much interest in other's success, because I can use it for my own. Cooperation acts as leverage and atractor. The more some gain, so gain others, and others still by that until the originators are all the more wealthy. And this repeats at higher and higher levels.

The irony of Western wealth is that it keeps getting attributed to "beating the other guy out:" the (assumed) *selfishness* of self-interest. Whereas if the rich had any brains, and wanted to be richer rather than just protect their privilege, they'd all be socialists: Give the greatest benefit to the greatest number, the greatest wealth will generate, including more to them. But we call them rich, not smart. (The old adage is, if you want to know what God thinks of money, look at the people he gives it to.)

Money is a surrogate for real things, the underlying wealth of life. The multiplying does not only happen with money, but, having much less basis in physical resources, all the more so for social and all other forms of wealth. I take joy in your self-esteem, you in mine, for we each gain by the other's. If you are strong and independent, so much stronger am I, being more able to fulfill my dreams as you are more able to contribute to them, so then the more I can contribute to yours. *More* common interests, not fewer. Communities of any sort just naturally work this way, when allowed to.

Understand the implication. You are important. Very important to everyone who knows you. It is not just *your* reliance on *others* at work, it is equally theirs on you. For they are relying on you for something. Maybe it is only a small thing, and maybe they can live without it if they had to. But they are the wealthier for knowing you, for having you there to give what you have. This multiplies your importance, your power, if you will.

Take pride in yourself, not *from* others.

This also implies eternal life. You live on in all you have touched and affected, themselves influencing and affecting others, so on forever. This is part of the Indian concept of karma. Not so foreign or unnatural, then, is it?

And your forefathers live on in you. Japanese Shintoism. Also not so foreign.

8) Teamwork and Joint Decisions

Any discussion of operational equality and cooperation must lead to one on group or joint decisions, and teamwork. This is especially true when proposing parents have equal and independent involvement with their children in an enmeshment, uni-paradigmistic culture, not comfortable with separation and personal independence. Aren't a lot of joint decisions necessary, or at least coordination as though from one mind?

Not necessarily. More important is that each parent be true to them self and consistent with their children, not consistency *between* the parents (sameness). Self-consistency is important, which most of us find hard enough without looking over our shoulder for what someone else is doing, whether married to them or not. Still, let us examine some of our society's myths about group decisions and teamwork.

My experience has been that the one who complains that others are not team players is the one having trouble being part of a team. They are having trouble with the fact that a team must consist of very different people, each with their own vision. Misconceptions abound about joint or mutual or group decisions and teamwork. Teamwork does not necessarily require much or even any of the others, though this should already be clear from the discussion on cooperation and equality, where independence is required before interdependence freely flows and multiplies. Furthermore, while many embrace the pretense of joint or group decisions and insist everyone do the same, they probably don't exist. Rather, we are witnessing our anxiety over mind control (everyone must think the same).

Teamwork requires common loyalty, not common thought. Each will have their own something to contribute, and their own way of doing so, however apparently at odds with the efforts of some others.

When someone in a group says, "Let's make this a group decision," they are not likely interested in what anyone else has to say. They are not seeking dissent or alternate views, but recruiting to their agenda, hoping to repress dissent by peer pressure. This is bullying. By the same token, when someone urges you to do something, "for the sake of the team," or to "be a team player," they are using the same peer pressure to get you to do what conveniences them. This is a disregard for your equal membership in the group, your equal voice, and your validity as part of the team. Such a person does not believe in the group, but uni-paradigm-ism.

Another way to grab power is to promote an individual's matter or decision to the group level, where *I* have influence. Take it out of an individual's hands; suddenly grab something private and shine a spotlight on it. This is startling, so the perpetrator gets the upper hand. The media and social workers are famous for this, but you'll see it in corporate meetings as well. It is a personal violation to make the attacked individual vulnerable – another form of bullying.

All the above are common means of coercion. They are uses of force as violent as any physical form, and acquiescence is not agreement. A price will be paid. Simply insisting there be a group or unanimous decision can be coercive.

(I might add that, "for the team" is a common male ploy, "Let's do this together" and violating privacy, common female ones. Either gender is equally prone to bullying, simply in their own way. Assault is not just physical, and, again, propensity toward bullying is not gender-specific, but cultural-specific.)

Just as common as using a "group decision" to misappropriate power is using it to abdicate responsibility. "I'll go along with whatever you guys say." One may seek the input of others before making a final decision, but if the position you hold says it is up to you, don't pretend it isn't. In any situation where we are hierarchically organized (which, like anything, has its time and place), that structure says which person is responsible for any one decision, however they may go about making it. While it is very good to seek input, it's still up to you.

Co-parenting, however, is not hierarchical, any more than is marriage. (Nor has marriage ever been for any society, whatever myths feminists concoct.) That alone makes it difficult for North Europe-rooted people to deal with, much less articulate in a non-marriage situation. So we'd better be clear on what a group or mutual or, more precisely, non-hierarchical decision may or may not be.

Group Decision

Before Europeans arrived, Native American cultures did not have "majority rule," which we confuse with democracy.[62] When there was an issue of consequence to many tribes (families), the chiefs would gather in one place and sit in a circle, at least as aware of their responsibility to their family as any leader of any society.[63] All members of the group determined a decision would be sought by the group, but not necessarily made.

Each had their turn to speak. They spoke as long as they wished, interruption unthinkable, each quietly and respectfully given full attention. When all had given their initial position and view, all would have their turn to speak again, addressing what had been raised. This would go on as long as it took to arrive at a *unanimous* decision, or arrive at none. The majority did not force all others along.

Sameness was not required, but true agreement was. Each individual had to come to the same conclusion, entirely on their own. This process requires complete respect for each member – that each is of equal significance and entitled to their own thought and action – and acceptance, even welcoming of each holding different perspectives, having something unique and important to contribute.

In our culture, when people say they want a group decision, they usually don't. They want uniformity. At the very least, let's dispense with any myth

---

[62] Majority rule can be majority oppression. It is not democracy *per se*. This is why, to my mind, democracy can only be predicated on everyone's equal significance. But since the word democracy has come to only refer to a mechanism for choosing a government, those of us who believe in classic democracy – in the equal significance of all people, irrespective of form of government – must call ourselves socialists, not simply democrats.

[63] One way or another, a chief, or any leader, is always derived by consensus, however much it may appear on the surface as inherited or forced. We have our way of gaining consensus on leadership (elections); others have always had theirs, sometimes including what we would call intrigue. It still comes down to the tolerance of those "ruled," still comes down to those ruled choosing their so-called ruler, or spokesman. Indeed, our method is very much a short-circuiting of more natural selection methods, due to time constraints and the size of the population involved.

about there being joint decisions. There are none. Everyone makes their own, and may come to the same conclusion *on their own,* for their own reasons. Or they may come to none, leaving what action is taken as a separate issue.

A common way to deal with every individual having their own angle on a problem, is division of responsibility. Delegation. This minimizes the amount of actual agreement required by a group to accomplish something that is multi-tasked. It has long been a normal mechanism employed by societies, called "organization" or "structure." Specializations need not be hierarchical. Indeed, they rarely are.

Teamwork

Teamwork is a delimited set of cooperation. Group decisions are not required, only common interest. What must be done and who will do it is made self-evident by the circumstance, and the differing skills and interests of the individuals. How any one task is done is up to the one doing it..

John Romer is considered the world's foremost Egyptologist. He has a wonderful empathy with his subjects. In his television mini-series on Egypt, *Ancient Lives,* there is a scene where he's sitting atop a large fallen Egyptian statue:

> This is the shoulder. It would have taken three stonemasons, working in unison, to produce this uniform curve.
> We [modern Euro-rooted peoples] can't do this kind of work.

He left it at that.

He was referring to ensemble work: a group of people working as one. It is cooperation in its purest form. If you've seen films of African workers digging a trench, dozens of people in a line, all tools lifting and plunging in unison to a song sung by all, that is ensemble work. Or a dozen women at a river pounding their clothes together, again by music. It is how Arab teams make Oriental rugs: a team of three to five, depending on its width, has an intricate pattern to follow. Each takes a strip of yarn and ties one knot at a time, each having to get exactly the right colour at exactly the right place, moving up the rug in a line together. Each only does their own section, while the sections are seamless. You can see it in a steel drum band in Trinidad where, with no conductor, a mass of people are swaying and playing as one instrument, like an active lake surface. There is one underlying force, many expressions of it.

Contrast the Trinidad steel band to the European orchestra, which thinks it must have a single conductor, to whom nobody pays attention anyway.

Other people work in ensemble automatically. We, hardly at all.

Mr. Romer is not quite right saying we can't or don't ever work like this. We can find this in our own culture in a hockey or baseball team in the playoffs when the team is playing at their peak. You can tell when the magic takes hold: everything is just happening to them, there is an inevitability. On rare occasions this happens to a work team. Usually the same people have been working together for two or more years. Some crisis arises and suddenly all act in unison to accomplish something quickly, each doing something entirely different but each piece fitting perfectly with the others. It is clear from the outset what must be done and who will do what; no group decisions are required. It just happens; it's a wonderful, spiritual experience. You don't realise until afterward how automatic everything was. This magic also happens for performing artists, though rarely in classic orchestras because of all the formal training.

What is this magic?

It only happens when each individual is so totally concentrating on only their own work, not on others', on what they are doing, that they take everyone and everything else for granted, and the individual mind is transcended. This level of teamwork requires only one group decision: get this done (whatever it is). No one needs to decide how. It is left to each individual to know their part and play it to their full.

Also, notice that, on a championship team, each member considers themselves pivotal, the most important member.

Why is this so rare for us? How did we lose it?

We are too busy minding everyone else's business to apply ourselves to our own. We are "helping" others rather than ourselves. Meddling. Though the magic is experienced as losing oneself, it is, in fact, ceasing to pay attention to externals (such as what others are doing) and concentrating solely on one's own senses and work. In the magic, we take everyone else's skills and expertise for granted, knowing they will be there. It is trust. Faith. Only then can the work act as the inter-connectivity.

There are two reasons for this loss of faith:

1. We have lost touch with the fact that our mind is but an organ. Instead, we identify with it as our very self. This the reason we describe the work magic as losing oneself. (I refer the reader back to the previous discussion about linear thinking, where we traced how we came to exclude everything but the mind from reality.) We live only in our heads. We try to do everything with only our mind, however inappropriate; we consider the conscious mind the only way anything can validly be done. Some actually propose one could live forever by digitizing the mind's contents, as though we are only knowledge and memories. This presupposes life occurs only in the brain. I fear they will be disappointed. The mind only exists as it does, because the body exists as it does.

   This mind identity makes it difficult to convince a Euro-rooted person to lose their mind, to let it be transcended and become "one with the Brahman." It would be losing one's self, leaving nothing to unite with any Brahman. We think we must *use* our mind to do anything, rather than let it be something else's instrument, like any other organ.

   Another way to describe it is: Ensemble workers are aware of the life of the thing on which they work, and allow its life to guide each member. Our scientific views and mass-production are either caused by or the effect of removing the life from the objects upon which we work. Thinking life only in our heads, we do not see the mass of it around us.

2. We do not consider ourselves worthy of our own full attention. This leaves us to occupy that mind with what others are doing and whether what *they* are doing is right or beneficial. The external orientation: turning without – other people – rather than regarding one's self.

We rarely perform ensemble work because we don't trust ourselves and don't trust others, one manifesting in the other. But when the hockey player is "on," he is making use of the familiar idiosyncrasies of his line-mates, irrespective of how irritating they were during the season, perceived as "not what he's *supposed* to do." He is concentrating on his own efforts, his own goals and objectives, using whatever exists.

If I want to improve the world or make society better, society is not others. It is me. I am as much a part of society as anyone (strong self-image), and the only part over which I have dominion. Improve myself – make sure my behaviour is what I think is right; tend only to myself – and I have improved society. Let others have their own opinions and ways, make their own contribution, play their own part. This is faith, and more "faith in God" than many North European so-called Christians often show.

Notice the *I*-ness instead of *you*-ness. Enmeshment – seeking identity in others – is one of our society's greatest illnesses. It makes us try to control others as though they were ourselves. The solution is not sitting around saying, "Am I bad for doing that." Self-condemnation is the problem, not the solution. The solution to meddling is to realise how important *I* am, and pay myself full attention. Pay attention to your own being, your own goals and purpose, and how you might treat others. Not what others think of you, nor you of them. How can one see the validity and significance of others until one has grasped one's own? How can one love another without loving oneself? It is only my love of myself I have to give. And can you imagine what a wonderful society this would be if people paid nearly as much attention to themselves as is currently paid to others? (What would the Sally Jessies of the world do?)

The North European-rooted myth of group or joint decisions is a manifestation of mind control – the desire for everyone to think the same – itself a manifestation of intolerance of separation, intolerance of differences, lack of acceptance of one's own uniqueness. It is our enmeshment illness, and persistent violation of individual-hood.

Instead of trying to make everything a group decision, have the courage to make your own. Have faith that this will naturally synchronize (not en-mesh, but synchronize) with the rest of the universe.

Epilogue

Teamwork's most fundamental requirement is that each member knows they are essential to the team's success, that the whole effort depends on them. This is social equality: equal significance. It is the basis for any cooperation. Everyone doesn't have to do the same thing or do everything one way. The significance of each member comes first; the degree true ensemble work is attained, varies.

The second prerequisite is confidence that you and your work will not be violated. Each person must know it will not be usurped or redone, but respected. This amounts to the same thing: you are essential, your essentiality unassailable. Because people mind their own business, not yours.

No one is a team player until they are secure in their turf. Teamwork only begins with clearly defined roles and responsibility, only happens when these things are honoured and protected.

Any post-separation child care must be predicated on this, or fail. If someone is divorcing, they mean to rid them self of the other party and will do so one way or another. Most cases of father abandonment are not abandonment. Fathers are forced away if only by having no structural assurance that their involvement with their children will be free of interference, will not be undermined. Abandoned children are created by our efforts to force the poor guy to live at a level of dependence on his ex to which marriage never subjected him, not a mutual interdependence on which each can securely stand. This precludes free involvement with his own children, on his own terms.

So it would behoove us to implement the independence of both ex-spouses, each from the other. This is not a separation for the child, who retains two fully involved parents and an integrated world.

None of this means a need for any amount of group or joint decision, or people thinking alike, so let's get out of the enmeshment and mind control businesses. Once responsibilities are defined, teamwork is silent, each caring for and relating to the children in their own way. (Communication of choices, yes. Joint decisions, no. Respecting the other's decisions, yes.) For the few things that require both parents' action, it will be things that are obvious what action must be taken. That kind of decision is situational, the situation carries people with it. Teamwork only requires a common loyalty. Each may disagree all they like with how the other expresses that loyalty, but must respect that expression.

Mind your own business. It is Yoga: The Way; the true path (to self-knowledge).

(A corollary: in wondering what post-divorce childcare arrangements society should provide, don't ask what would be best for society. Ask what you would want for yourself. Society is not other people. It is you.)

9) Implementation

Given North Europe-rooted peoples' fixation on mechanics, few are likely to accept this equality stuff until the mechanics of implementing it are discussed. (Probably to death!) Following are some of the author's thoughts.

How do you keep two people equally accountable to each other, without enmeshment, but ensuring separation? How do you implement the principles of cooperation revealed in Appendix I?

Scheduling

Take scheduling of time with the children: Who gets what time when? For the first five months (or five weeks, or three months or whatever), parent A determines the exact schedule. For the next same length of time, B does. Whoever is in charge must ensure equal time for the other on a twenty-day (or some agreed-to) moving average.[64] Each is responsible for ensuring equal time with the other.

For instance, parent A arranges a week at Disney World during her five-month scheduling period. As long as the average after three weeks still shows both parents having roughly equal time, there is no violation. Parent A must arrange equal time with the other sufficiently in advance to accommodate the week at Disney. A range can be declared within which the moving average can roam before a violation is declared. This provides each parent with considerable freedom. You can plan your proverbial quality time without fear of violating or angering someone, whether the courts or your ex.

Rather tends to keep them both honest, wouldn't you say? Because if I cheat her, I just gave her license to jerk me around. If I want her to be

---

[64] In a twenty-day moving average, you calculate the average each day with the twenty-first day falling off the end of the period as the new day adds in. This makes it "move."

considerate of my needs when she's in charge, I'd better consider hers when I am. We are accountable to each other, not the court or other agent of society.

Other advantages include:

- The schedule can be more readily adjusted to the child's need, as it is in the hands of those closest to him. Some children respond better with regular bouts of long periods with either parent, others with short spirts. This changes over time.

- The courts or social workers do not decide schedules. When they do, it dis-empowers *both* parents as though they are being grounded for bad behaviour. Who do the courts or social workers think they are, making themselves the parents by even participating in schedule definition? Give the parents a scheduling mechanism they run. It's not up to others to decide what constitutes a reasonable schedule for any family. Each family is unique; put it in their hands.

- The schedule is not fixed, but "flex." Consider the rigidity of, "every Wednesday from five to seven and every second weekend . . ." However much we try, few lives slot in so conveniently, including children's. Exceptions arise without a mechanisms for handling them. But this mechanism readily adapts to life's exceptions. It is always clear who is responsible for actual timings and that one will be in the other's place come their turn. If the time span and moving averages are wide enough (say five months; twenty or more days), even vacations can be enjoyed without court appearances or renegotiations.

- Easier for each to use the other as their babysitter of first choice, rather than feeling compelled to make every use of whatever precious seconds for only *their* relatives, never giving an inch.

- Tension is reduced around exact pick-up and delivery times. Lateness adds automatically, reducing future entitlement. The cause is irrelevant. No blaming.

- Don't you suppose the kids will be happy to see their parents working to accommodate each other?

▸ Easier to let the children decide, or accommodate their wishes and changing needs. One has control over one's own compensation. If I volunteer the other more time, that was my decision, not imposed.

▸ The implied sunset clause: Use it or lose it. A moving average means time not exercised within the aging period, and whose loss is not objected to, is lost. This can easily be a non-loss if both, however tacitly, agree the child should be more with one than the other during certain periods.

The list is endless.

An odd number of time units (five or seven months or weeks) should be used so no one parent monopolizes special days like Christmas, as would happen were the unit, say, six months. Sway over such special days must rotate. If the child(ren) come to be especially attached to Christmas at one place (one grandmother's, for instance), whoever has dominion over one Christmas can feel free to accommodate that, knowing they arrange their own compensation. There is far less motivation to try to disrupt existing traditions as such things are not hard-set against them.

All the things that can be varied in this formula allow the couple to do their own tailoring rather than the "one fits all" currently imposed. Further, the children are freer to increasingly influence the schedule and all arrangements as they naturally do in any family. Their doing so does not comprise a threat to any one parent. With clear definition of ultimate responsibilities, each parent is much freer to adjust to the children's needs and wishes, rather than make it a point of contention.

Responsibilities

Don't divide expenses. Divide responsibilities. Expenses are a symptom; stop treating them.

To a child, a parent is a person with whom to interact, ask things, learn intimacy, see how things work, do things. Parenting is not time or money. Those are only physical manifestations and thoroughly unreliable measures of anything.

Parenting is doing. Got that? Doing.

A family is not a financial balance sheet, and the current practice of only treating it as one is the main thing that makes all parties feel soiled. When the Great White Government comes up with some national average cost for raising a child, it may fit the nation, but no one member. By contrast, if I am responsible for my daughter's clothing, or her schooling, I can be doing things for her without her physical presence. Exact dollar amounts and time are practically irrelevant, as a need is being satisfied and interaction occurring.

Witness, again, our mechanics fixation. The only facet of family with which we attempt to deal is, in fact, the least significant but most visible: money. This promotes it to prominence at the expense of need. It is treating the symptom, and this disassociation has a large, negative, ripple effect.

A couple may readily agree to many areas being in one or the other's permanent charge. Where contention exists, the responsibility can rotate. A longer time frame may be preferred for this than for scheduling. For the first year, Mother may be in charge of medical care, Dad, schooling. The second year, they switch. Negotiations stop being who does what and become simply when: seven months, a year, two years?

Rotating responsibilities guarantees against anyone ever having grounds to feel cheated. Now you have the environment for cooperation, without anyone having to "get along" with someone they hate, or agree with anything the other does.

Some will point to the possibility of greater inconsistencies in the child's life, like changing doctors every year. That is correct. Some cases will generate the inconvenience (to the doctors) of sending medical records back and forth. How awful. It also would give the child greater basis for his own decisions and more room for the child's voice in these matters. (Wouldn't listening to the child be a shock?)

With responsibilities divided, the exact amount of time spent with the children loses its significance. Both parent and child know the other's role and feel the constant presence in their lives irrespective of physical presence. A lot like normal parents. Which I suggest we ensure divorced parents are guaranteed of being, and know they can expect. Accomplishing this requires that each knows they will have equal involvement in the children's lives, something not provided by "visitation" and the strife that turns out to mean, and paying half a national average dollar amount to someone you are trying to make a stranger.

When one first mentions dividing parental responsibilities equally, one hears objections about dividing the child, as though a child *is* responsibility for his care. This failure to distinguish context from content is the confusion of the adults, not the children. Division of responsibility naturally occurs in any family. Children know very well who controls what, always have, and always will. They know exactly who to go to for what, not to mention when they can play one against the other because division has never been made clear. In fact, dividing responsibilities stands a good chance of solving the cause of many divorces: one partner that dominates. Divorce becomes a safe haven one turns to for strength, not a process of humiliation that permanently diminishes all parties.

A so-called traditional household even divides into physical territories. Hers may be the kitchen and diningroom and half the bedroom; his the other half of the bedroom, the den or workroom. The children also have their own, and nobody messes with anyone else's. (Or nobody should. To violate someone else's realm of competence or solitude is to violate their identity, their individuality.) The divisions may be very different in different households, but divisions into personal spaces exist. Likewise for responsibilities. These are natural laws, played out in any family, however that family is organized. Why are we ignoring them?

Co-Parenting Versus Joint Everything

Clear division of responsibilities solves a common problem in some of the current joint custody arrangements. Sometimes both parents assume the other is monitoring something they are not, so neither does. Also, sometimes in existing shared-parenting situations, the child feels equally at a loss in – equally not part of – both households. This *will* lead to identity problems as much as losing one parent, for the child has effectively lost both. Everyone should be clear about who's in charge of what, or nobody winds up looking after anything.

The large body of work by social workers on negotiating joint-parenting agreements describes involving both parents in all decisions. None that I've seen describes implementing, "You must respect her choices if you want her to respect yours," which assumes each has an equally important though different set of choices. The first problem with both making all decisions is that there are a hundred ways to bully. The party that can whine the loudest, wins, increasingly squeezing out the other. The same happens with tantrums or strong feelings about everything. Why do you think they are getting divorced? Indeed, social workers' penchant for making everything into a joint decision seems only to make themselves boss. Playing one against the other gives the power to the broker in the middle.

The second problem is that "let's all come to a decision" assumes that any decision is final. None ever is. Any decision is always situational, and must be made again and again. So the least important issue in any decision-making is what the decision is (content). The most important issue is, whose is it to make (structure)? Because the same decision will have to be made many times with changing circumstances, it is rarely made once, and is never final or absolute. This is one reason one can and maybe should rotate them.

The danger of joint decisions cannot be overemphasised. Minimize them. Delegation empowers each party, and if you rotate contentious ones, nobody can feel cheated, but there will always be clear responsibility.

Finally, if we have a law that says both parents must have equal say in all significant areas of the child's life, we have enmeshment (confusing sameness for equality). It is unenforceable and fails the objective of separation. Consider the principal at the child's school. He just became responsible for deciding to which parent to listen. And how can either parent prove a violation of equal say? Under such a law, two things are inclined to happen: Some areas of the child's life become opportunities for intrusion between the parents; others are ignored.

When there is one piece of pie left, you don't share it. You split it. We should stop allowing our language's misnomers to drive notions of conflict resolution. The word sharing is without substance. What it is intended to mean, when not used to grab ownership for oneself, is that something gets either divided (delegation), or, when not divisible, it is yours at this time or situation, mine under different ones (need- or time-rotation). These are natural laws played out time after time in any number of circumstances, in any number of ways. It's all in the structure.

More on Division

What responsibilities can be delegated or rotated? This, too, is situational. Some of the obvious ones:

- ► After school activity
- ► Clothing
- ► Medical care
- ► Dental care may be separated from medical
- ► Religious activities
- ► Education
- ► Weekly allowance

One could start by asking each to list what they see as important areas of their children's lives. We might be surprised at how much agreement already exists, the extent to which each values different things, the extent they values each other's contributions and roles (*they* might be surprised by this), how easily a division can be arranged.

Minimize the flow of information required so it can be smooth. Some must happen so both know what decisions have been made and can have input from the perspective of their own duties. They have to accommodate each other. No matter how much they may not be on speaking terms, so long as no one is at any disadvantage, information can easily flow any number of ways. (Which might be something to define.) It is in the best interests of both to ensure it does, lest they do some harm in their own parenting. That's the whole point: they need each other, without having to like or deal closely with each other. There is information, not intrusion (behaviour).

Some things cannot be easily assigned. (Never say never.) Daycare is both very expensive and benefits both parents equally. It equally allows each to earn a living. This could be an item for equal say (each holding a veto over who provides the daycare) and equal payment. Not necessarily equal dollar amounts, but according to benefit: what it's worth to the party. When each of two sides holds a veto, both are compelled to find a solution that satisfies both. Still, this sort of thing must be minimized for all the reasons given above. (One is usually more prone to just giving in; becoming a battlefield; mistaken neglect; and so forth.) Disposition of a house is another issue too large for one person to handle, and affecting both, but this could be an area with degrees of say, not always 50:50.

Divisions of responsibilities must be enforceable. Not only must each parent honour the decisions of the other, but so must members of the community. Say parent A is in charge of schooling, but is male. The principal is aware that A makes schooling decisions, but ignores his instructions, deferring to B, because the principal thinks it should be that way. This is an outrage. A violation. This principal should be charged with contempt of court. Any parenting arrangement will need to carry recognition as court ordered, readily enforceable without large amounts of time or money, or justice will only exist for the rich.

The same goes for the parents. Quickly slapping contempt of court charges on a violator should soon curtail any wanton cheating. Court action also demands the normal requirements of proof, not paranoia nor jealousy, and subjects all parties to the same process. Currently, we have one institution that enforces payments from one parent, leaving the other defenceless.

Clearly, all this requires negotiation, and more so for some cases than others. Although social workers are clamouring to provide mediation services, there may be a better choice. Professional facilitators are found among management consultants. Their job – their training and profession – is to NOT take a stand on any issue, but explicitly only facilitate the parties coming to an agreement with which both are equally happy. Social workers, on the other hand, are commonly trained in intervention. They may be more inclined to ensure a role for themselves, or influence decisions by contributing their own values or agenda, be it under the guise "child's advocate" (which everyone loves to presume), or whatever other way of making themselves sole parent. This usurps both real parents who are the ones who must live with whatever result.

In these kinds of negotiations, one would want to take all reasonable steps to maximize neutrality in the intermediary. One way or another, both parties must be able to interview and authorize the facilitator. The parents must control the process, or risk being its victim.

If anything must go to a court for arbitration, the judgement needs to be open to appeal to at least one level on grounds of fairness and equity. Judges are as fallible as anyone, and we are not dealing with mere property issues or business contracts. Grounds for overturning a lower court's ruling in such matters cannot be restricted to the decision being outside the lower court's jurisdiction, lest we have one ultra-conservative or ultra-anything judge imposing his values to the permanent damage of all parties. Naturally, it would have to be something blatantly one-sided without good reason given, or the lower court would be robbed of all power. But appeal there must be. It is not a property settlement: These are human lives.

Society's Role

Some may say, "So now you want the state to divide intimate family functions, exactly what we've been trying to avoid all these years, exactly why we've dealt with as little of the real issues as we can."

In the first place, the point is to stop avoiding these issues. The current narrow scope is much of the injustice.

As to the state assigning functions, this is another confusion between context and content. There is a large difference between facilitating or ensuring something happens (context management), and doing it oneself (content). The state should ensure an equitable division of responsibility, not do it unless agreement is not reached, or if directly appealed to, and only for those functions appealed. Indeed, the author definitely favours the state (society) staying out of the content, which this structure does to a far greater degree than does CAS. CAS explicitly dictates content, even personal schedules.

Specific divisions of responsibilities cannot be written as hard rules to be applied to all cases; this is not a science. The state need simply assure that the division of responsibilities is as satisfactory as possible to all parties, and as close to a balance as common human judgement can manage. This is the structure; we cannot define the content.

However mechanics- or technology-driven we make our society, all things still come down to human judgment. Always have; always will. It is time to stop denying it. Success in this can only be measured by degree of satisfaction felt by the parties, especially the children. Malleability must be built in. Everyone should have a while to live with an initial agreement, and revisit it if desired. This is defining structure, not content, not how the child gets raised, but who does what of the raising. The way any healthy family is organized.

(In fact, very much a point of this is that if we commonly provide the structure of a healthy family, much more health for all members with naturally follow. This is exactly the opposite to what we are doing now: imposing a dysfunctional structure, producing dysfunctional behaviour.)

The driving principle is equal involvement in the children's lives. Not counting pennies. If we are as concerned for the children's well-being as we pretend, we will stop measuring everything in dollars and only consider the degree of parental involvement in the children's lives.

And replacing science with human judgment and expenses with responsibilities may provide the addition benefit of eliminating lawyers, who cannot cope with anything that is not dogmatic or in a formula.

Transfer Payments ("Support")

Women who are anxious to defend the status quo often accuse men who strive for co-custody of "just wanting out of support payments." It may be more justified to say that the women who make this argument are only interested in the money, not the welfare of their children. Again, we see that women's use of children for their power base may have turned into their greatest social abuse.

Yes, men do want "out of" support payments, and back in to the normal parenting hitherto only accorded mothers. There is absolutely no reason this should not happen.

If the driving force for non-marital child-care is involvement with the children, money follows. Not the reverse. All my resources are available to my children, not to those who are only someone else's. Until society decides to regulate exactly how much each married parent spends on their children, it has no business doing so to unmarried ones, especially only unmarried males. Each will naturally contribute the same amount: all they can. On what basis do we assume otherwise? Is it just to have government agencies? Who else in society has their personal lives so regulated except convicts? Which says a lot for our regard for divorced men.

If both are equally running a household for the children, how can you justify transfer payments from any one to any other? Having financially "equal" households is an attempt at sameness, not equality. We must stop being afraid of being different.

The obvious exception is where one parent voluntarily relinquishes their share of responsibility. The extra burden to the other must be compensated. Voluntary relinquishment can be overt or tacit, and may be temporary or permanent. It could happen for short periods of a few months due to distance (one takes an assignment in another city), or be permanent. It can be in degrees. But given the emotional confusion of anyone undergoing divorce, any relinquishment should be suspect, easily open to review for at least three years. As earlier stated, in a divorce, one is the initiator and the other is in some mode of giving in or trying not to. Still, some do divorce to remove their children from their lives, not only their spouse. A distinction can be made.

But start from 50:50, a presumption of equality. Not 0:100.

The current stated purpose of support is to perpetuate the single pre-divorce household. It is not support of the children. It is support of what is perceived to *remain* of the marriage, as though it is not over, as though it carries on, just without the father, who "left." Or was made to leave, or whom we force out, for not sufficiently pleasing his wife.

The purpose of support is to not allow the natural material manifestations of a change that is, in fact, occurring: to not allow divorce; pretend it isn't happening. Although the traditional reason is to force him to his contractual life-long care of *her*, the current rational is to minimize the impact on the children. It fails at the later miserably, maximizing it. It fails exactly because of its denial of change. Support fails because it is a euphemism for alimony, *in place of* preserving the spiritual-emotional ties between the children and each parent. It fails because we are still worshipping the god of marriage and really still trying to make its material ties permanent, not the god of family and its non-material bonds.

This is how we create single-parent families, abandoned children, and impoverished children. Not because these people are evil or do not love their children, but because it is the only way we leave them to end a single relationship, and because their ability to directly express their love of their children is frustrated. It may well be that many fathers who "abandon" their children are the *best* parents, who care most deeply, who therefore cannot bear the frustrations of mere visitation, so must turn away completely.

To eliminate transfer payments, we would have to accept that everyone is responsible for their own resources, irrespective of gender. Irrespective of individual means, each parent will contribute what they reasonably can to their children with only extreme cases as exceptions. Marriage should not be allowed to be, *per se,* an entitlement to the other's physical resources, certainly not for life or large parts thereof (marrying for money). Marriage would be better enshrined as a personal union. After all, the children will be living equally with both parents, with whatever each has to give. This does not mean just money. Each parent would run a household as they would if they were never married.

As far as the children are concerned, both parents are equally coping as best they can with the costs. Those who think this gives unfair advantage to the higher-income parent are assuming money the only or most important thing to children: all any parent has to offer. But every individual is different, each having something of their own to give. We might stop thinking money a cure-all or even a measure-all, certainly not what creates or constitutes equality, just because it's the only thing lawyers can grasp. If anything, the children are more likely to favour the household to which they can make the greatest contribution of their own. We all want to be where we are most needed, most useful, most important. This will not necessarily mean the more or less *financially* endowed household, money a poor measure of anything.

If we want parents to live up to the real sacred obligation to the children, free them each to do so as best each can. Each equally. Stop preventing it by removing the ability of one parent to even offer their own household, being burdened with the expenses of two. Two households cannot enjoy the same standard of living as one on the same total income. Period. Never will. Why should one parent be forced to bear all the burden of a breakup under any pretense; especially if it was *she* who divorced *him*?

Upon divorce, where is the lingering obligation, one to the other, or to a now hollow and meaningless household? Eliminate the "preserved household" paradigm, realize that a child's home can span multiple households, allow the change that is happening in any case, allow the child to continue to be part of both parent's life, allow divorce and that each are again as much on their own as before the marriage, and you eliminate any justification for child support. Let the two new households be different. Wherein the horror? We all have different incomes as we all have different eyes. Is it outrageous to expect women to stand on their own feet and make equal contribution? It may not be materially equal (the same amount of money), though it will often be that or better. It is equal responsibility for the child's care, and for providing their share.

This advocates gender equality. Feminist opposition is curious.

I suggest we replace today's, "Look, darling, Daddy is leaving us," with "Come help Daddy (or Mommy) find us a second home," and, "Come help Daddy (or Mommy) move and build it so you know this one, too, is as much yours as the current one, and we will remain as much or even more part of each other's lives." There should never be any leaving of the children, we must stop turning divorcing a spouse into divorcing the children. Rather, natural, organic changes need accommodation. While the transition remains unsettling to the children, it is nothing as traumatic as the current leaving we impose.

Conclusions

This chapter is by no means a definitive discussion of co-parenting. It barely introduces its structure. There are problems and traps in co-parenting, as there are in anything. It is simply the author's contention that there are far fewer and far less severe ones here than with any structure predicated on in-equality. If this book has helped open just a few minds to the notion of equality of parenthood – that equality works, having its own way of working; once it is understood what it truly is, that it is not in sameness but in complementing differences – its mission is fulfilled.

What are some of the traps in co-parenting? One is the shuttle-child who has no sense of permanent home. In this case, the objective of assuring a child permanence, while at one level is met by always having both parents, at another is undermined, however less traumatic it may be. When is this how much of a problem? Some children are more flexible than others, some parents more able to adjust and accommodate. Clear separation of responsibilities between the parents so the child knows to whom to turn for what, only partially addresses this. The rest is left up to the parents, and that's the point.

Because one thing the author knows very definitely to be true: If I know my prerogative will be backed by society – not simply my decisions, but my very right to them – if I know my role as parent is protected as much as is my co-parent's and that I can count on that, then I am strong enough to be free to accommodate and be flexible. But if society continues to try to regulate parents and parenting, and to the extent the courts and social workers and laws still try to decide who does what in a family, we can be sure of rigidity, as people dependent on others for what they get will only cling the harder to their crumbs and play games around the laws that are only playing games with them.

For if there is anything we are after here – if there is anything that is *change* in what is herein proposed – it is freeing parents to be more able to listen to and be sensitive to their children's needs, able to themselves respond and adjust, rather than being forced to fight for only their own selves, using the children to do so, because their very parenthood is under siege, not just their marriage. This freeing of both parents can only be attained if all members of the family know that the only thing society will do is assure a level playing field – assure their equal involvement – not tell them who will do what and how, not tell them what equal involvement must mean in their case and for their children, as is done today. And I might warn, it will easily take two or more generations for the full benefits to be seen, simply for people to believe they will be supported, not hounded.

We are arguing for a presumption of strength, power, independence, and dignity for all, equally. Free people to be the humans we are. Stop imposing dysfunctional structures and our own narrow righteousness, and let natural humanness express itself, for it is good. Only in extreme cases must society step in to protect children, and that is so irrespective of marriage. Don't pre-empt.

Epilogue

*T*he Artist

    I had to choose the cover designer for this book. I wanted to be sure that anyone working on it had some affinity for the subject, or at least was not committed to some form of extremism, so I e-mailed a probing question to each candidate. Here is part of one very fine artist's response:

> Everyone in this office feels strongly about children living with the most appropriate (best parenting skilled) parent, regardless of gender.

I hate to jump all over this innocent when she saw herself being liberal and progressive, but that's the point: what passes for progressive. She is perfectly happy traumatizing children with the loss of a parent, so long as we are equally horrid to both male and female parents. While you have to concede the genuine lack of gender bias, this is feminist and left-wing social progress: Find a new victim. I am not seeing the progress, nor even change. (One has to admit, however, that if the same horrors were equally inflicted upon women as men, there'd be a presumption of co-parenting in a damn hurry.)

    This is uni-paradigm-ism. There isn't the slightest doubt that a child can and must have only one parent or household. It's perfectly all right to traumatize children with the loss of a parent, so long as we retain the one god for all things at all times; it just comes down to which parent you eliminate and on what basis.

    But there is more: "the best parenting skilled ."

    Never mind who is going to determine who has these "best parenting skills," much less determine what those skills are and that the choice does not reflect a gender bias. Rather, note the assumption that there is (there must be) one superior parent, and one inferior one, by some ("fair") measure or other. Obviously, if you have two things, such as parents, one has to be better; the better one, most deserving.

This is not equality. This is the Doctrine of Superiority, the doctrine that everything must be better or worse, not simply different. It presumes one parent will turn out "superior" overall, for everything, not that two parents are *more than twice* as good as either (the leverage inherent to a group or system: the whole greater than the sum of its parts), not that each parent is equally important, however much for different reasons or at different times. It ignores the fact a child needs different people (including uncles and grandparents) to freely turn to and talk to for different things at different times; that *variety* is critical to survival and to each individual. This is our mythology of *in*equality and uniformity; our Superiority Cult.

The narrowness of this common better-worse thinking is appalling, yet is held by many calling themselves experts in family and psychology. It is assumed true in the public thinking, even though few live their lives seeking dominance over others or to be dominated in all things just because of one talent, one skill set, one expertise, or one body of knowledge, each one of which is only important in one context. Most of us are too busy simply clinging to each other for sheer survival (each needing others at different times for different things) to be bothered worrying about anyone being overall superior. This is why nobody ever has the "upper hand," some only deluding themselves that they do. The "superior-inferior, better than others" assumption is not social reality. But it is our deeply ingrained mythology, and is damaging.

The Senator

While writing this book I had occasion to write the New York state senator who chairs that state's Standing Committee on Children and Families. He kindly sent the requested information and, in response to my query about current state policy, wrote:

> ... I do not believe it is wise to establish a legal presumption that joint custody is in the best interest of a child particularly where there is acrimony between estranged parents.

I was barely able to refrain from replying:

> Thank you for your information.
> Sorry to hear you think so little of yourself as a parent. Do your children share this opinion: that you should be disposed of should your wife kick up the slightest fuss; that you matter so little to them they are happy to do without you so long as their mother is never upset (at least not by you)? Or are you one of those fathers who really does not care about his children or their welfare, or just feeling obliged to live up to some social cliché that you are supposed to be that way?
> Possibly you have fallen for the old party line that you have nothing, have never had anything, and cannot possibly have anything of value to contribute to your children, other than money. Just being their flesh and blood is not enough to make you matter to them, or vice versa. Either way, terribly sorry to see anyone suffer from such an awful self-image.
> Or perhaps you are gallànt. Some form of chivalry? A man must always defer to a woman, after all. Fairness, especially to children who really don't have any right of consideration, be damned. If a woman whines, she must be served.
> Is this chivalrous, or spineless?
> One way or another, you clearly believe you or your contribution to your children is not worth standing up for in the face of the slightest opposition. Again, do your children share this view?
> Awfully thoughtful of you, though, to force all others in your state to live by your self-image. Generations of children will undoubtedly applaud you for the loss of their fathers.

(Well, I'm sorry but there are limits to even my "understanding" for these nincompoops.)

You would be amazed at the casualness with which our judges, social workers, and lawyers – the whole divorce industry, not to mention the politicians – destroy families and people's lives, simply carrying out the execution, faithfully implementing our structure of "parentectomy." The callousness is astonishing. Many involved actually think themselves compassionate. Anyone who goes through this process has a sense of "what planet have I suddenly landed on?" it is so unreal. So unnatural. So wrong. Everything is so insane you haven't even the chance to figure out what is coming from where, much less sort out your own reactions.[65]

Neanderthal Man

In 1856, Europeans first discovered Neanderthal Man in their own backyard (Germany). The first skeleton was not complete and was in poor condition. Twenty years passed before it was examined, not by archeologists or anthropologists, but medical people. They immediately saw that this individual had been badly suffering from arthritis.

Too late. The original sketches remain our cliché "caveman." Neanderthal Man, with a twenty percent larger brain than ours, is forever condemned to dragging his knuckles and slouching in European images.

By the 1960s, anthropologist had uncovered more evidence, and finally had to come to what they called a "startling" conclusion: Neanderthals cared for their sick, old, and crippled. They even buried their dead with flowers, as though showing affection and attachments.

It is helpful to study developing discoveries in North European science: the discoveries of other peoples, races or societies, even of natural sciences. Not because you learn so much about Neanderthal or ancient Europeans or ancient Egypt or the creation of the universe. Because you learn so much about us.

Why have we been so amazed that others of even our own species have managed to build things like Stonehenge and pyramids? Have they not our brains, ingenuity, capacity for learning, thought, and knowledge? Do we

---

[65] Anyone who still does not believe this – who believes any industry, including the divorce one, the slightest "caring," who is not convinced that only structures can protect, that only fundamental structural change will help, that "changing people's attitudes" is meaningless, anyone who still believes even the psychologists and social workers in this industry are a help to anything but the status quo and protecting their role, projecting their own distorted beliefs – is advised to read Robert Mendelson's *A Family Divided*. Prometheus Books. ISBN 1-57392-151-3. It is a case study, the father's experiences entirely typical. His success in overcoming the obstacles is not typical, few having the resources. But having the resources, he was subjected to it all. It took ten years.

think there is something special about us? Were they not just as human, with identical physiology, including brains?

Why were Euro-scientists startled that Neanderthal or anyone else cared for their sick and elderly? Were we expecting them to simply discard those who could not "earn their keep"? Why? Because that is what we are like? Are we expecting others to be as or even more brutal and callous than us?

Perhaps our being startled at other's genius or kindness speaks more of our own brutality and ignorance than other's kindness. Perhaps Neanderthal Man would never have been as ruthless toward his families as we are now, valuing so little what cannot be measured in currency. Some years ago I started to realize that *we* are the oddities, distorted if not demented, not that others are.

While this book describes the five myths that seem to most contribute to the imposition of CAS, sheer apathy, sheer carelessness about blood ties and how we brutalize each other and ourselves, may be the greatest problem.

Feminism and Maleness

Fatherlessness – today most commonly caused by Custody-Access-Support and more rampant than ever, but can be the result of wars or workaholism – produces similar problems in girls and boys: high suicide rate, runaways, school dropouts, low self-esteem, etcetera. Children of either gender may experience the same problems, but display different symptoms.

Boys who have grown up without a father exhibit greater hostility, are 14 times more likely to commit an anger-displacement rape, 20 times more likely to wind up in jail, and on and on (*see inset page 8*). Basically, when you see a group of boys being wantonly destructive, like breaking school or community equipment just for "fun," you can be almost certain they do not have a father.

Manliness is responsibility. It is respect for others, honour (self-respect), and all the skills needed to work in a group to nurture the community. But one would think these boys learned their image of maleness from feminism.

Now there's an interesting thought. Could there be something to that? Could there be some connection, maybe a similar source?

The current wave of our society's woman's movements began in the 1970s as an attempt to reform society's lingering Victorian stereotypes of women. Men have always been men and women, women, and likely always will be, but a society's stereotypes, its conventions and images about its members as promoted (even manufactured) by the media, are important to an individual's self-expectations and self-image. They also form one's initial reaction to a new event or entity in their life.

The old Victorian images that fostered women's omission from business and politics were long inappropriate, and now dis-empowering in an industrial, consumer, mass production, leisure time, cash flow society. What was then called "women's liberation" was a move toward operational equality for women in this context. Specifically, it was to send women to the workforce (now the only source of social worth) as fully as men, from which the Industrial Revolution had initially banished them to increase society's specialization. (Because, at the Industrial Revolution's beginning, home still demanded as much in skills, dedication, and knowledge as did anything in industry. So someone competent had to tend to it. Industrialization itself came to undermined that need, the vitality of home.)

Since the 1970s, however, what is now "feminism" has increasingly revolved around male bashing: characterising men as inherently evil purely by being male, as all wife-beaters and child-molesters, citing testosterone as the source of all aggression, women as gentle, kind and naturally possessing the most desirable (best, superior) values. Men's only salvation is the degree to which they "get in touch with their female side."

Female is gentle and kind; male, vicious and brutal. More than anything, this bigotry is causing massive female defections from feminism, as most women *like* their fathers, husbands, sons, and brothers and do not see them as evil. Women are increasingly confused by this vilification, less able to endorse feminism as it has simply become far worse that anything it originally fought: barefaced sexism. (Men are pissed by it, but to say anything would be used to confirm the accusations. That is the beauty of accusing others of what one is most guilty.)

> [Fathers are] pathological bullies who abuse their children.
> — Letty Cottin Pogrebin, New York Times, June 17, 1990

I feel that 'man-hating' is an honorable and viable political act, that the oppressed have a right to class-hatred against the class that is oppressing them.

— Robin Morgan, former editor, Ms. magazine.

WHEREAS organizations advocating "father's rights," whose members consist of non-custodial parents, their attorneys and their allies, are a growing force in our country; and WHEREAS the objectives of these groups are to increase restrictions and limits on custodial parents' rights and to decrease child support obligations of non-custodial parents by using the abuse of power in order to control in the same fashion as do batterers; . . .

— National Organization for Women
Action Alert on "Fathers' Rights," 1996

Men are rapists, batterers, plunderers, killers . . .

— Andrea Dworkin, *Pornography: Men*
Possessing Women. Perigee, 1981. Pg 48

You see what I mean about fatherless boys acting out the feminist version of maleness. Is there a connection? Did each get this image and their own violent nature by the same means?

What happened to feminism? What went wrong with something that seemed not only appropriate and needed, but noble?

Certainly feminism saw itself the *cause* of the changes occurring in the 1970s, rather than simply one of their results, and was understandably pleased with itself. So you have this powerful movement (a social structure) flush with success. What do you think, it will suddenly disband?

To make yourself permanent when there is really nothing left to change, requires a permanent enemy. Continued belligerence needed justification, so men became inherently (hence, permanently) a threat to women. For instance, Susan Faludi's 1991 sensational book, *Backlash*, claimed continued, even worsening prejudice against women throughout all society. It later turned out based on entirely false or misrepresented information;

there was not only no backlash, the opposite was happening.[66] But being sensational it gained popular acceptance rather than critical assessment, as any who questioned it would prove its thesis. So the belief in a need for permanent militance was enshrined, any and all female anger and suspicion was not simply vindicated, it was required.

To become ruler, you have to be an alternative. This requires something from which to *be* an alternative (hence the myth of the male society as though there were never any women), and clearly superior. Nothing plays on male protectiveness (nurturing) like "victim women," so the myth of the inherent (and hence, eternal) evil of men and maleness, and the female need for special consideration, has thrived and been institutionalized; male-bashing flourished; all with the support of the many men anxious to be on the "right side," exactly as happened for the Temperance Movement.[67] Moral intimidation rules as much today as in Queen Victoria's time, with its convenience of not requiring much in the line of facts or truth.

But while one can understand a social entity seeking self-perpetuation – even dominance, when a North Europe-rooted one – this does not fully explain the targeting of men and maleness, much less its fury and bitterness. Such a generalized "evil male" motif is not Victorian. It is new, not to mention unique to North Europe-rooted culture. From where does its universal endorsement come?

Germain Grear was one of the early women's movement writers (*Female Eunuch*, 1970). She is a fascinating character. She is brilliant, has

---

[66] Cathy Young, *Ceasefire!.Why Women and Men must Join Forces to Achieve True Equality* (The Free Press, 1999), pp63 – 69. ISBN 0-684-83442-1.

[67] For those still not confident that gender bias has now simply reached a possibly greater, however opposite, extreme, consider the United States' Violence Against Women Act. Its target is not violence. It is not even violence against women. Its provisions are solely to protect against *male* violence toward *women*. Combine this with the so-called anti-domestic violence ads that only picture bruised women. Compare both to the fact that domestic violence is equally committed by men and women (*see inset page 111*), that for every bruised woman there is a scalded man, and that there are no provisions protecting men. Indeed, a man abused by a women is either a joke or applauded. The case for describing feminism as seeking superiority and special treatment at others' expense, very like racism, is difficult to rebut. (And for the same reason: the perception of having been abused oneself, or being somehow entitled to retribution.) Is feminism, at the very least, obsolete?

a doctorate from Cambridge in Victorian literature, and is very good with words and writing. She knows very little cultural anthropology or even history, but is a brilliant wordsmith.

She is an exhibitionist. If she has a choice of a dirty word and a clean one, she'll use the dirty one. One article she wrote was so filthy even the London underground paper for which she was writing refused to print it. She loves to shock; lives to shock people; does as much as she can with her writing, seemingly the point of most of her work. She has also been known to be spiteful toward men, blaming them for much of society's (or her, perceived) ills.

Then, late in her career, she came out with a stunningly poignant book: *Daddy, We Hardly Knew You.* Her father had recently died, and she had gone on a two-year quest across three continents to discover the man taken from her when she was six, whom she'd felt she'd never known.

Is there a particular anger to feminism, an anger of, "You men have abandoned us so we have to do everything ourselves," a pushing aside, a desire to hurt back? Is there an intent to drive men and maleness out of society altogether, like insisting children not have fathers, maybe because that is what already happened to them: their abandonment? Angry rejection is commonly how children react to losing a parent. "He doesn't love me, so I'll hate him."

Is feminism perpetuating the very forces that bore it? Is this how a society perpetuates, even increases its insanity?

Patriarchy has effectively been eliminated from family for generations in our culture, at least in our official view of ourselves, however much that can never completely be the reality. There are many ways to accomplish this: wars, work, imposing Custody-Access-Support upon divorce and increasing the divorce rate. What is the impact on society? Has a mother-centric culture, where 43 percent of children have only a mother, made us more genteel, softer, or more caring as per the feminist Victorian female stereotype. Or has there been an increase in violence: wonton violence, murder for attention? Are people increasingly willing to assume responsibility, or increasingly blaming others for their own actions or inaction, be it smoking (the tobacco companies), a diet pill, or feminists saying, "*Men* have airplanes, guns, bombs, poisonous gases . . .[italics mine],"[68] not that society has them, removing themselves from society and responsibility?

In how much of this are we seeing the bitterness of never having had the love and example of a father, or the insanity of a long imbalance? What is the social cost of billions of lost fathers?

The most disturbing question about CAS may be, how many generations to heal its scars?

---

[68] Feminist Andrea Dworkin, 1981.

APPENDIX I

Preface to
THE EVOLUTION OF COOPERATION

From THE EVOLUTION OF COOPERATION
by ROBERT AXELROD.
Copyright © 1984 by Robert Axelrod,
(Harper Collins Publishers ISBN 0-465-02121-2)
Reprinted by permission of Basic Books,
a member of Perseus Books, L.L.C.

This project began with a simple question: When should a person cooperate, and when should a person be selfish, in an ongoing interaction with another person? Should a friend keep providing favors to another friend who never reciprocates? Should a business provide prompt service to another business that is about to be bankrupt? How intensely should the United States try to punish the Soviet Union for a particular hostile act, and what pattern of behavior can the United States use to best elicit cooperative behavior from the Soviet Union?

There is a simple way to represent the type of situation that gives rise to these problems. This is to use a particular kind of game called the iterated Prisoner's Dilemma. The game allows the players to achieve mutual gains from cooperation, but is also allows for the possibility that one player will exploit the other, or the possibility that neither will cooperate. As in most realistic situations, the players do not have strictly opposing interests. To find a good strategy to use in such situations, I invited experts in game theory to submit programs for a Computer Prisoner's Dilemma Tournament—much like a computer chess tournament. Each program would have available to it the history of the interaction so far and could use this history in making its choice of whether or not to cooperate on the current move. Entries came from game theorists in economics, psychology, sociology, political science, and mathematics. I ran the fourteen entries and a random rule against each other in a round robin tournament. To my considerable surprise, the winner was the simplest of all the programs submitted, TIT FOR TAT. TIT FOR TAT is merely the strategy of starting with cooperation, and thereafter doing what the other player did on the previous move.

I then circulated the results and solicited entries for a second round of the tournament. This time I received sixty-two entries from six countries. Most of the contestants were computer hobbyists, but there were also professors of evolutionary biology, physics, and computer science, as well as the five disciplines represented in the first round. As in the first round, some very elaborate programs were submitted. There were also a number of attempts to improve on TIT FOR TAT itself. TIT FOR TAT was again sent in by the winner of the first round, Anatol Rapoport of the University of Toronto. Again it won.

Something very interesting was happening here. I suspected that the properties that made TIT FOR TAT so successful in the tournaments would work in a world where *any* strategy was possible. If so, then cooperation based solely on reciprocity seemed possible. But I wanted to know the exact conditions that would be needed to foster cooperation on these terms. This lead me to an evolutionary perspective: a consideration of how cooperation can emerge among egoists without central authority. The evolutionary perspective suggested three distinct questions. First, how can a potentially cooperative strategy get an initial foothold in an environment which is predominantly non-cooperative? Second, what type of strategy can thrive in a variegated environment composed of other individuals using a wide diversity of more or less sophisticated strategies? Third, under what conditions can such a strategy, once fully established among a group of people, resist invasion by a less cooperative strategy?

The tournament results were published in the *Journal of Conflict Resolution* (Axelrod 1980a and 1980b), and are presented here in revised form in chapter 2. The theoretical results about initial viability, robustness, and stability were published in the *American Political Science Review* (Axelrod 1981). These findings provide the basis for chapter 3.

After thinking about the evolution of cooperation in a social context, I realized that the findings also had implications for biological evolution. So I collaborated with a biologist—William Hamilton—to develop the biological implications of these strategic ideas. This resulted in a paper published in *Science* (Axelrod and Hamilton 1981) which appears here in revised form as chapter 5. The paper has been awarded the Newcomb Cleveland Prize of American Association for the Advancement of Science.

This gratifying response encouraged me to present these ideas in a form that would make them accessible not only to biologists and mathematically oriented social scientists but also to a broader audience interested in understanding the conditions that can foster cooperation among individuals, organizations, and nations. This in turn led me to see applications of the ideas in a great variety of concrete situations, and to appreciate how readily the results could be used to generate implications for private behavior and for public policy.

APPENDIX II

Divorce Fantasy

Assume for a moment that in divorce it is fair to divide equally between the two parties all that either has acquired during the marriage. (Though I don't know how you could assume this unless you assume they are one physical being while married, a rather striking unreality. And one could as easily claim the other *prevented* greater wealth in any area as helped attain what was acquired, but enough of logic.)

Assume, also, that when we say wealth or assets, we mean it: all the assets of the marriage, not just material wealth. I have a recurring dream: The judge leans down over the couple and says:

> John, you came to provide the intellectual strength of the union. Your wife having freed you from the constraints of social obligations, you became more methodical and thoughtful, your mind rich with knowledge and ideas.
>
> Give half your brain to Shirley.
>
> Shirley, you came to provide the social wealth of the union. You have acquired many friends for the two of you, John being somewhat dry and introverted.
>
> Stop seeing half of them. They are only for John now, whether he chooses to use them or not. And stop laughing by fifty percent. (With the security John provided, you discovered and provided that kind of joy thing. Knock it off.) We'll be keeping count.

Any human relationship is a balance of many dimensions: sex, humour, activities, and yes, even money and property. Any relationship is a large set of trade-offs, all dimensions combined and balanced between the parties. Divorce occurs when one party feels them out of balance.

If you are going to equally divide the assets, either those brought in at, or only those acquired during, the marriage, fairness only exists in dividing *all* such assets equally. For if you only take one – any one: the physical realm (property), social, or intellectual – and divide only that "equally," someone is going to be very cheated. There will be a winner and a loser.

This is the inherent, structural unfairness of current divorce practices. Either divide all assets of the relationship equally, not just the material ones, or divide none. Either way, both parties will come out even. Because should the relationship end, both will either lose equally (whatever was being received), which one might assume was the risk upon entering it, or both equally retain whatever was provided in exchange for half of what they were giving, though I don't know why anyone should expect this.

Dividing only one asset, cheats. It inevitably cheats. This creates cause for resentment, if not motivation for murder. Which one would think we are trying to do with the current structure.

If we cannot divide all assets, divide none. I suggest nobody be presumed to owe anyone anything, that each individual is always responsible for them self, that we remove the enmeshment view of a married couple. Marriage is a spiritual union. We have no business forcing it into the physical-only world of lawyers, or presupposing what exchanges may or may not have been taking place. The total balance sheet is solely up to the individuals, on which it is not for society to pass judgement. These are personal choices.

I would never suggest that a spiritual union does not have its physical expression. If it did not, it would not be so vital that fathers have as much involvement with their children as mothers. Any spiritual union must have its physical expression. I am saying you cannot divide such material expression alone, and assume you've fairly divided the marriage's assets.

There are situations where *alimony* is warranted: when a financial dependence has been created by the marital arrangements. For example, by mutual consent, a woman gives up any career for five or more years to exclusively raise the children, though one would have to establish the mutual consent. Or one leaves the workforce for an extended period for whatever reason in support of the marriage. It will take a little time for this spouse to re-enter the workforce. In rare cases, such as over age fifty, it may not be possible at all. The financial dependence was created by mutual consent; the working member must be obliged to assist until the other party can be reasonably expected to support them self. Rarely for life. The alimony may gradually taper off, not suddenly disappear. This is already the case in many jurisdictions.

Notice that I said until she can reasonably be expected to support herself. I said nothing about "kept in a manner to which she became accustomed," as though a pet. I'm not sure society should be supporting that. Notice also that the only criteria is a return to self-sufficiency. Not compensating career damage or time lost as it was as much her own choice, but only supporting the return. Dropping out of the workforce is not a prerequisite for marriage or family, so should not be so presumed.

Other than a case for limited alimony, you take out of a marriage only what material assets you brought in, both at the beginning and during. Nothing more or less. If it is otherwise – if we entitle people to any material thing to which they did not directly and materially contribute and to which they would not be legally entitled notwithstanding marriage – we are institutionalizing marrying for money and revenge in divorce. During marriage, both are as capable of accumulating material assets as they were before and after. If one chooses not to, that is a personal choice, not something about which society can pass judgement one way or the other, or we are institutionalizing freeloading.

Indeed, nothing is stopping a couple from signing a Dependency Agreement, where obligations both ways are clearly spelled out. This gives lawyers something to do. This would be separate from marriage, not a hidden, assumed part of it. Divorce has no business ever being punitive to anyone, in any form.

This essay is an assault on "marital property." There is no such thing. It is a figment of enmeshment, lawyers, and centuries-old traditions having no place today. An individual may own property; two or more may own specific percentages. But if I marry, suddenly half of anything I earn or otherwise acquire, is hers. Without her doing anything. I, for one, have difficulty seeing the logic in this, or any rationale. If I lose everything, she can walk away. She is not compelled to share in that, takes no share of debt on divorce.

If it is certain that the marriage will last for a lifetime, that both will always be married to the other, that both will always equally share in whatever fortune, then "all things equally owned by both" is a good description of marriage. But in our culture, right now, marriages are not for life; you cannot make that assumption. They have become amazingly transient. Marital property, then, becomes a money-grab, which may be contributing to that transience.[69]

Remove property from marriage. The two must be wholly independent of each another.

The furor feminists raise over the torching of wives in India is interesting. There have been a number of cases where the husband's mother kills his wife by setting fire to her in a way to make it look like a kitchen accident. This frees her son to marry again, reaping another dowry. These events are used as another opportunity to show women as victims of men (even though they are committed by their mothers), avoiding the real issue: marrying for money. These incidents occur because of the thousands-year-old tradition of exorbitant dowries. The groom's family is disappointed by what they got with one wife, so free themselves to seek new rewards.

If it is wrong for a society to systemically encourage marrying for money, it is as wrong for men to marry women for money (as in India) as for women to marry men for money (as is the custom here). Somehow we fail to see the same sins in our own culture.

---

[69] Women initiate two and a half times the number of divorces than do men. If there is an area in which one would expect equal percentages, seeking divorce is it. This statistic screams systemic cause, and a blatantly sexist one. It is not the individuals. They are simply and naturally responding to the structures in which they are placed. Have we made of marriage but a racket?

APPENDIX III

J ohn Guidubaldi is an Ohio psychologist. His career has largely been in child learning, and he headed what, at the time, was the largest study of divorce in America: *Growing Up in a Divorced Family: Initial and Long Term Perspectives in Children's Adjustment* (1987). In 1995 he was named to the below commission. I include his famous minority report (and there were others from this committee along similar lines) in its entirety for three reasons:

1. He does what I do not: present the professional research. (There is a reference list at the end.)
2. He gives a concise second perspective on all issues.
3. He provides some insights into the politics, which specifically means how, and the extent to which, feminists and politicians manage to hide or deny the facts.

At one point he indulges in some "old man" railing against the "Permissive Society." Be patient: there are some valid points. While he may be a small-*c* conservative in some ways, he is not a radical proponent of the traditional family. I do not support his suggested qualifiers for no-fault divorce, seeing the error of current divorce laws in their being structured to so strongly motivate one party. I would also be sure to assert that family may take many forms, be it a homosexual couple and children, a homosexual biological parent, cross-cultural, adoption, multiple-parent, or even polygamous. He does not deny this, I am just ensuring the point is made. Family is family; matriarchy and patriarchy equally important irrespective of their source (grandparents, for instance), perhaps more important simply is that there be a variety of permanent sources of nurturing.

That said, however small-*c* conservative he may or may not be, and from whatever different angle he may approach the same issues, it is striking the agreement between him and this socialist of the first wave of the Permissive Society. Some may claim our commonality in being male and a genetic pre-disposition toward oppressing women. Or possibly a commitment to children, family, fairness, and a healthy, balanced, nurturing community knows no political or gender lines.

KC

MINORITY REPORT AND POLICY RECOMMENDATIONS OF THE UNITED STATES COMMISSION ON CHILD & FAMILY WELFARE BY JOHN GUIDUBALDI, D.Ed., L.P., L.P.C.C.

A COMMISSION CREATED UNDER THE AUTHORITY OF: P.L. 102-521 10/25/92 U.S. Code Citation: 42 USC 12301

REPORT TO THE PRESIDENT AND THE CONGRESS OF THE UNITED STATES JULY 1996

"All our institutions, particularly government, must reexamine the ways in which they affect families... We've passed programs in housing that have helped to destroy neighborhoods. We've enacted tax policies that discriminate against families of average and lower income. And we've done most of this in a mindless way, not deliberately, but often unconsciously. All of us in public life must begin to examine the effect of proposed and existing laws and programs on family life." Vice President, Walter Mondale (1977)

Introduction

Our Commission began its deliberations in January, 1995, with a dedicated staff and a collaborative spirit, accepting a noble mission to enhance children's access to both parents' financial and emotional resources.

However, in our short tenure, we have had to cope with thorny issues that lie at the heart of gender conflict, family disruption, and the abdication of individual autonomy to the ever more cancerous intrusion of our judicial system. Frustrated attempts to resolve our disparate points of view sometimes led to political expediency and watered down recommendations. On several critical issues, rather than offering the President and Congress clear suggestions for change, the Commission majority made only small steps in the necessary direction. One could accept this posture on most issues, acknowledging that the wheels of government do indeed grind slowly. However, the issues facing this Commission are so central to children's mental health that impatience is a necessary virtue. Commissioner Harrington's minority report to this Commission, and a prior minority report to the U.S. Commission on Interstate Child Support by Don Chavez, provide excellent extensive analyses of central issues in our national family disruption crisis, and offer a number of cogent remedies. This minority report is intended to amplify and extend these analyses from my own professional perspective as a clinical and research psychologist.

This report identifies flaws and biases in Commission procedures and addresses the Commission's failure to critically evaluate testimony, particularly with regard to the interpretation of empirical research on the relationship of father involvement to healthy child development. It then offers perspective on several issues and central propositions that were either minimized or entirely excluded from consideration by the Commission majority. Finally, recommendations are proposed for legislative initiatives to supplement those offered in the majority report.

Procedural Deficiencies
Some of the problems of this Commission were no doubt attributable to the minimal funding available. For example, with only $250,000 allocated from a much larger initial authorization, the Commission was limited to three public hearings, and no Commissioner was permitted to participate in more than two hearings. At the hearings, Commissioners were limited to five minutes in questioning each panel and further limited to one question for individual witnesses. Severe restrictions on travel support precluded testimony from several witnesses who had a great deal to offer and were

willing to donate time but were unable or unwilling to fund their own travel expenses. Following our last meeting in September 1995, Commissioners were not involved in the creation of the final report and were not even provided with a draft until six months later in March, 1996. At that point we were offered our only opportunity to review the draft report, but were not provided with the critiques of other Commissioners. During that period of time, from September to March, and subsequently from March until July, 1996, the Commission staff worked solely with the Commission Chair, Mary Cathcart. Individual Commissioners were not consulted at all regarding material to be included, omitted or emphasized. At no time in our deliberations as a group did the Commission afford staff and the chair such wide latitude in determining the ultimate nature of our report. Beyond the liabilities of limited funding, this Commission failed on at least three other counts. First, the majority frequently minimized attention to its primary Congressional mandate to address issues of parental access. For example, although divorce and unwed motherhood are the central reasons for parental absence, almost no attention was directed to the specific societal factors that have created a nation of single parents. The majority report makes brief mention of family economic deficits, but no acknowledgment of the sweeping tide of individualism and accompanying values deficits. Consequently, only feeble preventative recommendations are observable in the final report. The Commission should have considered such issues as the financial and personal incentives to divorce, the reduction of social sanctions for divorce, the role of the "no-fault" legal standard, the explosive growth of the "divorce industry", the diminishing standards of personal accountability, the effects of government subsidy on the increase in unwed motherhood, and the deterrents to marriage inherent in our legal procedures for determining financial and child custody awards.

The second major omission was the Commission's unwillingness to critically evaluate the relative merits of conflicting testimony and submitted materials. Rather than exercising their responsibility to weigh the evidence when issues were contentious, the majority simply listed those in favor and those opposed. No attention was paid to the rigor of research methodology or the quality of empirical foundations underlying witness testimony. The Commission report notes that it was necessary to "retreat from" the responsibility to formulate a recommendation where Commissioner disagreements were apparent, exceptions to a rule existed or research evidence appeared to be contradictory. I strongly disagree with this posture and believe that the Commission "retreated" from its responsibility to invest effort in the discernment of truth. For example, no consideration was given to documents submitted by this Commissioner examining the validity of two fallacious arguments in opposition to joint custody -- one of which argues that joint custody should not be awarded where conflict exists between the parents, and the second argues that there is no bias in the courts against fathers since they are highly likely to be awarded custody when they request it. In each of these cases, the Commission was provided with clear and objective analysis of these false claims that exposed the absolute inadequacy of the data base supporting such blatant distortions. An even more grievous problem is the exercise of bias in the reporting of research evidence bearing on the central issue of shared parenting. Although our agreed upon mission statement focuses on children's access to both the financial <u>and</u> emotional resources of each parent, the majority refused to endorse any guideline for a presumption of shared parenting after divorce. Even with strong provisions for exceptions based on spousal violence, substance abuse, or other impediments, the Commission was unwilling to endorse a recommendation for a marginal 30 % -70 % time share standard. The bias against a presumption of joint custody was observable in several Commission actions. For example, bias was clear in the uncritical acceptance of testimony opposing joint custody, the attempt to limit testimony of those in favor, and the ignoring of substantial supportive documents. Commission procedure for each hearing was to create "balance," resulting in the search for those who would speak against shared parenting, typically using the subterfuge of conflict or spousal violence. While the word "balance" appears to connote our even-handedness, this approach reinforced a polarization of the Commission, subverting our Congressional mandate and dilution our efforts to maximize children's access to their fathers. Rather than seeking testimony that would suggest ways to expand post-divorce father involvement, the Commission solicited a considerable amount of testimony to preserve the sole-mother-custody status quo in divorce, while focusing on increasing father involvement in unmarried rather than divorced conditions. Another exercise of bias was the Commission's inconsistency about the linkage between payment of child support and access to children. On the one hand, on pages 12 and 13, the Majority Report notes that child support payments are much more likely when children have contact with their noncustodial parent, whether that parent is the mother or the father. Yet on page 14, the report asserts that "...payment of child support and access to children are separate and distinct issues." The attempt to artificially separate two forms of parental support that ordinarily go hand in hand is a distortion of modern society. Rather than allowing direct support from a caring parent, it requires one parent to pay a middleman (often an adversarial one) financial support (with no accountability) in order to care for the child. Joint custody presents an interesting dilemma to those who promote sole custody. If the child enjoys both greater financial support and greater emotional assistance from both parents, how can one justify continuation of sole mother custody? Yet, if joint custody becomes widespread and fathers are directly supporting their children, how can one justify payment of full child support awards to mothers? In the final report, only two authors were cited in favor of a presumption of joint custody and five others were cited as opposed. An objective characterization of the full range of testimony would have included the support of several outstanding researchers and child development experts, including strong endorsement from an extensive review of literature submitted by Division 16 of the American Psychological Association. Acknowledging that all research evidence is probabilistic, it is nonetheless quite possible to arrive at conclusions to guide public policy based on the currently available research literature. This Commissioner generated the Commission recommendation that the government should sponsor needed research to clarify critical issues regarding the family and child welfare. However, I do not believe that government officials should delay legislative action in anticipation of future research findings. To do so would jeopardize the well-being of at least two million children who experience either divorce or unwed motherhood each year, as well as countless others who are currently struggling to cope with the confusion and adversity foisted on them by misguided adults. We now have had the advantage of approximately 20 years of research studies to inform our legislative decisions. It is time to act on this accumulated wisdom.

Research Evidence

Socialization Failure: What We've Done For 20 Years Has Not Worked In the "Best Interests of the Child".

Widespread and well recognized evidence now documents the decline in socially responsible behavior of our nation's youth. This decline markedly coincided with the rapidly escalating divorce rate from the mid-sixties and with the movement toward a matriarchal society. I first heard the alarm bells when Senator Birch Baye's Senate Subcommittee issued its report on juvenile crime and violence more than 20 years ago. The 1975 Subcommittee report described unprecedented increases in several areas of juvenile crime over a three-year period, 1970-73. For example, serious assaults on peers increased by 85.3 %, serious assaults on teachers by 77.4 %, rapes and attempted rapes by 40.1 %, and homicides by 18.5 %. Drug and alcohol offenses on school property increased by 37.5 % and the number of weapons confiscated in schools increased by 54.4 %. The divorce rate was in the process of doubling between 1965 and 1978.

Simultaneously, new research by Wiley (1977) had illustrated a steady decline in nationally administered standardized test scores, beginning in the mid-sixties and becoming more pronounced in the late seventies. According to Wiley, these substantial declines in a wide array of measures, from SAT and ACT tests for high-school seniors to Iowa Tests of Basic Skills for middle-elementary students, could not be explained by differences across the years in pupil composition or alterations in tests. Having reviewed these data, in 1980 I concluded a special issue of the School Psychology Review, entitled "Families: Current Status and Emerging Trends" with the following statement: We are beginning to recognize the impact of pervasive family disruption on a wide range of children's school behaviors. We are becoming uncomfortably aware that the increasing divorce rate isn't just a passing fad or a temporary artifact of the post World War II baby boom. Most importantly, we are beginning to understand that the growing lack of commitment to child- rearing may be one of the most significant societal changes in our lifetimes. (pp. 378, 379) Continuing evidence of socialization failure was cited seven years later by U.S. Secretary of Education, William J. Bennett, in an issue of the American Psychologist (1987). After describing massive expansion of federal spending during the

1960's and 1970's to improve the well-being of American children, Bennett asks, "How did American children fare during those 20 years of unparalleled financial commitment?" He then reported that the birthrate for unwed teenagers rose 200%, the rate of homicide among young people more than doubled, juvenile arrests more than doubled, and that there was no way to even estimate the proliferation of drug use (p. 247). Bennett concluded that the absence of fathers was a likely cause of these juvenile problems. To illustrate these trends from my own state level perspective, during the period when the divorce rate and subsequent father absence was more than doubling from the 1970's to 1990, Ohio experienced a 35 % increase in cases of child and adolescent serious emotional disturbance, a 158% increase in learning disabilities cases, a 65% increase in state facilities' juvenile confinement rate for crime and violence, and a 175% increase in confinement rate in private facilities for juveniles. More recent information from the Annie E. Casey Foundation (Kids Count Data Book, 1994) documents that, in the very brief period from 1985 to 1991, we Ohioans experienced a 74 % increase in juvenile violent crime arrest rates, a 31 % increase in births to single teenagers, and an 8 % increase in teen violent deaths. During that same six-year time period, the percent of Ohio children in single parent families rose 9 % to a current level of 22.5 % of all Ohio families. We have been witnessing these horrific increases in problems of children and youth without relief for at least two decades. They are not conveniently explained away by demographic bulges in the size of the youth population. Yet, we have steadfastly adhered to the same adversarial gender-biased judicial procedures with preferential maternal custody and disgruntled absent fathers as the rule. Our Commission recommends movement in the corrective direction, but timidly shies away from the needed endorsement of gender equity.

Divorce and Father Absence: How much Evidence do We Need?
From a scientific point of view, statistics demonstrating what now amounts to 30 years of strongly parallel increases in divorce rate, single parenting, father absence, and children's maladjustment are highly suggestive but not definitive in determining causal relations. However, it would be foolhardy and against all rules of common sense to ignore such a strong association. Moreover, a wealth of research studies have now been conducted to

strengthen the conclusion that divorce, single parenting, and father absence are strongly related to adverse child and adolescent outcomes. From the perspective of child psychology, what does the accumulated research evidence conclude? First, it is abundantly clear that existing divorce procedures have not worked "in the best interests of the child." Repeatedly, in study after study since the mid- 1970's, divorced-family children have been shown to function more poorly than children from biologically intact two-parent families on a wide range of academic, social, and emotional measures. My own research studies, on the first nationwide sample of 699 children from 38 states, strongly confirm the substantial decrements in performance of divorced family children on standardized tests, self-reports, and independent ratings by parents and teachers. (e.g., Guidubaldi, 1989; Guidubaldi, 1988; Guidubaldi, Perry, & Nastasi, 1987) These results are also confirmed at two follow-up periods in sub-samples from the original study -- one that included 220 subjects at 2 and 3-year follow-ups and another that included 81 adolescents and young adults in a 7 and 8-year follow-up study. This study also concluded that (a) the effects of divorce are not temporary stressors but rather long-term influences, (b) boys have more difficulties adjusting to divorce, particularly as they approach adolescence, (c) contrary to the position of some professionals (e.g., Bane,1979) the decline in socioeconomic status after divorce is not a sufficient explanation for children's decreased performance, and (d) authoritative child-rearing style and structure in home routines such as bedtimes, mealtimes, and television viewing habits relate to better child outcomes. One of the most striking findings was that 51 % of children from sole mother custody families see their fathers "once or twice a year or never." In our smaller 7 and 8-year follow-up sample we found that even after an average of 11 or 12 years following the divorce event, adolescents who have good relationships with their noncustodial fathers have fewer teacher-ratings of behavior problems, fewer attention or aggression problems, higher grades in Language and Social Studies, and are less likely to abuse drugs or alcohol according to their own self-ratings. In the only other nationwide study, Furstenberg and Nord found almost the exact percentage (50%) of father absent cases. One can speculate whether this high incidence of absence stems from fathers' selfish interests in pursuing less responsible lifestyles, or whether their parenting efforts are thwarted by restrictions imposed by custodial moms or gender biassed court orders. This interpretation is supported by Kruk (1992) who notes the most frequent reason for fathers' disengagement (90%) was obstruction of paternal access by the child's mother and her desire to break contact between father and child. Interestingly, this explanation is not even considered in the Commission's listing of possible reasons on page 14 of the majority report. Fathers also mentioned that they ceased contact because of their inability to adapt to the constraints of the visiting situation (33%). Regardless of interpretation of motives, the fact remains that sole maternal custody relates strongly to ultimate father absence. Another salient research issue is the highly replicated finding that boys fare much more poorly than girls in post-divorce households. Since more than 88 % of divorced-family children are in sole mother-custody homes, and as explained earlier, half of these have almost no contact with dads, it is clear that many boys are being reared without benefit of a same-sex parental figure. Thus father absence may reasonably be hypothesized as an explanation for the strong gender differences in post-divorce child adjustment -- a condition not easily ameliorated by the school environment which is populated by female role models for at least the first seven years of formal schooling. The relationship of father absence to child adjustment in unmarried mother households presents additional evidence for a policy of shared parenting. In our studies of urban children in special education (e.g., Guidubaldi & Duckworth, 1996), we find that 70% of children (mostly boys) with severe behavioral handicaps have no father contact at all according to the mothers' ratings. These children and adolescents are often the most disturbed or potentially dangerous students in school. One is compelled to ask how many of them would exhibit more cooperative behavior if their fathers were available and influencing their daily lives. Research summaries previously provided to Commission members document an impressive array of significant relationships between father involvement and better child adjustment for the total sample of urban children in special education, including categories such as learning disability, mental retardation, severe behavior problems, and sensory handicaps. Once again, the Commission majority failed to respond to highly pertinent data.

Joint Custody: A Win-Win Proposition

The overwhelming weight of testimony and printed material presented to the Commission supports the notion of increasing the involvement of parents in the child's, life. Our mission statement embodies this challenge to ensure that children receive not only financial support but also emotional support from both parents. We have heard consistent support for more father involvement from respected researchers and child development specialists such as Sanford Braver, Joan Kelly, Richard Warshak, Henry Biller, Nicholas Zill, and others. Why then is there still Commission opposition to a recommendation that would, by definition, increase father involvement opportunity for those seeking to maintain parenting roles after divorce?

As Richard Warshak's testimony indicates, no study has found that joint physical custody is disadvantageous to children. Where researchers have found significant differences, they favor the joint custody arrangement. Only a few empirical studies raise any concerns at all about joint custody and these have been given an unwarranted anti joint custody "spin." These studies merit a closer look. For example, Janet Johnston's work has been cited as opposing joint custody. She notes in her article, "Court-ordered joint physical custody and frequent visitation arrangements in high-conflict divorce tend to be associated with poorer child outcomes, especially for girls" (High Conflict Divorce,1994, p. 165).

A closer look at her definition of high conflict families reveals that she estimated the incidence from Maccoby and Mnookin's California study where 25 % of the divorcing families where judged to have high conflict, but only 10 % of these (2.5 %) show an association between joint custody/frequent visitation access and poorer child adjustment. Clearly, such an extreme population should not serve as the basis for policy that affects the welfare of the other 97.5 % of the population. Johnston, herself, acknowledges that joint physical custody and frequent visitation are not detrimental to the majority of children. She notes that, "In some cases, especially where parents are cooperative, they are more beneficial" (p. 176). Maccoby and Mnookin's work is also sometimes cited as evidence against joint custody. However, closer scrutiny of their article about joint legal custody (Albiston, Maccoby, & Mnookin, 1990) reveals no negative effects and, conversely, a positive effect between joint legal custody and decreasing discord between the parents for families in which the children visited both parents. The authors conclude that, "Thus the retention of joint legal custody as an option for its affirmation of the involvement of nonresidential parents and its potential impact on perceptions of gender roles may be warranted" (p. 177).

In addition to Maccoby's conclusion that joint custody provides a "symbol of the expectation that both parents are to continue in their role as parents after the divorce," we should recognize that the presumption of joint custody has another equally powerful anticipatory effect. Mindful of the fact that equality of parenting privilege will be the cornerstone of court decisions, parents are likely to be far more cooperative in pre-trial mediation, and may avoid litigation all together. If on the other hand, either of the potential litigants forecasts an advantageous position in court, their involvement in meaningful mediation may be severely compromised, and the efforts of even the most skilled mediators may be thwarted. Political extrapolations have sometimes resulted in the conclusion that where there is conflict at the time of divorce (when isn't there?) joint custody should be precluded. If this conclusion were allowed to stand, it would serve as incentive to promote conflict by those desiring sole custody. Conflict is certainly present in most divorcing situations, but it usually subsides with time. Temporary anger is common in reaction to such a powerful psychosocial stressor. It is not ordinarily indicative of pathology and should not result in an abrogation of parenting rights. Moreover, the expansion of the definition of spousal abuse has further confused the issue. Rather well defined rules of evidence pertaining to occurrences of physical abuse provide necessary safeguards against false claims, as well as protecting those who are truly victims.

However, in recent years, more amorphous claims of "psychological abuse" have been elevated to the same level of consequence and have become widespread in divorce actions. Often rules of evidence are cast aside and the simplistic "guilty until proven innocent" orientation is exercised by confused judges who have limited ability to distinguish between truly menacing verbal behavior and harmless verbal expressions of anger (which flow both ways in marital discord). These distortions have fueled the controversy over what might otherwise appear to be an obviously fair proposition -- that neither parent should lose parenting privileges or responsibilities as a result of divorce. A frequently heard rationale for sole mother custody concerns the issue of pre-divorce parenting role performance serving as a precedent for post-divorce parenting roles In response, it should be noted that during the marriage, traditional role complementary provides for efficient childrearing, wherein one of the parents usually serves as the primary bread-winner, providing for the child's food shelter, clothing, etc. while the other parent's main focus is on utilizing these resources in providing direct services for the child. Neither contribution should be denigrated in determining post-divorce childrearing privileges or responsibilities. Since both roles were essential for child welfare, since both parties may be presumed to have had at least a tacit agreement to these role divisions, and since in many families the roles are not mutually exclusive and may involve a considerable amount of overlap, the pre-divorce parenting roles should not be the basis for post-divorce parenting time and should not place either parent at a disadvantage in custody conflicts.

Furthermore, it is blatantly clear that post-divorce lifestyles are markedly changed for all parties concerned, and a consequent redefinition of roles and privileges is essential. For example, to expect mothers to be dependent economically on their divorced spouses neglects their capabilities to become self sufficient, productive wage earners, and in fact may promote attitudes of learned helplessness. To expect fathers to continue to provide for the child's well- being through child support payments to their ex-spouses neglects the father's capacity to contribute directly to the child's well-being and may promote anger, resentment and a sense of "taxation without representation". For many fathers, the orientation is that of a second class citizen placed outside the child's mainstream, useful only as a source of continued financial support. For many mothers, this unequal post-divorce situation results in the feeling of continued economic dependency, a need to support the child on a reduced financial base since two households must now be maintained, and the inability to move forward into new employment opportunities because of the heavy childrearing burden essential in sole custody. Another argument frequently heard against joint custody is that children are unable to make transitions from one parent's home to another. No evidence is brought to bear on this assumption, and indeed ample evidence exists to support the alternative conclusion that developmental capabilities, of even young children, enable them to make healthy transitions from one environment to another (as in movement from home to daycare, baby-sitter's residence, and grandparent's homes). On what basis then, should we conclude that even young children cannot make the transition from one loving parent to another? Do the minor inconveniences outweigh the positive contributions of a highly involved caring parent?

Considering the controversy over the issue of joint custody and the distortions of research findings in the service of preserving the sole-mother custody status quo, I asked two officials of the American Psychological Association, who gave testimony, to provide the Commission with an objective analysis of this body of research. I requested this openly in the Cleveland, Ohio Commission hearing on April 20th, and no objections were raised by other Commissioners. Following its approval by the Division 16 Operating Committee, the subsequent report was submitted on June 14, 1995 by Beth Doll, the Division Vice President for Social Council and Ethical Responsibility and Ethnic Minority Affairs. It began with the following statement:

> A search of the empirical research specific to joint custody was conducted. Major data-based studies available at the time of this review have been individually summarized and evaluated relevant to findings and adequacy of the methodology as requested. While flawless studies on such a complex subject are extremely rare as indicated by the evaluations, the goal of this report is to provide a synthesis so that the Commission's policy recommendations may be predicated on the best available empirical base. To minimize some of the confusion in such a highly charged area of study, this review focused on the weight of evidence as determined

by both replication of findings and consideration of methodological rigor. This document then reviewed results from 23 studies, providing abstracts of each and summary findings according to criteria of (a) father involvement, (b) best interests of the child standard, (c) financial child support, (d) relitigation and costs to the family, and (e) parental conflict. On each of these criteria, the report supports the conclusion that joint custody is associated with favorable outcomes.

Regrettably, this objective analysis from the world's largest organization of psychologists was ignored in our Commission meetings and in our final report. As an authoritative source of information on the social and emotional well-being of our citizenry, the APA has consistently promoted standards of gender equity. In its Council meeting in 1977, almost 20 years ago, it recognized the centrality of these issues: Be it resolved that the Council of Representatives recognizes officially and makes suitable promulgation of the fact that it is scientifically and psychologically baseless, as well as a violation of human rights, to discriminate against men because of their sex in assignment of children's custody, in adoption, in the staffing of child-care services, and personnel practices providing for parental leave in relation to childbirth and emergencies involving children and in similar laws and procedures.

Cultural Context
Parents' Constitutional Rights: A Biological Imperative
Any meaningful attempt to reestablish stability of marital relationships s must begin with a careful analysis of cultural factors that contributed to the etiology of family disruption. The commission failed to address these issues, and thus its report, replete with recommendations, lacks a conceptual core. At a minimum, we must comprehend and adhere to rights guaranteed by our U.S. Constitution. Secondly, we need to examine historically the events that psychologically predisposed many to view marriage as an unnecessary obstruction of their freedom, and thirdly, we must consider those factors that currently serve as enticements to divorce and unwed motherhood. A comprehensive analysis of these issues cannot

be offered in this brief report; however, excerpts to illustrate the rights of parents and the erosion of traditional fatherhood provide prerequisite elements. The primacy of parenthood has been safeguarded by the United States Constitution as illustrated in the following citations:

The rights of parents to the care, custody and nurturance of their children is of such character that it cannot be denied without violating those fundamental principles of liberty and justice which lie at the base of all our civil and political institution, and such right is a fundamental right protected by this Amendment (First) and Amendments 5, 9 and 14. **Doe v Irwin** 441 F Supp 1247; U.S. D.C. of Michigan, (1985).

A parent's right to care and companionship of his or her children are so fundamental, as to be guaranteed protection under the First, Ninth, and Fourteenth Amendments of the United States Constitution. **In re: J.S. and C.**, 324 A 2d 90; supra 129 NJ Super, at 489.

Federal courts (and State Courts), under Griswold can protect under the "life, liberty, and pursuit of happiness" phrase of the Declaration of Independence, the right of a man to enjoy the mutual care, company, love and affection of his children, and this cannot be taken away from him without due process of law. There is a family right to privacy which the state cannot invade or it becomes actionable for civil rights damages. **Griswold v Connecticut**, 381 US 479, (1965).

The U.S. Supreme Court has made it clear that a "parent's right to custody and companionship of a natural child has been specifically accorded protection under the Constitution. "Smith v. Organization of Foster Families" 431 US 816, 53 Led 2d 14, 97 S ct. 2094 (1977); Stanley v Illinois supra; Caban v. Mohammed 441 US 380, 99 S ct. 60 Led 2d 296 (1979).

The Permissive Society: Psychologically Enabling Divorce

In the face of a father's constitutional guarantees of parental rights, as well as clear psychological research evidence documenting the benefits to the child of continuing father involvement, regardless of marital status, how has it come to pass that father absence now characterizes the lives of millions? Our Commission report appears to suggest that the failure of marriage in American culture is largely the outcome of low wages, unemployment, and general economic difficulties. However, as noted by Islamic authors at a recent inter-religious colloquium in Rome: Several studies in the U.S.A. prove that the divorce rates declined in times of economic depression and rose during the time of economic prosperity. The depression of 1932 to 1933 had the lowest rate of divorce and the highest rate in the 1980's during the period of economic achievement. Mothers are leaving home to earn money for a better living, but in many cases at the cost of a very high price. Money is definitely essential for the maintenance of a family. But one should not forget that money can buy a bed but not sleep, finery but not beauty, a house but not a home, medicine but not health, luxuries but not culture, sex but not love, and amusements but not happiness. (1995, p.74)

Our search for underlying causes of family disintegration and father absence must begin with an acute awareness of a process we might describe as the "dethronement of authority." That process had its inception during the tumultuous 1960's and flourished in the 1970's. Its theoretical roots were in the humanistic psychology movement that taught self actualization, in Kohlberg's rejection of the boy scout bag of virtues in favor of moral reasoning, and in the process of civil disobedience that led to success of the civil rights movement. In each case, the authority of traditional mores was challenged. The exposure of abuses and deceptions by authorities in the Vietnam War, Watergate, and other scandals to follow, nourished anti-authority sentiment which was expressed in a generalized manner to such divergent targets as the President of our country, university officials, policemen, clergy, and to fathers who traditionally represented the ultimate authority within the family. Time and time again, traditional authority was characterized as outdated, insensitive, and so dedicate to self preservation that it was not open to needed change.

On the other hand, the impatience of change agents oversimplified the virtues of change and ignored the society's need for a well- anchored foundation of tested values. Gender role complementarily gave way to role redundancy; parental authority roles were undermined by declining religious influence, desensitizing of taboos by the rock music industry, and by the new phenomenon of widespread divorce. Confrontation politics reigned and "Times were a changin." Several corollaries to this anti-authority movement soon became obvious and ultimately assumed the mantle of political correctness. Slogans such as "I'm OK, you're OK " "Do our own thing, " "Don't worry, be happy, and "Different strokes for different folks" all reflected the new legitimacy of socially approved egocentrism.

America's traditional sympathies for the underdog mutated into a fetish of inflated entitlements, and millions of Americans compromised their dignity for nurturance. Accountability for personal failures was conveniently transplanted to the educational system, the nation's economy, and to a disease model that provided convenient exoneration from guilt for sins of excessive indulgence. This was the context in which cultural civility declined, family stability began to erode, and socialization of our children failed. It is not surprising that the father's traditional role as head of household was severely challenged by their children who were encouraged to be more rebellious by permissive media, negative peer group models, and on occasion, by mothers who were themselves alienated from their spouse or ex-spouse. Equally undermining paternal authority was the new "liberated" woman's role.

Several factors contributed to increased autonomy from the homemaker and mother roles. Expanding maternal employment opportunities and a new movement to provide "equal pay for equal work" brought about greater economic independence. Simultaneously, widespread use of the birth control pill brought about greater independence from child-rearing permitting women to govern their own fertility. In the absence of compelling social mores, and with declining influence of religious prescriptions, marital loyalty bonds were seen as less obligatory. These were the circumstances existing when "no-fault divorce" rulings emerged. Coupled with economic independence, fertility control, and cultural permissiveness, the "no-fault" divorce option provided the enabling legal vehicle for quick and easy exits from unfulfilling marriages. Henceforth, parents could leave their spouses with minimal guilt using the convenient rubric of incompatibility. However, if children were involved, and if they too must be left behind, divorce-initiating parents could be overwhelmed by guilt. Thus, in order to psychologically manage, the termination of the marriage, the initiator must have some assurance of continued salience as a parent. The judicial sole-mother custody award enabled millions of mothers to divorce with absolution.

In today's world, if one investigates the simple question, "Who initiates divorce?" we find from <u>Monthly Vital Statistics Report, May 21, 1991</u>, that from 1975 to 1988, in families with children present, wives filed for divorce in approximately two-thirds of the cases each year. In 1975, 71.4 % of the cases were filed by women, and in 1988 65 % were filed by women. While these statistics alone do not compel a conclusion that women anticipate advantages to being single rather than remaining in the marriage, the do raise that reasonable hypothesis -- one that the Commission majority refused to consider. If women can anticipate a clear gender bias in the courts regarding custody, they can expect to be the primary residential parent for their children. If they can anticipate enforcement of child support by the courts, they can expect a high probability of support moneys without the need to account for their expenditures. Clearly, they can also anticipate maintaining the marital residence, receiving half of all marital property, and gaining total freedom to establish new social connections and intimacy relationships. Weighing these gains against the alternative of remaining in the marriage with a spouse who may, in the wife's judgment, be oppressive, unfaithful, or just plain boring, could result in a seductive enticement to obtain a divorce. Solutions to this hypothesized scenario are elusive, but without question, should include reconsideration of the ease with which divorces are granted when children are involved.

The Divorce Industry: The Fox in the Hen House

Once the decision to divorce is seriously considered, a powerful set of forces that enable and promote this process is brought to bear. Some have referred to this as the "divorce industry." It includes judges, attorneys, psychologists, social workers, property appraisers, accountants, and others who stand ready to make a profit from the misfortunes of the divorcing couple. The divorce industry is now so vast and so profitable that it may be impervious to change without major legislative intervention; yet, lawyers are typically the most influential forces in drafting legislation. To date, our tripartite government has defaulted on this topic to a monopolistic judiciary.

Even with ample evidence of violations of Constitutional rights, Congress has been reluctant to act in defense of children's right to their fathers' nurturance. Does this inaction result from a fear of alienating the entire female electorate? If asked, this myth would easily be dispelled by the paternal grandmother who has lost her grandchildren; the new wife who must cope with excessive child support payments to an ex-wife, as well as her husband's frustrated attempts to see his children; the daughter who is now grown, but remembers vividly the pain of father loss; and the many women who want to marry and have children, but find men unable to make a commitment. Of all the parties in the divorce process, domestic court judges clearly play the most influential roles.

In an era when half of the married population may be expected to divorce, the procedures for electing and assigning judicial personnel to domestic court responsibilities need to be examined. Domestic court judges, at this moment in our history, are extremely powerful persons, controlling the most important decisions of childrearing privilege and asset distribution for millions of families. An individual's basic rights of parenting his or her own offspring, and enjoying the fruits of his or her own labor, have been seriously compromised in our society. The courts entrusted with these potentially earth-shattering decisions are among our lowest status courts, and judicial personnel are often elected without regard to their level of knowledge and understanding of family dynamics, home economics, or child development. Moreover, they are often on the bench for extended periods of time, and have little likelihood of public criticism from attorneys in their communities since these players in the divorce game depend on the goodwill of their local judges to ensure their success rate and financial livelihood. Finally, their decisions -- good or bad, fair or unfair -- are largely impervious to modification.

Appeals courts are yet another expensive layer of judicial bureaucracy for litigants, and even if litigants are not deterred by financial, mental energy, and exorbitant time costs, the likelihood of appeals court reversals are minimal given the use of the ambiguous and extremely broad, "abuse of judicial discretion" test. Successful modification of trial court judge's rulings in state supreme courts is an even more unlikely probability. Thus, citizens desperately require a more effective set of remedies for bad judicial decisions, and a more efficient and viable procedure for removal of judges who repeatedly abuse their power. Regardless of whether the abuse stems from gender bias, idiosyncratic or whimsical personality preferences, ignorance, or indifference, judges must be held accountable for the drastic changes they mandate in the lives of their constituents.

Throughout the past 20 years, my experiences as a Licensed Psychologist and Counselor have provided a first-hand view of family disruption and afforded the opportunity to witness dozens of cases of severe judicial abuse. From my professional experience, it seems that the combination of sympathy for the perceived underdog and envy for those more successful than ourselves has led to a Robin Hood approach that pilfers funds from those with deep pockets, extracts an exorbitant commission, and distributes the rest to those considered too weak to fend for themselves. A few brief examples (with modified names for anonymity) may illustrate the greed, exploitation, and injustice that occur in courts across this count on a daily basis:

> While serving as a counselor for Gordy, the owner of an auto body repair shop, his new wife informed me that she falsely accused her ex-husband of sexually abusing their eight-year-old daughter. After his arrest, she dropped charges, but only after he agreed not to be involved in the daughter's life, and to not meddle in her new marriage.

> A ten-year-old boy, Billy, and his 12-year-old sister, Vera, were brought by their mother to my office because of severe school discipline problems. They had recently experienced the divorce of their parents and both were severely alienated from

their father. When dad came to visit, they would refuse, slamming the door in his face and cursing with the ugliest of epithets. Mother supported their abusive behavior and explained that father was only getting what he deserved since he had been sexually unfaithful with his secretary.

Paul was going through a divorce process, but on the advice of his attorney, was living in the family home under a temporary separation order. He was contesting custody of his twin 5-year-old boys and had previously seen three psychologists, spending more than $6,000 for court ordered psychological assessments of himself, his wife, and their children. One evening, without warning, his wife hit him over the head with a heavy scotch tape dispenser, knocking him unconscious. When he regained consciousness he called an ambulance. In the emergency ward, as he was receiving 26 sutures, he told the medical staff what happened. They laughed.

Gino, who owned several restaurants, was divorced from his wife. Later, he impregnated a woman he was dating and offered to marry her. She refused saying she didn't love him. After the baby was born, Gino established paternity and regularly paid $1,500 per month child support. Five years later, the child's mother brought Gino to court stipulating that because his income was higher than the maximum used in state child-support guidelines, he should pay the same percentage but based upon his actual income so that the "child" could be kept in the style he would have been entitled to if a marriage had occurred. Her motion demanded $1,000,000 back child support, interest, and attorney's fees, as well as $100,000 per year in future child support.

Jim, who had custody of his daughter, came to counseling because he was considering a second marriage, but could not rid himself of the fear of financial exploitation, which he experienced at the hands of his first wife. His ex-wife had two college degrees, was in good health and received a large cash settlement in the divorce. She claimed she could not obtain a job commensurate with her credentials, but had filed only four applications in nine years. At the divorce trial, Jim had been ordered to pay $1,300 per month alimony. He was still paying that amount nine years and three appeals later. The appeals court continued to rule that circumstances had not changed and that the trial court judge was operating within his "breadth of judicial discretion."

Marvin is an Orthodox Jewish man who had married Svetlana, a Russian immigrant. She fell in love with another man and would not return from her nightclub singing job until morning. She filed for divorce and was moving to another state with her new man. She insisted on taking their 5-year old son with her. Marvin refused, asserting that the son, Sheldon, had many ties in the Orthodox community where he lived. Svetlana won custody and moved from St. Louis to Tacoma.

Sam is a self-made millionaire, having developed patents for innovation of manufacturing procedures in a major industry. He married late in his forties and had a prenuptial agreement. Four years and two children later, his wife filed for a divorce. Sam had bought a house for her and the children, was paying private school tuition for both children, and had established a substantial enrichment fund for the children's use in travel and recreational activities. A long 9-year period of court battles ensued over the issue of child support, his ex-wife demanding more than the $6,000 per month she was currently receiving, as well as more than $120,000 for her own legal expenses. Sam refused, was thrown in jail, and humiliated on the T.V. news as a millionaire "deadbeat dad." His children watched the T.V. coverage of their father's incarceration.

Recommendations

The Commission has stated 23 recommendations. Operating on the assumption that 10% of a loaf is better than none, all of these are further endorsed by this minority report. This Commissioner contributed to the framing of several of these recommendations, but believes that the Commission majority has strayed from its original mandate, omitted major issues, and moved only marginally in other areas. The recommendations by Commissioner Don Chavez, in his aforementioned minority report to the Interstate Child Support Enforcement Commission, are also endorsed as substantial remedies to the financial plight of children from divorced and unwed parent families. Most pertinent of all are the extensive array of 53 well-conceived recommendations drafted by Commissioner Bill Harrington in his minority report from this Commission. These recommendations are jointly endorsed by this Commissioner, including especially Harrington's recommendations:

- (#1) establishing a White House "Council on Father Involvement;"
- (#14)Congressional hearings on the "Campaign of Misinformation" regarding punitive child support schedules and standards for alimony payments;
- (#20) abolishing father-excluding welfare policies and creating welfare policies to encourage family togetherness;
- (#24) establishing a three-year plan designed to provide incentives to earn a living and to remove the child from welfare dependency;
- (#27) establishing a new policy of rebuttable presumption of shared parenting/joint custody for AFDC cases;
- (#36) establishing statewide commissions on the status of fatherhood and child welfare;
- (#43) establishing education and sensitivity training for judicial officers and support staff regarding anti-father gender bias;
- (#44) establishing rules of professional conduct for lawyers that reduce the tendency to over-litigate for family law clients; and
- (#46) promoting and encouraging men to be elementary school teachers

Recommendations specifically stemming from the arguments in this report are as follows:

10. In order to maximize children's adult nurturance and safeguard both parents' constitutional rights of parenthood, thus increasing the attractiveness of marriage by assurance of fair treatment in the event of marriage failure, the President and Congress should promote legislation to ensure gender equity in divorce and unwed-parent child custody and financial settlements. This legislation should incorporate a rebuttable presumption of joint legal and physical custody, and should include provisions for determining fair child support awards to eliminate the phenomenon of disguised alimony.

11. In order to provide needed reforms in our domestic courts, the President and Congress should promote legislation to improve the accountability and responsible decision making of domestic court judges, including term limits, annual reviews by superior courts, and measures to make the appeals process less costly and less time consuming for litigants. Specifically, this minority report recommends:

   A. That a system of state supreme court routine monitoring of local domestic court judges be implemented.

   B. That a standardized procedure be made available for monitoring of local domestic court judges by citizen groups, with reports given to state supreme courts for remedial action where warranted.

   C. That the term of office for domestic court judges be limited to four years, with option for renewal by election or reappointment not to exceed two consecutive terms.

   D. That each domestic court judge be required to keep an independent file of all rulings relating to children in divorce, paternity, or adoption proceedings. Such file should be available for public review as an expected part of judicial accountability.

   E. That the "breadth of judicial discretion" standard be modified to require domestic court judges to issue rulings based on the preponderance of established evidence. Accountability should ensure that rulings are not predicated on hearsay or unfounded character assassination. Findings of fact and conclusions of law should be reviewed by appellate court judges to ensure that rulings are consistent with established evidence.

12. Considering the child's right to enjoy the support of both parents, and also the strong relationship between effective child rearing and the culture's level of civility and socially responsible behavior, the President and Congress should enact legislation that places restrictions on the use of "no-fault" divorces when children are involved.

13. Acknowledging that American Public Schools have been historically entrusted with the tax supported mission to enhance both the academic capability <u>and</u> the good citizenship of our children, and recognizing the efficiency of utilizing a well established agency of government rather than generating a new bureaucracy to address a critical societal problem, the President and Congress should enact legislation that restores the school's ability to work effectively with parents as partners in the socialization process. Such legislation should include restoration of neighborhood schools, incentives for effective school-based parent organizations, utilization of school mental health professionals to assist families in distress, and effective school-based parent education programs.

14. In order to restore responsibility as a prerequisite to parenting, the President and Congress should enact legislation that would remove incentives and provide deterrents to the selfish practice of reproduction without obligation. Both fathers and mothers should be held to a standard that requires diligent effort on behalf of their children, rather than relying on taxpayers and governmental compensation for their own delinquency.

15. In order to address more specifically the declining popularity of marriage and pervasive father absence, the President and Congress should establish a new Commission to explore ways to reinforce stable co-parenting relationships in the interests of our nation s children.

Personal Perspective

In closing this report, I have sought the counsel of a friend from inside the beltway. I respect him greatly for he has been one of the most eloquent spokespersons for children's and fathers rights during the past decade. Hearing only a few passages of this report by phone, he has advised me to soften my tone, expressing not anger, but sorrow at the Commission's missed opportunity to rectify major societal problems. His well-intentioned advice is politically sound and it has given me pause, but being neither attorney nor politician, I find it difficult to stifle my passion about these problems. They are of such magnitude that they are strangling the potential of a whole generation of Americans. The strident voices of some of us informed observers need to be heard above the slow hum of politics as usual. Passion and a sense of urgency must guide our nation's lawmakers, for the lives of children truly hang in the balance. To preempt the potential critic who is forever searching for personal information to defuse another's logical argument, I'll close by sharing a few personal experiences that have indeed shaped my thinking -- in the direction of realism. My own father was hospitalized when I was five years old, and he never returned. My mother, who had only an eighth grade education, struggled with low level laboring jobs to rear all four of us children. Her religious values, hard work ethic, and her personal qualities of honesty and nurturance toward others provided each of her children with a strong foundation to meet our own challenges. Some may claim this proves the case for sole mother custody; however, my mother defied the odds and my father loss was through illness and death, not divorce or unwed motherhood. More powerfully, I can personally attest to the many years of grieving for his lost guidance and support, and I know first-hand the vulnerability to male peer group influence as a compensatory source of masculine guidance.

The greatest of my personal adult challenges was my own divorce. When my long-term wife decided that she wanted her "freedom," I learned first-hand what so many of my male clients had grieved about in my private psychologist office -- the absolute loss of power to control the two most important things in one's life: parenting privilege and the fruits of one's own labor. I was fortunate because of my daughter's choice, to have the privilege of Mr. Mom status for the past nine years, I know full well the nurturing capability of fatherhood. I also understand how financial injustice, imposed by judicial injustice, can generate a legacy that places unnecessary long-term burdens on both adults and their children. As I write my final sentences, I'm preparing to leave for the hospital here in Tallahassee, to visit my newly arrived second granddaughter and baby sit with my first. Please Mr. President and members of Congress, do all that you can to restore civility and justice to this society so that the children of this new generation will be stable and secure. Do this for all our nation's children -- and especially for Bailey Page and Madison Emma.

ORIGINAL SIGNED John Guidubaldi, D.Ed,, L,P, L,P,C,C. Commissioner, U.S. Commission on Child and Family Welfare

References

Albistoma, C. R., Maccoby, E. E., & Mnookin, R. R. (1990). Does joint legal custody matter? Stanford Law and Policy Review, 2, 167-179

American Psychological Association. (1995). Preliminary summary: Empirical research describing outcomes of joint custody. Washington, DC.

Annie E. Casey Foundation. (1994). Kids Count Data Book.

Bane, M. J. (1976). Marital disruption and the lives of children. Journal of Social Issues, 32, 109-110.

Bennett, W. J. (1987). The role of the family in the nurture and protection of the young. American Psychologist, 42, 246-250.

Committee on the Judiciary of the United States Senate. (1975). Our Nation's schools-a report card: "A" in school violence and vandalism (Preliminary report of the Subcommittee to investigate juvenile delinquency). Washin ton DC, Government Printing Office.

Furstenberg, F., Nord, C., & Zill, N. (1983). The life course of children of divorce: Marital disruption and parental contact. American Sociological Review, 48, (Oct), 656-668.

Guidubaldi, J. (1989), Differences in children's divorce adjustment across grade level and gender: A report from the NASP-Kent State nationwide project In S. Wolchik & Karoly (Eds.) Children of Divoce: Perspectives and adjustment (pp. 185-231). Lexington, MA: Lexington Books

Guidubaldi, J. (1988), The legacy of lost families: Divorce and the next generation. The World & I, Nov, 520-534. T

Guidubaldi, J. (1980). The status report extended: Further elaboration's the American family. School Psychology Review, 9(4), 374-379.

Guidubaldi, J., & Duckworth J, (1996, March). Enhancing fathers' involvement in child rearing: An empirical basis for consultation and parent education, Symposium presented at the National Association of School Psychologists Annual Convention Atlanta, GA

Guidubaldi, J., Perry, J., & Nastasi, B. (1987), Growing up in a divorced family: Initial and long- term perspectives on children's adjustment In S. Oskamp (Ed.). Applied social psycological annual: Volume 7 family processes and problems: Social psychology aspects, Newbury Park, CA: Sage.

Johnston, J. R. (1994). High-Conllict Divorce. In R. E. Behrman The Future of Children 4(1) (pp.165-182), The Center for the Future of Children, The David and Lucile _ Packard Foundation

Kazi, N. I., & Azizun, N. I. (1994). Islam. Marriage and the Family in today's world: Interreligious colloquium, (pp. 65-74), Pontifical Council for Interreligious Dialogue, Pontifical Council for the Family, Vatican City, Rome.

Kohlberg, L. (1976). Moral stages and moralization. In T. Lickona (Ed.), Moral development and behavior: Theory, research and social issues. New York: Holt, Rhinehart & Winston.,

Kohlberg, L. (1969). Stage and sequence: The cognitive developmental approach to socialization. In D. A. Goslin (Ed.), Handbook of socialization theory and research. Chicago: Rand McNally.

Mondale, W. F. (1977). Introducing a special report: The family in trouble. Psychology Today, May, 39.

Wiley, D. (1977). Declining achievement scores: Do we need to worry? St. Louis: CEMRELL

APPENDIX IV

No study of sole custody versus joint custody has ever concluded with a preference for sole custody. The author of one, often cited by opponents of co-custody, concluded there *may* be problems under extreme circumstances. (Janet Johnston's *High Conflict Divorce*, 1994.) But any second look has concluded too casual a use of too little data for such a conclusion, and more thorough studies have failed to confirm it.

Following is an extensive list of many of these studies. It is lifted verbatim from the web pages of The Children's Rights Council (www.vix.com/crc; 300 I Street NE, Suite 400, Washington, DC, 20002, (202) 547-6227). This is a non-profit, non-gender organization of parents founded in 1985. They promote a children's bill of rights which includes the right to both parents.

KC

Research on Shared Parenting and Joint Custody

*Joint custody and shared parenting have been studied for more than a quarter-century, with the **majority of studies indicating significant benefits for children.** About a third of existing studies show no difference between joint and sole custody for children's adjustment to divorce. **The critical factor appears to be conflict between parents. When parents cooperate and minimize conflict, children do better with shared parenting. If there is significant conflict between parents, however, shared parenting provides no benefits and children do no better (and no worse) than they do in sole custody.** This section summarizes some of the research published in the past decade.*

Joint Physical Custody

Adolescents After Divorce, Buchanan, C., Maccoby, and Dornbusch, Harvard University Press, 1996.
A study of 517 families with children ranging in age from 10.5 years to 18 years, across a four and a half year period. Measures were: assessed depression, deviance, school effort, and school grades. *Children in shared parenting arrangements were found to have better adjustment on these measures than those in sole custody.*

Division 16, School Psychology, American Psychological Association, Report to the U.S. Commission on Child and Family Welfare, June 14, 1995.
This report "summarizes and evaluates the major research concerning joint custody and its impact on children's welfare." The report concludes that *"The research reviewed supports the conclusion that joint custody is associated with certain favorable outcomes for children including father involvement, best interest of the child for adjustment outcomes, child support, reduced relitigation costs, and sometimes reduced parental conflict."* The APA also noted that "The need for improved policy to reduce the present adversarial approach that has resulted in primarily sole maternal custody, limited father involvement and maladjustment of both children and parents is critical. *Increased mediation, joint custody, and parent education are supported for this policy."*
Note: This report was approved and submitted by Division 16 of the APA, and is a part of the public record. However, it is not listed among official APA publications; it was quashed because it did not fit the political ideology of those at the top of the APA.

Wilkinson, Ronald Richard, "A Comparison of Children's Post-divorce Adjustment in Sole and Joint Physical Custody Arrangements Matched for Types of Parental Conflict" Doctoral dissertation, 1992; Texas Woman's University
This study included "forty boys and girls, ages 8 to 12, in attendance at selected private secular and parochial schools in a large Southwestern metropolitan area participated, along with their middle to upper-class

parents." The study compared adjustment of children in joint and sole physical custody, controlling for level of conflict between parents, to determine if parental conflict would be more detrimental to children in joint or sole custody. The author summarized findings as follows: "Overall, no significant difference between joint and sole physical custody groups was found."

Rockwell-Evans, Kim Evonne, "Parental and Children's Experiences and Adjustment in Maternal Versus Joint Custody Families " Doctoral dissertation, 1991. North Texas State U.
This study compared 21 joint custody and 21 maternal custody families, with children between the ages of 4-15.
Results showed that mis-behavior and "acting out" were more common among sole custody children: *"A multiple regression analysis of these data found children in joint custody families had fewer behavioral adjustment problems with externalizing behavior than children in mother custody families."* "Regardless of custody arrangement, parents with low self esteem were more likely to have children with behavioral adjustment problems when predicting the child's overall behavioral adjustment and internalized behavior."

J. Pearson and N. Thoennes,"Custody After Divorce: Demographic and Attitudinal Patterns", *American Journal of Orthopsychiatry,* Vol. 60, 1990.
"Consistent with other studies of joint and sole custody [citations], our joint legal and residential non-custodians were decidedly more involved with their children following divorce than were non-custodians in sole custody arrangements. . . . Lastly, respondents in joint custody arrangements were more apt to perceive their ex-spouse as having a good relationship with the children and to report satisfaction with that person's performance as a parent."
" . . . conflict between divorcing parents in our sample did not appear to worsen as a result of the increased demand for inter-parental cooperation and communication in joint legal or joint residential custody arrangements. *To the contrary, parents with sole maternal custody reported the greatest deterioration in the relationships over time."*

Glover, R. and C. Steele, "Comparing the Effects on the Child of Post-divorce Parenting Arrangements," *Journal of Divorce,* Vol. 12, No. 2-3 (1989).

This study evaluated children aged 6 to 15 in the areas of locus of control, self-concept, and family relationships. The children were divided into three groups: shared custody, maternal custody, and intact families. Intact family children had averaged higher than divorced family children on self-concept and father relationships, and shared custody children averaged higher the sole custody children in these areas. Intact family children had fewer least-positive responses in all areas than divorced family children, and shared custody children had fewer least-positive responses than sole custody children in all areas except mother relationship. This study indicates that, on average, a two parent intact family is the best arrangement for children, and a shared parenting arrangement is better than a sole custody arrangement, i.e., a two-parent family is better even if parents are divorced.

Ilfeld, Holly Zingale "Children's perceptions of their relationship with their fathers in three family constellations: mother sole custody, joint custody and intact families" Doctoral dissertation, U. of California, Davis 1989

This study evaluated children's perceptions of their fathers at least four years post-divorce, comparing joint custody, sole custody and intact families. The subjects were 43 latency-age children: 11 from maternal custody families, 14 from joint custody families and 18 controls from intact homes.

Results: "There was a significant difference in the perceptions of children in sole and joint custody. Joint custody children reported spending more time with their fathers in child-centered activities, activities which were considered pleasurable and important to children. " And: "No differences were found [from intact] as a function of custody arrangements in children's perceptions of emotional closeness to the father, acceptance by the father, or fathers's potency or activity. "

Lerman, Isabel A. "Adjustment of latency age children in joint and single custody arrangements" California School of Professional Psychology, San Diego, 1989

This study evaluated 90 children, aged 7 to 12, divided equally among maternal, joint legal, and joint physical custody groups.

Results showed negative effects for sole custody: "Single custody subjects evidenced greater self-hate and perceived more rejection from their fathers than joint physical custody subjects." Conflict between parents was found to be a significant factor, which may explain the better adjustment for joint physical custody children: "Degree of interparental conflict was a significant predictor of child self-hate. Higher conflict was associated with greater self-hate; lower conflict was associated with lower self-hate." "Higher father-child contact was associated with better adjustment, lower self-hate, and lower perceived rejection from father; lower father-child contact was associated with poorer adjustment, higher self-hate, and higher perceived rejection from father. "

Extreme Situations

In situations with high levels of conflict, mental illness, or domestic violence, joint physical custody is no better (and no worse) than sole custody.

Surviving the Breakup, J. Wallerstein and J. Kelly; Second Chances, J. Wallerstein and S. Blakeslee; and other publications.

Judith Wallerstein and colleagues have produced many publications on a 20+ year study of 184 families that had been referred to her clinic for therapy. The parents were predominantly mentally ill, with approximately half the men and half the women "moderately disturbed or frequently incapacitated by disabling neuroses and addictions," including some who were "sometimes suicidal." An additional 20% of the women and 15% of the men were categorized as "severely disturbed." Approximately one third of the sample were considered to have "adequate psychological functioning" before divorce. Although there was a significant level of attrition, with families dropping out of the study when problems were resolved, some conclusions emerged from the remaining families. Children in joint custody situations did no better than those in sole custody, indicating that parents must be reasonably psychologically healthy for shared parenting to benefit children.

Johnston, Janet R., Marsha Kline, and Jeanne M. Tschann, "Ongoing Postdivorce Conflict: Effects on Children of Joint Custody and Frequent Access," American Journal of Orthopsychiatry, Vol. 59, No. 4 (Oct. 1989).
Johnston et al. studied 100 low income families involved in ongoing custody disputes that included frequent verbal and physical aggression. Approximately one third of the children were in joint physical custody arrangements averaging 12 days per month with the less-seen parent, with the others in either mother or father sole physical custody averaging 4 days a month with the less-seen parent. The study found that "there was no clear evidence that children are better adjusted in either custody type", and that "mean scores for the Child Behavior Checklist lie within the normal range for all custody types." Also, "there was no evidence that the clinically disturbed children were more likely to be in joint than in sole custody." However, the study did find that more frequent contact between parents in either joint or sole custody arrangements was "associated with more emotional and behavioral problems in the children."
Johnston's study indicates that shared parenting may not reduce disputes between parents in extreme high-conflict situations, but also shows that sole custody does not protect children from the effects of conflict between parents. In high conflict situations, it is probably better to reduce interaction between parents. For example, parents can pick up children from school instead of from the other parent's house.
The study did find one significant benefit from shared parenting even in these cases: "Only one parent with joint custody ceased contact with her child, whereas 12 parents of sole custody children 'dropped out'." Thus joint custody does appear to protect children from the complete loss of a parent, even in high conflict situations. Joint Legal Custody

Although not as beneficial to children as equal shared parenting (joint physical custody), joint legal custody helps to some extent. The main benefits of joint legal custody are in reducing visitation interference and improving child support compliance.

Joint legal custody has been consistently linked with more parental involvement, higher child support compliance, and less conflict between parents. Until recently, however, it was not clear whether these benefits occurred as a <u>result</u> of joint legal custody, or simply because more cooperative parents chose joint custody in the first place. The 1997 study by Seltzer provides strong evidence for a cause and effect relationship between joint legal custody and the benefits associated with it.

Seltzer, J. "Father by Law: Effects of Joint Legal Custody on Non-residential Fathers Involvement with Children," NSFH Paper No. 75, Feb., 1997, U. of Wisconsin-Madison, http://ssc.wisc.edu/cde/nsfhwp/home.htm
Seltzer used data from the National Survey of Families and Households, a survey of over 13,000 families that collected data in two waves, 1987-88 and 1992-94. Because the study included data on the quality of family relationships, it was possible to study the effects of joint legal custody while controlling from pre-separation family relationships by analysing data on families that had separated between the survey waves. Seltzer concluded that "Controlling for the quality of family relationships before separation and socioeconomic status, fathers with joint legal custody see their children more frequently, have more overnight visits, and pay more child support than fathers in families in which mothers have sole legal custody." She suggests that joint legal custody helps reduce visitation denial: "By clarifying that divorced fathers are 'by law' still fathers, parents' negotiations about fathers' participation in child rearing after divorce may shift from trying to resolve *whether* fathers will be involved in child rearing to the matter of *how* fathers will be involved." [emphasis in original]

Gunnoe, M.L., and S.L. Braver, "The Effects of Joint Legal Custody on Family Functioning, Controlling for Factors that Predispose a joint award," *Child Development.*

This study evaluated 273 families, controlling for 28 variables that influence a predisposition to agree on joint legal custody. Controlling for these factors, children in joint legal custody families had more time with their fathers and fewer adjustment and behavior problems. The custody type, however, did not affect the adjustment of fathers or mothers post-divorce, conflict between ex-spouses, or child support compliance.

Sanford Braver,"Determining the Impact of Joint Custody on Divorcing Families",

Study consisted of 378 families; some with unmatched partners, in various custody arrangements.

". . .Sharlene Wolchik, Iwrin Sandler and I found in 1985 that children in joint custody had higher feelings of self-worth than children in sole maternal custody."

"Our results showed considerable benefits for joint custody, even when equating predisposing factors. After this adjustment, children in joint custody were found to be significantly better adjusted, and to exhibit less antisocial and impulsive behavior than sole custody families. Fathers also visited more, and were more involved in child care, as well as more satisfied with the divorce settlement. Mothers, however, were significantly less satisfied with the custody arrangements in joint custody families."

"When the couple disagrees initially, which is better for the family, for the father to get his preference (joint [custody]) or for the mother to get her preference (sole [custody])? We found that the groups differed significantly in terms of how much financial child support was paid: when sole custody was that arrangement despite the fathers' wishes, 80% was paid (according to what the father reported; the figure was 64% by mothers' report), while when joint custody was awarded despite the mothers' preference, it zoomed to almost perfect compliance (97% by fathers' report; 94% by mothers' report) . . . A similar relationship was found for fathers' contact with the child. It was significantly highest for the group in which joint custody was awarded despite the mothers' preference." "Joint custody, even when awarded despite the contrary preference of the mother, leads to more involved fathers, and almost perfect of financial child support; controlling for predisposing factors, it leads to better adjusted children. . . We believe these findings call for policy makers, in the best interest of the children, to adopt a presumption that is rebuttable for joint legal custody, that is, a judicial preference that both parents retain their right and responsibilities toward their children post divorce."

INDEX

Additional Copies

Phone: 1-800-247-6553 / 419-281-1802
Web: http://www.atlasbooks.com/marktplc/00397.htm
E-mail: order@bookmaster.com
Fax: 1-419-281-6883
Mail: BookMasters, Inc.
P.O. Box 388
Ashland, OH 44805
USA

For e-mail, fax or mail, fill in and submit the following.
Cheques (by mail order) may be in US or Canadian dollars, payable to
BookMasters Inc.

Where's Daddy? ISBN 0-9674736-5-9
US: $26.50   Can: $37.00
Plus shipping and handling, amount varies with destination.*
Virginia and Ohio residents, add state sales tax.

Number of Copies: ____

Name: _____

Address: _____

_____

City: _____ State / Province: _____

Zip / Postal Code: _____ Country: _____

Charge Card: **G**VISA   **G**MastrCard   **G**AmerExpr   **G**Discover

Card Number: _____ Expiry: _____
mm/yy

Name on card if different from above: _____

* S&H for up to 3 copies: within US, $3.95 US$; to Canada, $7.95 Can$; overseas, $8.00 US$.

Additional Copies

Phone: 1-800-247-6553 / 419-281-1802
Web: http://www.atlasbooks.com/marktplc/00397.htm
E-mail: order@bookmaster.com
Fax: 1-419-281-6883
Mail: BookMasters, Inc.
P.O. Box 388
Ashland, OH 44805
USA

For e-mail, fax or mail, fill in and submit the following.
Cheques (by mail order) may be in US or Canadian dollars, payable to
BookMasters Inc.

Where's Daddy? ISBN 0-9674736-5-9
US: $26.50   Can: $37.00
Plus shipping and handling, amount varies with destination.*
Virginia and Ohio residents, add state sales tax.

Number of Copies: ____

Name: _____

Address: _____

_____

City: _____   State / Province: _____

Zip / Postal Code: _____   Country: _____

Charge Card: **G**VISA   **G**MastrCard   **G**AmerExpr   **G**Discover

Card Number: _____   Expiry: _____
                                                                    mm/yy

Name on card if different from above: _____

* S&H for up to 3 copies: within US, $3.95 US$; to Canada, $7.95 Can$; overseas, $8.00 US$.

Additional Copies

Phone:	1-800-247-6553 / 419-281-1802
Web:	http://www.atlasbooks.com/marktplc/00397.htm
E-mail:	order@bookmaster.com
Fax:	1-419-281-6883
Mail:	BookMasters, Inc.
	P.O. Box 388
	Ashland, OH 44805
	USA

For e-mail, fax or mail, fill in and submit the following.
Cheques (by mail order) may be in US or Canadian dollars, payable to
BookMasters Inc.

Where's Daddy? ISBN 0-9674736-5-9
US: $26.50   Can: $37.00
Plus shipping and handling, amount varies with destination.*
Virginia and Ohio residents, add state sales tax.

Number of Copies: ____

Name: _____

Address: _____

_____

City: _____   State / Province: _____

Zip / Postal Code: _____   Country: _____

Charge Card: **G**VISA   **G**MastrCard   **G**AmerExpr   **G**Discover

Card Number: _____   Expiry: _____
mm/yy

Name on card if different from above: _____

* S&H for up to 3 copies: within US, $3.95 US$; to Canada, $7.95 Can$; overseas, $8.00 US$.

Additional Copies

Phone: 1-800-247-6553 / 419-281-1802
Web: http://www.atlasbooks.com/marktplc/00397.htm
E-mail: order@bookmaster.com
Fax: 1-419-281-6883
Mail: BookMasters, Inc.
P.O. Box 388
Ashland, OH 44805
USA

For e-mail, fax or mail, fill in and submit the following.
Cheques (by mail order) may be in US or Canadian dollars, payable to
BookMasters Inc.

Where's Daddy? ISBN 0-9674736-5-9
US: $26.50 Can: $37.00
Plus shipping and handling, amount varies with destination.*
Virginia and Ohio residents, add state sales tax.

Number of Copies: ____

Name: _____

Address: _____

_____

City: _____ State / Province: _____

Zip / Postal Code: _____ Country: _____

Charge Card: **G**VISA **G**MastrCard **G**AmerExpr **G**Discover

Card Number: _____ Expiry:_____
mm/yy

Name on card if different from above: _____

* S&H for up to 3 copies: within US, $3.95 US$; to Canada, $7.95 Can$; overseas, $8.00 US$.